Token Ring Troubleshooting Guide

About the Author

Daniel J. Nassar is president of LAN Scope Incorporated, a Philadelphia area-based Local Area Networking consulting firm that specializes in high-end LAN/WAN services. He specifically specializes in protocol analysis, performance tuning, disaster recovery planning, LAN inventory analysis, high-end integration design, and project management/engineering to the LAN/WAN marketplace. Nassar is experienced in an extensive range of computer system areas. He is proficient in LAN layout and design and in all phases of LAN problem analysis and performance tuning, especially in the Token Ring environment. Computer system maintenance and diagnostics also is a specialty.

He can be reached for questions concerning this book at:

LAN Scope, Inc. (610)359-3573 or (610) 446-3831

Token Ring Troubleshooting Guide

Daniel J. Nassar

toExcel
San Jose   New York   Lincoln   Shanghai

Token Ring Troubleshooting Guide

Published by toExcel

For information address:
toExcel
165 West 95th Street, Suite B-N
New York, NY 10025
www.toExcel.com

ISBN: 1-58348-012-9

LCCN: 98-88994

Printed in the United States of America

TRADEMARKS

Contents

Preface

I've worked in the LAN industry for many years. For a number of those years, I worked in environments in which I had to troubleshoot Token Ring networks daily. I decided to write this book because I have not found a solid, comprehensive, easy-to-read manual on the Token Ring. Hopefully this book provides the good, in-depth understanding of the Token Ring topology that I could never find.

The main purpose of this book is to provide the necessary reference material you need to effectively troubleshoot LAN problems in the Token Ring environment. The Token Ring network topology offers a sophisticated option to the local area network arena, but that sophistication can make it difficult to troubleshoot.

This book is geared to the following readers:

- LAN system engineers and technical support engineers who must deal with day-to-day Token Ring troubleshooting problems

- LAN designers and consultants who need a solid guide to rely on as they work in the Token Ring environment

- LAN managers who must perform the daily administration and monitoring of Token Ring LANs

- Users on Token Ring LANs who want a better understanding of Token Ring and the problems that they may encounter

- Computer science and electronic engineering technology students who want a good understanding of the Token Ring topology

chapter 1

INTRODUCTION TO TOKEN RING

Although you may be familiar with the basic theory of Token Ring operation, you probably realize that basic theory is insufficient when complex problems develop on your Token Ring networks. If you know the basics about Token Ring, you may want to skip to Chapter 2, which contains a nitty-gritty discussion on the inner workings of Token Ring and Token Ring network troubleshooting. If your familiarity with Token Ring stops with the name and, perhaps, some familiarity with the pieces that are plugged together to create a Token Ring network, you may want to stick around, however.

This introductory chapter describes Token Ring theory as gently as possible and gives you some analogies onto which you can hang the many terms you encounter starting in Chapter 2.

WHY TOKEN RING?

Of the dozens of types of network wiring systems, two standards predominate in local area networks: 802.3 (popularly, but inaccurately, called EtherNet) and 802.5 (Token Ring). The numbers 802.3 and 802.5 are the identifiers for the standards that describe the detailed workings of the networks. These standards are established by committees of the Institute of Electrical and Electronic Engineers (IEEE).

The popularity of these network types arises because they are open standards, not systems that are under the control of a particular equipment manufacturer.

802.3, currently the most popular network standard, was derived from a networking system developed jointly by Xerox and Digital Equipment Corporation. The original system was called EtherNet, and that name has been commonly applied to the 802.3 standard as well, despite some differences. Over the years, new versions of 802.3 have been standardized to reduce the cost of installation and to improve manageability. At least three reasons explain the popularity of EtherNet:

- EtherNet has been standardized longer than Token Ring.

- EtherNet offers high performance at low cost.

- EtherNet has become an integral component of many vendors' computer network architectures.

Token Ring was developed by IBM and Texas Instruments and was defined as IEEE standard 802.5 in 1985. IBM probably developed Token Ring, at least in part, so that it would have a networking system that was unique and that could be clearly differentiated from the 802.3/EtherNet network standards. Besides marketing considerations, however, several engineering goals motivated the development of Token Ring. To understand some of these goals, you need a little background in the theoretical workings of 802.3 and 802.5.

Token Ring and EtherNet are similar because they are both baseband networks. Baseband networks are restricted to transmitting one message at a time through the network cabling medium.

Token Ring and EtherNet differ in at least two significant respects:

- In the method they use to ensure that only one message at a time is transmitted and that each message is transmitted correctly.

- In the cabling arrangement that carries their electrical signals.

By understanding these differences, you can understand the reasons for the complicated cabling and signaling designs that engineers developed for Token Ring.

UNDERSTANDING 802.3/ETHERNET

The technical term that describes the control mechanism of this standard is impressive: Carrier Sense Multiple Access with Collision Detection (CSMA/CD). That mouthful of a term is easy to understand in the context of a simple analogy.

The CSMA part of the standard means that the network operates like a telephone party line with everyone listening in. Multiple Access simply means that each person on the party line can originate a conversation at any time. Carrier Sense means that a speaker is expected to listen for silence on the line before beginning to speak. (The carrier is a signal that indicates that the line is idle.)

Collision Detection comes in when, despite efforts to start talking on a quiet line, two conversations begin at once and interfere with each other. The rules of CD instruct all parties to stop talking, clear the line, and wait for a random period of time. Then new attempts can be made to initiate messages. Collisions are a fact of life in CSMA/CD networks.

Under the 802.3 standard, conversations are transmitted through the wire at 10Mbits per second (10 mega or million bits per second). Because the average message is only about a thousand bytes long, collisions are actually fairly unlikely unless a very high number of messages need to be transmitted by a large number of stations.

Theoretically, when enough transmitters attempt to send enough messages on a CSMA/CD network, the percentage of collisions can become so high that most of the network's available capacity is lost to collisions detection and recovery. In practice, however, high data rates are required for this to take place. Nevertheless, there is a random aspect to CSMA/CD, and any given station may need to make several attempts to transmit a message. This characteristic results in some criticism of CSMA/CD networks in situations when messages must be reliably transmitted at specific times.

A potential criticism of 802.3/EtherNet, therefore, is that network traffic is managed statistically. Network managers cannot ensure that critical messages do not encounter delays.

A second criticism of 802.3/EtherNet derives from the cabling system that is commonly employed. Technically, EtherNet is a bus topology, meaning that its physical arrangement (its topology) puts every network station in a position to transmit through a common wire to every other network station. In fact, every message transmitted on the network is received at every node simultaneously; it is simply ignored except by the intended recipient.

The 802.3/EtherNet cabling system is typically a long coaxial cable that loops past each workstation, connecting to the network port of the workstation through a tap connector. Coax is an excellent medium for transmitting data at high data rates, offering high performance at reasonable cost. The nature of a bus network wired with coax, however, can make it difficult to isolate the cause of a problem. A crimp or break in the cable at one location can disable the entire network because interfering signals may be reflected back into the cable.

The second criticism of 802.3/EtherNet, therefore, is that it can be difficult to isolate the problem to a particular location on the network. The recently popular 10BaseT wiring standard for 802.3 networks was designed to make it easier to isolate problems, but vestiges of the problem remain.

UNDERSTANDING TOKEN RING

Token Ring was developed to address the two mentioned criticisms of 802.3/EtherNet technology. The design of Token Ring guarantees that each station on the network has an opportunity to transmit at regular intervals. Plus the cabling design for Token Ring makes it easy to isolate most problems to a particular part of the network—to a fault domain.

The control method for Token Ring is called Token Access. The telephone analogy doesn't work well for Token Access. It is more effective to describe Token Ring in terms of a somewhat artificial parlor game.

In the game, the participants are seated in a ring. Each participant is eager to send written messages to other players. Each player writes down the message and passes the message to the neighbor on the left. Players receive messages from their neighbor on the right.

If everyone were writing and transmitting messages at once, however, a player might be too busy writing and sending messages to pass others' messages around the ring. Therefore, a control mechanism is required. The players pass a marble (a "token") around the ring. Only the person currently holding the marble can write a message and pass it to the left. The message is passed hand-to-hand around the ring until it reaches the intended recipient who reads it, marks it as received, and then sends it on its way until it returns to the original sender. The originator notes that the message was read and releases the marble to the ring so that other players can have their turns to transmit.

Because only the person holding the token can transmit, collisions cannot occur. Although the collision problem of CSMA/CD is obvious, numerous problems must also be anticipated in the Token Access method.

Suppose that the marble token is dropped and lost. How can the players be assured that they need not remain forever silent? One player on the ring is designated as an Active Monitor; the AM monitors the token status by maintaining a master clock. Numerous timers monitor events on the ring and determine when the AM should generate a new token. One, called T(ANY_TOKEN), indicates whether a token of any time has passed through the AM within a specific period of time.

Suppose that a new player wants to enter or leave the game and does so exactly at the point a message is passing. During the shuffling of chairs to make room, the message may be lost or damaged. How do the players reestablish the ring and the smooth transfer of messages between the neighbors? Token Ring defines a ring insertion process that ensures an orderly reconfiguration of the ring.

Suppose that a player falls asleep and the token stops in his lap. How can the other players detect this failure and resume normal operation. (Oh, yes. You weren't told that the players are blindfolded. Token Access is pretty complicated, and the required analogies can get fairly strained.) After losing contact with a neighbor for a certain period of time, a player can send out a distress signal called a beacon that initiates an attempt to recover proper ring function.

Suppose that a message is smudged while being handed around. How can the sender and receiver know that the message was garbled? Each message contains an error checking component (called a Cyclic Redundancy Check) that enables the recipients to determine whether the message has been damaged.

These potential problems required the designers of Token Ring to put in numerous, complicated safeguards to cover the many possible error conditions. The mechanisms of Token Ring are more complicated than CSMA/CD.

The token-passing mechanism ensures that each station on the ring has an opportunity to transmit at regular intervals. If the station holds the token, it has exclusive access to the network. This advantage of Token Ring becomes significant under conditions of high network traffic; therefore token access is regarded as a deterministic system whereas CSMA/CD is probabalistic. The complexity of Token Access control is, therefore, necessary if precise transmission control is required.

The design of Token Ring also makes it far easier to isolate the causes of a network failure. In the parlor game, players expect all messages to arrive from the player to the right (in Token Ring, that player is the Nearest Active Upstream Neighbor, the NAUN). If neither a token or a message arrives within a reasonable period of time, the player can raise an alarm. The game moderator, knowing the order of the players in the ring, can start addressing the problem by checking on the NAUN of the complaining player. In fact, for any given player, the likely cause of failure can be isolated to the player and to the NAUN. This feature is the troubleshooting fault domain for Token Ring.

The second advantage of Token Ring, therefore, is that you usually can isolate problems to fault domains. As mentioned in EtherNet, many problems affect the entire network and are difficult to isolate.

A third advantage of Token Ring is that the network components are designed with a high level of diagnostic capability. Components can perform self-checks and checks on the cables to which they are attached; a component may automatically remove itself from the network if an error is found. Further, components can exchange management data with monitor stations; the monitors can often determine the health of a network component and take corrective action.

The reliability of deterministic control and the ease of troubleshooting fault domains have made Token Ring the fastest growing type of network. Although 802.3/EtherNet remains popular, Token Ring is increasingly being chosen for more critical networks.

Why Do You Need this Book?

An automobile usually works properly as you drive it from the showroom. Similarly, a Token Ring often works properly right out of the box. The network may operate properly for a considerable period of time. Eventually, however, both automobiles and networks experience performance problems or out-and-out failure. At those times the owner has two options: to hire an outside troubleshooter at an expert's hourly rate or to solve the problem using in-house tools and skills. If the rates for auto repair are high, rates for network technicians are even higher. Rates frequently exceed $100 per hour, with every hour causing expensive losses in business productivity. You cannot rent a network while yours is under repair. Wise network administrators plan for network failures by becoming familiar with network troubleshooting techniques before a crisis arises.

As you can see, the desirable features of Token Ring come at a cost. Many complicated mechanisms are necessary for Token Ring's performance. If a Token Ring fails, the troubleshooter comes face-to-face with those mechanisms.

Unfortunately, international standards are not written in terms of analogies. Although the standards would certainly be more fun to read if they were expressed in terms of parlor game analogies, the standards are written for precision by engineers who are comfortable with complex terms and formulas. Network administrators who need to troubleshoot Token Ring networks eventually must face up to the terminology and the complexities, at least to some degree.

This book doesn't attempt to turn you into an electronic engineer. Its goal is to distill the complications of Token Ring, transmitting to you only what you need to know as a network administrator or technician. The emphasis is on troubleshooting methodologies and techniques that systematize your Token Ring problem solving.

The most powerful tools are the troubleshooting flow guides in Chapter 7. Armed with some basic knowledge about Token Ring and these flow guides, you can quickly resolve most of your Token Ring problems.

Don't wait until you experience a network failure to start using this book. The time to start is now, while your network is working well. By doing so, you learn how your network functions normally; this is the baseline against which you will compare your network when it is in trouble.

The skills you need to troubleshoot Token Ring cannot be acquired in a day. Learning to troubleshoot is nearly impossible when the network is down and the users are complaining. Don't wait! Read this book. Beg, borrow, or steal the budget for some diagnostic tools.

chapter 2 ARCHITECTURE

To become effective at troubleshooting a Token Ring network, you must first thoroughly understand how Token Ring is composed. Token Ring's design is one of the most complex in the LAN arena. This chapter leads you through the Token Ring design and layout and describes how the main functions work. You look in detail at the management roles of the network, and the Token Ring communication processes. Finally you examine the Token Ring frame types, to provide you with an overall understanding of the architecture.

THE OSI MODEL FOR LAN COMMUNICATION

The Open Systems Interconnection (OSI) model for LANs was defined by the International Organization for Standardization (IOS). The model was originally developed as a platform on which network vendors could standardize uniform protocol communication on networks. The IEEE also uses the OSI model when developing IEEE LAN standards.

The model is a hierarchical-structure model that defines and relates seven layers of communication protocols. The seven layers operate interactively with each other to provide a method for end-to-end communication between source and destination roles and functions. The bottom three layers are intended for transmission and routing definition. The top three layers are intended for communication for user and host applications. The middle layer acts as an interface between the top and bottom layers (see fig. 1.1).

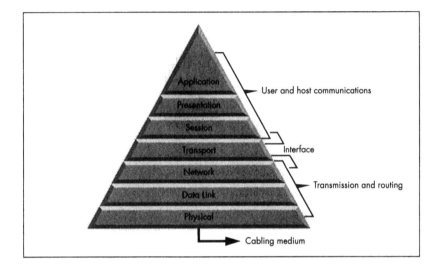

The OSI Seven-Layer Design

The seven layers of the OSI model are detailed next. Note how each of the seven layers depends on the others for key elements of its operation.

Physical Layer. The Physical layer is responsible for actually transmitting the bitstream on the medium. This layer is concerned with the actual coding of the data signal, and how it is composed with relation to the following hardware elements: current, voltage, connectors, interface layouts, and the network card.

Data Link Layer. This layer is responsible for communicating with the actual bitstream at the Physical layer. The Data Link layer is where the bitstream is assembled and disassembled into data frames. This layer decodes all the necessary flags and error-checking data to provide accurate data transmission. This is also the layer where the addressing of the data frame occurs.

Network Layer. The Network layer is where a virtual data path is defined between two network nodes. The data frames are actually assembled into packets at this layer. Addressing and routing for the packet are assigned at the Network layer.

Transport Layer. The Transport layer handles communications between the Network layer and the Session layer. But the Transport layer is mainly defined to handle host-to-host communications. This layer takes packets at the Network layer and assembles and disassembles them into larger transmission segments for communication to the higher layers.

Session Layer. The Session layer is responsible for establishing and terminating host-to-host communications. This layer provides timing and control for communicating between hosts within the model. Overall host session management takes place at this layer.

Presentation Layer. This layer takes the actual data that is transmitted between two nodes and encodes and decodes it into the proper syntax for presentation to the Application layer. Actual code conversion and compression occurs at this layer.

Application Layer. This layer communicates with the end user. At this layer you find end-user applications such as electronic mail, file transfer, and networking programs.

OSI and the Token Ring Network

Every LAN topology relates to the OSI model a little differently. So as not to confuse the differences between the topologies, let's call the Token Ring version the Token Ring Protocol model.

Overall the Token Ring Protocol model relates closely to the OSI model (see fig. 2.2).

FIGURE 2.2
The individual pieces of the Token Ring Protocol model relate quite closely to the seven layers of the OSI model for LANs.

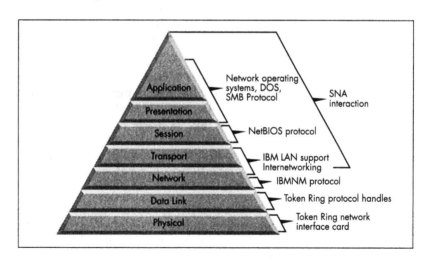

DESIGN AND LAYOUT

In this chapter and throughout this book, several key terms are used repeatedly. These terms include topology, network protocol, and network architecture.

Topology is the physical and logical layout of a network. The Token Ring topology has a unique layout.

Network protocol is an orderly, predefined method by which devices on a LAN communicate with each other.

Network architecture is the design that integrates the network topology with the network protocols. The Token Ring architecture has the same physical components as any other local area network (LAN) architecture.

Most of the devices that will be connected to the network are PCs, or workstations. One of the PCs will serve as a file server, which is where the network operating system resides. Peripherals such as printers and modems are connected to either the workstations or the file server.

The file server and workstations talk to each other through network interface cards (NICs). Every device connected to the network must have a NIC installed. The NICs connect to the multistation access units (MAUs), which serve as the network wiring hubs.

Every device that is connected to the network will have a NIC installed. The NIC has a nine-pin port that connects to a cable that connects to a MAU port. (Note that it is possible to have a twisted-pair port if the NIC is made for unshielded twisted pair (UTP) cabling medium. UTP is discussed in Chapter 3.) The NIC is primarily responsible for handling all the network communication that takes place between a network device and the rest of the network.

The NIC actually contains the Token Ring chipset, which contains routines called the Agent. The Agent interprets and routes all the data frames that are transferred between the device and the network.

The Agent works with the Network Basic Input/Output System (NetBIOS) that is loaded with the Token Ring device drivers via the

IBM LAN Support Program disk. The NetBIOS handles Session-layer protocol communication, allowing the operating system on the PC to talk to the network protocols that the NIC receives from other devices on the network.

Next let's look at the MAUs. This discussion uses the IBM 8228 MAU (see fig. 2.3). Chapter 3 details other wiring hubs.

FIGURE 2.3
The eight available ports and the Ring In and Ring Out ports of a multistation access unit.

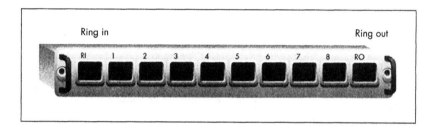

Each MAU has eight available ports for network devices. The network devices are connected to the MAU ports via cables called lobe cables. Each port on the MAU has an internal relay that opens when the network device that is cabled to it attempts to access the network. The NIC sends a DC current to open the relay. If the device is not using the network, the relay remains closed.

On each end of an MAU is a port for cabling it to another MAU, for the purpose of expanding the network. On the left side of the MAU is a port called RING IN (RI); on the right side of the MAU is a port called RING OUT (RO).

Expanding the network from, for example, eight to 16 devices entails simply connecting the RO port of the existing MAU to the RI port of the new MAU.

The unused RI and RO ports on the MAUs have self-shorting data connectors that automatically loop the cabling back to form an electrical ring. All the ports on the MAU have the self-shorting feature: When there is no device connected to the port, it self-shorts to close the ring. This makes it easy to add and remove network devices from the MAU.

The cabling path that connects the MAUs and follows through the MAUs is called the main ring path. This path is different from the lobe cable, which connects the MAU ports to the network devices.

The MAU configuration makes the Token Ring network easy to expand. All you have to do is run all the network lobe cables to one area. Any time you need to add devices you simply connect a new MAU to the existing chain of MAUs.

When you run a large group of cables to one area, the cables are usually connected to a patch panel (see fig. 2.4). A patch panel allows the flexibility of moving lobe cables from one MAU to another MAU easily. The area in which the patch panel is located is called a wiring closet. Some Token Ring network installations are so large that they require multiple wiring closets.

FIGURE 2.4
The Token Ring topology allows the network to form a physical star but an electrical ring, providing great flexibility for network design and layout.

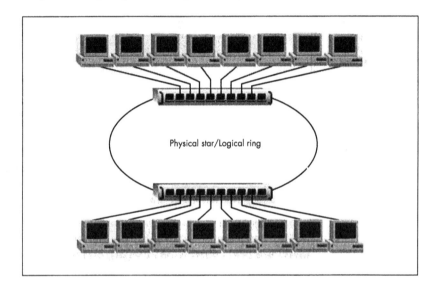

Physical star/Logical ring

In the case of long-distance cable runs between wiring closets, devices called repeaters may be needed to compensate for the distance.

Some Token Ring networks are connected to other LANs, requiring the use of a bridge or router. Bridges and routers are hardware and software devices that connect individual networks.

Now let's look at the actual cabling. Please refer to Figure 2.3.

The cable used is four-wire, which consists of two shielded twisted pairs. One pair is the main ring path, and the second pair is a secondary or backup path.

If you find a bad cable between two MAUs, remove the cable and the respective RI and RO ports will automatically self-short. Data will automatically flow on the backup path.

This feature makes the Token Ring topology so fault tolerant. The backup path allows for the quick, continued operation of the ring if there is just a bad cable on the main cabling backbone. It also is a great aid for troubleshooting ring problems.

Figure 2.4 shows how the Token Ring network layout is a physical star but an electrical ring. This layout allows for great flexibility when designing and laying out the network.

Overall the physical star/logical ring concept is the most sophisticated LAN topology on the market.

HOW THE TOKEN RING NETWORK WORKS

Token-Passing Theory

Stations (PCs) gain access to the cabling medium via a token that is passed around the ring. The token is actually a three-byte frame that is passed sequentially around the ring. The token circulates the ring, remaining in an idle state until a station needs to transmit on the ring. A station needing to transmit data waits to grab the token (see fig. 2.5). Every station on the ring has the opportunity to grab the token, but a station can only grab the token when the token is not being used by another station.

FIGURE 2.5
A patch panel allows connecting many lobe cables from the network ring stations in a single location. These patch panels are in a wiring closet, which includes the MAUs.

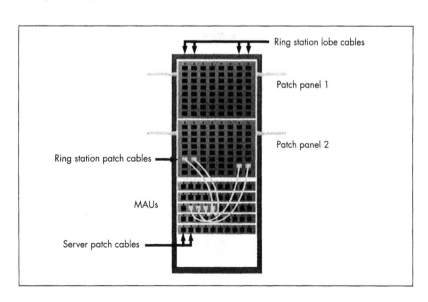

Ring station lobe cables

Patch panel 1

Patch panel 2

Ring station patch cables

MAUs

Server patch cables

Before the station retransmits the token it appends an information frame to the token frame. When this occurs the token becomes either a medium access control (MAC) or a logical link control (LLC) frame. Part of the information will be the destination address or addresses for the information being sent.

After the destination station or stations receive the data, the token returns to the originating source station.

If the source station is done transmitting, it resets the token frame by removing any additional information that it appended to the packet (called "stripping") and passes the token back onto the ring.

Downstream and Upstream

The two logical directions of travel on the ring are upstream and downstream. The direction of travel for data on the ring is always downstream.

A token is always transmitted to the next station in a downstream direction. A station that transmits the token is called the nearest active upstream neighbor (NAUN) with respect to the next active downstream station to which it transmits a token (see fig. 2.6).

FIGURE 2.6
Token Ring cabling is four-wire, consisting of two shielded twisted pairs. The RI and RO ports are automatically self-shorting.

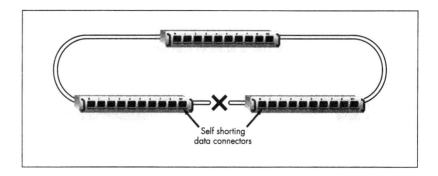

Self shorting
data connectors

NAUNs

The concept of the NAUN is important in the Token Ring environment, because it is a direct reference point for controlling communications and addressing stations on the ring. One of the NAUN's most important roles is in the Neighbor Notification process. The Neighbor Notification process allows a ring station (RS) to learn its NAUN's address and then to let its respective nearest active downstream neighbor know its address. See the Neighbor Notification section below for more detail.

Another important NAUN role is isolating a ring failure to a fault area called the fault domain. When a failure occurs on the ring, the Token Ring architecture inherently locates the problem to the fault domain. The NAUN is used in Token Ring processes to locate the fault domain.

Addressing Schemes

Token Ring architecture dictates that each station on the ring be uniquely identified by a separate defined address. Three different address types are: individual, group, and functional.

Individual addressing is when each station is addressed uniquely across the ring.

Group addressing is when one or more stations are addressed. Stations defined as part of a common group address can be addressed by a broadcast to their group address. Broadcasting is a method by which a station on the ring communicates with one or more stations through a common address that the destination stations share.

Functional addressing is used when stations need to communicate with a station that provides common functions. Some functional addresses are predefined by the Token Ring architecture, and some are reserved for definition by the user as needed. The predefined functional addresses are as follows:

Configuration Report Server	C00000000010
Ring Error Monitor	C00000000008
Ring Parameter Server	C00000000002
Active Monitor	C00000000001
Bridge	C00000000100
LAN Manager	C00000002000

User-defined functional addresses can be assigned to C00000080000 through C00040000000.

Addresses can be defined by two different methods: *universal administration* and *local administration*. Universal administration means that stations on the ring are assigned unique individual addresses by the IEEE. Local administration means that stations on the ring are assigned unique individual addresses by a group or person other than the IEEE.

4Mbps versus 16Mbps and ETR

The main difference between 4Mbps and 16Mbps Token Ring is bandwidth. The 4Mbps Token Ring frames are about 4500 bytes, and 16Mbps Token Ring frames are four times that size—18000 bytes. This increase in bandwidth allows for higher throughput of data. This makes good sense for today's complicated environments, with applications such as database client/servers that need a larger network bandwidth.

Another noticeable difference in the 16Mbps speed is the introduction of early token release (ETR) into the Token Ring architecture. ETR allows two frames to travel on the ring at the same time. At 4Mbps only one frame travels on the ring at any given time (see fig. 2.7).

FIGURE 2.7
For 16Mbps Token Ring networks, early token release (ETR) allows two data frames to travel on the ring at the same time.

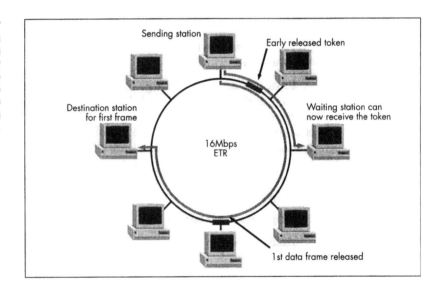

ETR allows two frames on the ring because, at 16Mbps, data frames spend less time on the ring, and more open bandwidth is available. The Token Ring architecture transmits idle characters called *null characters* to fill the open bandwidth. This is still a waste of bandwidth, but with 16Mbps/ETR the sending station releases the token immediately after it sends the data frame. This differs from 4Mbps, which holds the token until it receives the old data frame back from the receiving station. A station waiting to transmit data can do so faster.

Currently 16Mbps networks are most often used for backbone situations within large Token Ring topology environments.

The FDDI/Token Ring Relationship

The Fiber Data Distributed Interface (FDDI) is a network topology that uses a fiber optic medium and runs at 100Mbps. The topology is a token-passing network very similar to 802.5. IEEE is looking closely at FDDI as a possible new standard.

FDDI lends itself to being a great backbone topology for general Token Ring. With some of the newest technologies being introduced in the hubbing bridge modules, we will see FDDI and 802.5 Token Ring become more interoperable. (The scope of this book doesn't allow a detailed discussion of the FDDI protocol. For more information on FDDI, see reference 8 in Appendix A.)

Differential Manchester Encoding

Data transmission on the ring medium is actually coded in a symbol format called *Differential Manchester Encoding* (see fig. 2.8). Occurring at the Physical layer, the code is produced by synchronizing a half-bit clock signal against a bit slot. A standard digital 0 and 1 pulse form can be represented.

A 0 is represented when a positive or negative transition is at the beginning of a bit slot; a 1 is represented when no transition at all is at the beginning of a bit slot. A transition will always be at the middle of a bit slot because of the half-bit clock.

FIGURE 2.8
The symbol coding for data transmission on a Token Ring network is according to Differential Manchester Encoding.

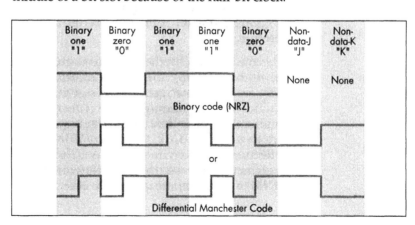

The resulting symbol is a blended code that provides a unique framing method critical to the starting and ending delimiter frame sequence timing.

Frame Types

Token Ring architecture has three different frame types: the token frame, the data frame, and the abort sequence.

The token frame is a three-byte frame. The token circulates the ring as a control signal.

A data frame carries either MAC information or LLC information. MAC information is used to manage the flow of traffic on the ring. LLC information is the user data information to be transmitted on the ring.

An abort sequence frame is used to clear the ring when there is a problem with a frame. The station that currently has control of the token (the originating station) transmits an abort sequence frame if it detects a problem with the current data frame.

The *802.5 IEEE Standard Frame Format* section below discusses these frame types in detail.

CONTROL OF THE RING ENVIRONMENT

Management Roles of the Ring

Every station on the ring includes a NIC which contains an Agent. The Agent communicates with certain Token Ring management stations on the ring through MAC frame transmissions. The management station roles are predefined by the Token Ring architecture.

The roles played by these stations are very important when it comes to maintaining ring communication integrity. These roles include local ring management roles and ring management server roles. Local ring management roles serve to synchronize communications on a local ring. The ring management server roles interact with the LAN Manager/IBM Systems Networking Architecture (SNA) environment. As Chapter 1 discusses, the ring management roles use the IBM Network Management protocol (IBMNM) to communicate with each other.

Some of the management roles do not restrict the stations to only the management role assigned. Those stations can also function as general ring stations. The individual role descriptions below specify for which management roles this is true.

The ring management roles are standby monitor (SM), active monitor (AM), configuration report server (CRS), ring parameter server (RPS), ring error monitor (REM), LAN bridge server (LBS), and the LAN reporting mechanism (LRM).

Standby Monitors (SMs)

SMs are not solely defined by management functions, but rather they are all general RSes on the ring. Standby monitors do act in local management roles at times, because they are responsible for detecting failures that may occur with the active monitor. If the SMs do not detect an Active Monitor Present MAC frame on the ring, they go into contention for the active monitor role. (See the Token Claiming section below.)

The important point is that the Agent on the NIC of every RS is involved in MAC conversations with key management stations, such as the AM, CRS, RPS, REM, LBS, and the LRM.

SMs communicate with the management stations when they need to engage in ring control conversations. The management stations themselves may also initiate the conversation, to access certain information from an SM about the station itself or to inquire about the current frame it is controlling.

SMs may also request certain important ring parameters from one of the management stations, as discussed below.

Active Monitor (AM)

The leading local management role is that of the AM. The AM also can function as a general RS on the ring.

The AM is the main communication manager on the ring. It is responsible for maintaining key transfer of data and control information balanced between all the stations on the ring. Token Ring architecture looks to the AM continually for stabilization reference points to maintain ring integrity (see fig. 2.9).

FIGURE 2.9
One station on the
ring serves as the
active monitor
(AM). Other active
stations on the
ring serve as
standby monitors.

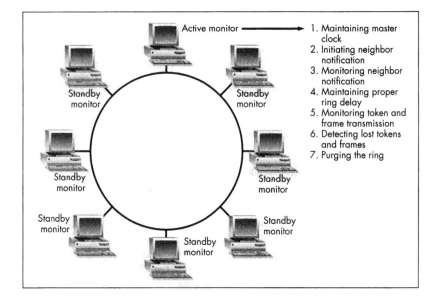

The AM has seven main responsibilities:

- Maintaining the master clock

- Initiating Neighbor Notification

- Monitoring Neighbor Notification

- Maintaining proper ring delay

- Monitoring token and frame transmission

- Detecting lost token and frames

- Purging the ring

Maintaining the Master Clock. The AM is responsible for maintaining the ring's master clock, which controls timing on the Token Ring network by making sure all station clocks are synchronized. The master clock references Token Ring protocol timers inherent to the Token Ring architecture.

Initiating Neighbor Notification. The AM regularly transmits an Active Monitor Present MAC frame. The frame is transmitted minimally every 7 seconds by T(NEIGHBOR_NOTIFICATION), one of the Token Ring protocol timers built into the Token Ring architecture.

The AM is responsible for broadcasting the frame to every station on the ring. The transmission of this frame starts the Neighbor Notification process.

Monitoring Neighbor Notification. The AM maintains a constant status of the Neighbor Notification process as it occurs on the ring. It uses the Token Ring protocol timers to monitor the process. If any interruptions occur during the process, the AM takes appropriate management steps via MAC frame communication to stabilize the ring.

Maintaining proper ring delay. The AM injects a 24-bit delay pattern into the ring. This ensures that a token sent from an originating station is completely transmitted to the destination station before returning to the originating station. Without the 24-bit delay, ring overlap could occur. The 24-bit delay sent by the AM ensures proper ring delay.

Monitoring token and frame transmission. The AM interrogates the monitor bit in the Access Control field of every token and frame it intercepts. The AM uses the monitor bit as a reference point to check for completed frame transmission between stations on the ring. The AM checks whether the bit has been reset by the last transmission on the ring. If the status is not correct, the AM purges the ring, as discussed later in this section.

Detecting lost token and frames. The Token Ring architecture dictates that it should not take any longer than 10 milliseconds for a frame to circle the ring. The AM references a Token Ring protocol timer called T(ANY_TOKEN) for the 10-millisecond interval. The AM checks to make sure that it detects a starting delimiter from a frame or token within that timer period. If it does not see a frame, and the timer expires, the AM purges the ring.

Purging the ring. The AM broadcasts a Ring Purge frame when it has to clear the ring to originate a new token. This occurs when the AM detects a disruption on the ring in the active timing between stations or the improper execution of a Token Ring process. When the AM generates the frame it resets all the RSes to Normal Repeat mode and resets all Token Ring protocol timers. This restarts the Neighbor Notification process.

Only one station on the ring plays the role of AM at any given time. The role is assigned dynamically according to Token Ring actions on the ring. Any RS on the ring can be assigned the role. The active RS with the current highest active address on the ring that wins a process called Token Claiming becomes the AM.

Configuration Report Server (CRS)

The configuration report server is a ring management server role played by one RS in a multiple-ring environment where ring management is to be accomplished from a central point. The central point is the Token Ring LAN Manager console. (LAN Manager is discussed later in this section.) Every ring in a multiple-ring environment has one CRS present. The CRS can also act as a general RS.

The main responsibility of the CRS is to collect important statistical information from the ring and forward that information to the LAN Manager console. The information includes individual RS statistics such as NAUN changes and New Monitor MAC frame transmissions.

The CRS can also change and set individual RS parameters on a ring as requested by the LAN Manager console. For instance, the LAN Manager console can request that the CRS remove an RS from the ring.

Ring Parameter Server (RPS)

The RPS plays a local management and a ring management server role. Every ring usually has one RS that acts as an RPS. This role is also critical in a multiple-ring environment, because the RPS communicates certain local ring information to the Token Ring LAN Manager console. The RPS can also act as a general RS.

The RPS provides three main services:

- The RPS is responsible for sending ring initialization parameters to all new RSes attaching to the ring. This information includes the logical ring number, the RPS version level, and the soft-error timer value.

- The RPS monitors the RSes by requesting their ring station address, their ring station microcode level, and their NAUN's address. The RPS uses this information to monitor all RSes to ensure that their attachment status is consistent with normal ring operational parameters.

- The RPS communicates regularly with the LAN Manager console to forward all the current RS status information that it collects.

Ring Error Monitor (REM)

When it comes to important roles in troubleshooting, none is more important than that of the REM. The REM's sole purpose is gathering ring errors, as a reference for troubleshooting ring problems. The REM can play both local management and ring management server roles. The REM usually does not act as a general RS; it is dedicated to the process of gathering error statistics.

The REM has three main functions:

- The REM collects soft and hard errors from all stations that generate errors on the ring. Each RS's Agent must transmit any errors to the functional address of the REM.

- The REM analyzes the soft errors it receives and decides whether Token Ring thresholds are exceeded. If it determines that they have been, it attempts to isolate the error to a fault domain.

- The REM is responsible for forwarding all errors it receives to the LAN Manager functional address.

The REM is the role that most Token Ring protocol analyzers assume when they are used on the ring for troubleshooting.

LAN Bridge Server (LBS)

The LBS monitors important statistical information about data routed between two or more rings connected by a bridge. The LBS is a ring management server role.

The LBS communicates the statistics it gathers to the Token Ring LAN Manager console. The LBS can also act as a general RS.

Most multiple-ring environments use the LBS function to keep the LAN Manager updated about dynamic changes that occur on the routing channels between RSes on different rings. The LBS also monitors the actual performance of a bridge on the ring by counting the number of frames actually transmitted through the bridge, and by detecting any lost or discarded frames that travel through the bridge.

LAN Reporting Mechanism (LRM)

The LRM is a ring management server function responsible for maintaining communication between a LAN Manager console and any remote management servers.

Even though the LRM is defined as a ring management server itself, the LRM is usually collocated within each of the other ring management servers (see fig. 2.10).

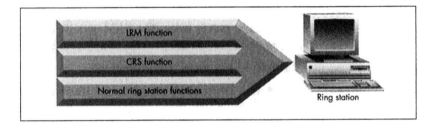

LAN Manager and SNA Relationship

It should now be apparent that the main purpose of the Token Ring management components is to provide a centralized point from which to comprehensively manage a complete Token Ring environment.

The central point is a function called the LAN Manager. The LAN Manager interacts with all the ring management servers described above to collect, analyze, and log statistical data about the whole Token Ring environment. In a multiple-ring configuration, the ring management servers communicate through the LRM to constantly update the LAN Manager with vital ring statistics. The LAN Manager can take necessary management actions based upon the information it receives from the other management servers.

The LAN Manager function usually resides within a dedicated console, but the function can be collocated within other ring management servers. IBM has a LAN Manager product called "LAN Manager" that provides a ring with both the REM and LAN Manager functional addressees. Some third-party companies have developed products that use the LAN Manager functional address so their products can collect and manipulate the data addressed to a LAN Manager console.

The LAN Manager function also illustrates that IBM has created a function that blends directly into its Systems Networking Architecture (SNA). SNA is IBM's ultimate design scheme for how IBM hardware and software should communicate over a data communications network. SNA was originally conceived for IBM's mainframe arena, but with the birth of LANs it has become the key access method for LAN-to-IBM host communications.

An SNA network has certain defined communication points, the main three being systems services control points (SSCPs), physical units (PUs), and logical units (LUs). An SNA network uses these points to establish communication throughout the mix of software and hardware entities within a computing environment (see fig. 2.11).

FIGURE 2.11
The three main communication points in an SNA network: system services control points (SSCPs), physical units (PUs), and logical units (LUs).

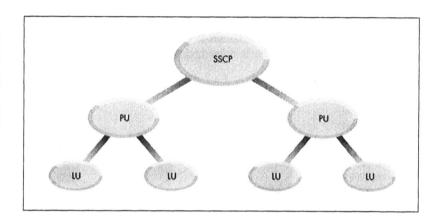

The SSCP is the main control point in an SNA network. It controls communication to a PU, which in turn can communicate with LUs. Through updates in the SNA structure two LUs can now communicate with each other through multiple SSCPs. This is called an LU-LU session. It allows two remote PCs on remotely different LANs to communicate with each other directly through the SNA architecture (see fig. 2.12).

FIGURE 2.12
LU-to-LU sessions allow remote PCs on different LANs to communicate with each other by means of the SNA architecture.

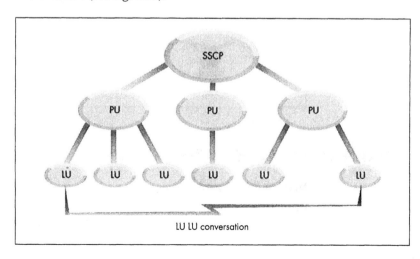

This book does not cover SNA. To get a full understanding of the SNA architecture and concepts, refer to the SNA source listed in Appendix A.

What is important for our discussion is that the Token Ring architecture provides for the LAN Manager to communicate with the SNA environment via an SSCP. This makes the Token Ring architecture the most comfortable way to interface with an IBM host environment.

Figure 2.13 shows an overall view of how all the Token Ring management roles and the LAN management roles interact.

FIGURE 2.13
Interaction of Token Ring and LAN management roles: LAN manager, system services control point (SSCP), active monitor (AM), configuration report server (CRS), ring parameter server (RPS), and LAN bridge server (LBS).

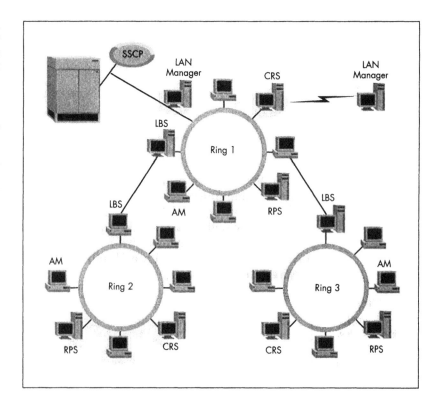

TOKEN RING COMMUNICATION

Ring Insertion

Ring Insertion is the process every station must go through to actively attach itself to a Token Ring network. This process usually begins when activated by either a software or a hardware process initiated by the station user—either turning on a station or activating a network start program. (Ring Recovery may also start the process, as discussed later in this section.)

A station is not considered an active SM until it has completed a five-phase process, Ring Insertion.

Phase 0: Lobe Media Check/Physical Insertion. The lobe media check test is when the NIC transmits the Lobe Test MAC frame to the MAU port, which will test the loop bit error rate between the NIC and the MAU port. If the frame is received back okay, the NIC sends the station attach signal (phantom DC current) through the station lobe cable to activate the MAU port it is going to attach to. During this phase you will actually hear the MAU port click. The click is the sound of a relay opening in the port hardware. When this occurs the station physically connects to the ring via the MAU port (see fig. 2.14).

FIGURE 2.14
A ring station physically attaches to the ring at the MAU during Phase 0 of the ring insertion process.

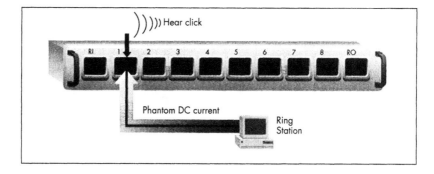

Phase 1: Monitor Check. A station that has just connected to the ring will next start its T(Attach) Token Ring protocol timer. While this timer is running the station looks to see if there is an AM on the ring. The station waits to see if it receives one of three MAC frames: Active Monitor Present, Standby Monitor Present, or Ring Purge.

If the station detects one of the three MAC frames before the timer expires, it assumes an AM is present on the ring, and it moves to Phase 2. If the station does not detect one of the three frames, it initiates the Token Claiming process.

Phase 2: Duplicate Address Verification. The main purpose of this phase is to ensure that no other station on the ring has the same address as the station that is trying to attach. The station generates a Duplicate Address Test MAC frame onto the ring. The MAC frame is addressed to the station that transmits it, so the same station should receive the frame back; if it does, no other station on the ring has the same address. It also tests the ability of the station to receive frames. If the station does not receive the frame back, it removes itself from the ring and restarts the Ring Insertion process (see fig. 2.15).

FIGURE 2.15
Duplicate address verification occurs during Phase 2 of the ring insertion process. If a new station receives its Duplicate Address Test frame back, it knows no other station on the ring has its address.

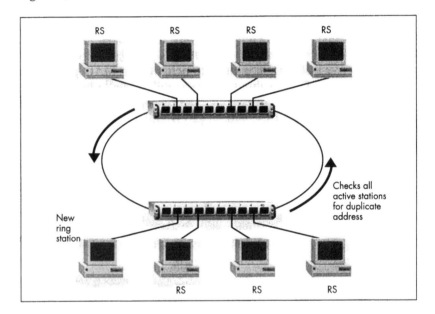

Phase 3: Neighbor Notification. During this phase the station participates in the Neighbor Notification process for the first time. The station learns the address of its NAUN and notifies its nearest active downstream neighbor of its own address. If there is any interruption in this process (such as beaconing), the station removes itself from the ring and restarts the Ring Insertion process (see fig. 2.16).

Phase 4: Request Initialization. Every RS has its own preconfigured default operational parameters for the local ring number and soft error report timer values. The Request Initialization phase—Phase 4—allows an RPS if present on the ring to check the integrity of every new station attempting Ring Insertion.

FIGURE 2.16
A new ring station participates in neighbor notification for the first time, learning the address of its NAUN and notifying its nearest active downstream neighbor of its own address.

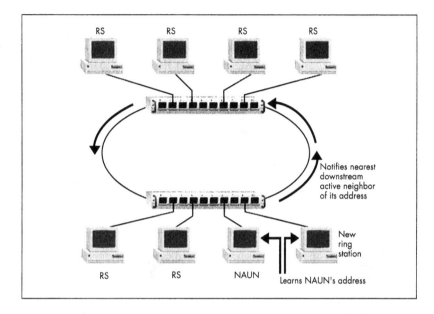

During this phase, the new station generates a Request Initialization MAC frame on the ring addressed to the RPS. This frame lets the RPS know that a station has attached to the ring and is ready to accept any special operational parameters that the RPS has available for the ring. The RPS then sends an Initialize Ring Station MAC frame, which will set the new station for the correct ring number and soft error report timer values. If the RPS does have any special parameters, it transmits them to the new station.

Note that if the RPS sees any problem with the information included in the Request Initialization MAC frame or if too many stations are on the ring, it notifies a LAN Manager console. The LAN Manager console then notifies the CRS to transmit a Remove Ring Station MAC frame to the new RS, which causes the RS to be removed from the ring.

When all five phases are complete, the new station becomes a physically and logically attached RS (see fig. 2.17).

Token Claiming

Only one RS on the ring is designated as the AM. Token Claiming is the process during which SMs go into contention to win the AM role. Token Claiming occurs on the ring when one of three conditions arises:

- A new station attaches to the ring but does not detect an AM on the ring. This can occur if the new station does not receive an Active Monitor Present MAC frame on the ring during the Ring Insertion process.

- The AM cannot detect any frames on the ring and its T(Receive_Notification) Token Ring protocol timer expires.

- An SM detects the absence of an AM or cannot detect any frames on the ring, and its T(Good_Token) or T(Receive_Notification) protocol timers expire.

FIGURE 2.17
When the ring insertion process is complete, the new station becomes a physically and logically attached ring station active on the network.

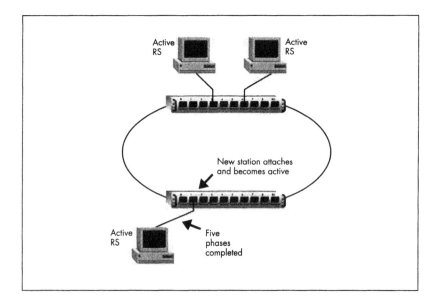

Not all stations participate in the Token Claiming process, because the default mode is for a station not to participate. There are two main modes that stations will operate under during the process: Claim Token Transmit mode and Claim Token Repeat mode.

All stations participating in the process go into contention to win the AM role. The station with the highest Token Ring address wins the process. When one of the three conditions above occurs, the process is initiated by either an SM or the AM.

The stations that participate are in the Claim Token Transmit mode. Stations that are not participants are in Claim Token Repeat mode. The station that first initiates the process enters the Claim Token Transmit mode by generating a Claim Token MAC frame addressed to itself onto the ring. Each station that receives the frame enters the Claim Token Repeat mode.

Every station in the Claim Token Repeat mode compares its address to the address in the Claim Token MAC frame it receives. If its address is higher, it also becomes a participant in the Token Claiming process by generating its own Claim Token MAC frame. This process continues around the ring until a Token Claiming participant receives its own Claim Token MAC frame back three times. When this occurs, that station assumes that it has the highest address, and it wins the AM role (see fig. 2.18).

FIGURE 2.18
During the token claiming process, all the participating ring stations on the network vie for the active monitor role. The station with the highest address assumes the AM role.

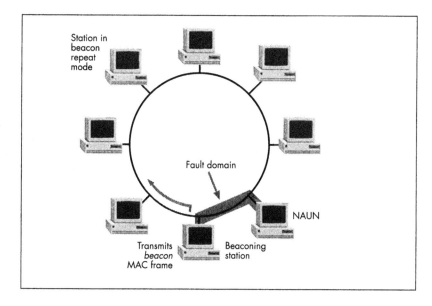

Priority Access

Priority Access is the qualifying method by which all RSes attain a certain priority for their turn to gain control of the token. Only one station at a time can have control of the token. In the token frame and MAC/LLC frames is a field called the Access Control field. The Access Control field is a one-byte field that controls how a station actually references a frame or token for access to the ring.

In the Access Control field, the first three bits are the priority bits, which indicate the current priority of a certain token or frame. The last three bits of the Access Control field are the reservation bits, which an RS uses to request a certain priority to gain access to the ring. The priority bits and reservation bits range from 111 (the highest priority) to 000 (the lowest priority). All RSes can request and raise the priority level of the ring.

The Access Control field also contains a bit called the monitor bit, which is used to prevent a frame or token from controlling the ring by continuously circling the ring. The monitor bit can be set to either a 0 or a 1 state. When any RS transmits a frame or token onto the ring it sets the monitor bit to the 0 state. One of the checks that occurs when an AM interrogates a frame or token is to check the state of the monitor bit. The AM sets this bit to the 1 state if it is in a 0 state.

But if the bit is received at the AM in a 1 state, the AM assumes that the frame or token has circled the ring at least once without being received back at its originating station. The AM resets the bit to a 0 state and generates the Ring Purge process to establish ring recovery. This helps to ensure priority fairness on the ring.

The priority access method truly is a fair system. The mechanism ensures that all stations have an equal chance to access the ring. This is enforced in that a station that raises the priority level of the ring has to return the priority level back to its original state.

Again, RSes use the Access Control fields to look at both the priority of a given frame or token and to reserve the use of a frame or token for a certain priority.

Neighbor Notification

Neighbor Notification is a logical consecutive process by which every RS is informed of its NAUN's address.

Every MAC/LLC frame has in its structure a Frame Status (FS) field. The FS field is a one-byte field that reflects the current status of the respective frame. Within the FS field are two important bits: the addressed recognized bits (A bits) and the frame copied bits (C bits). The Neighbor Notification process then:

- Looks at the A bits to verify if the frame is currently recognized by the last station source address (SA) included in the frame

- Looks at the C bits to see if the SA copied the frame successfully

The AM initiates the Neighbor Notification process. The following events occur during the Neighbor Notification process:

- The AM initiates the process by generating an Active Monitor Present (AMP) MAC frame onto the ring. When it starts the process it sets an internal flag signaling that the process is starting. The frame is broadcast on the ring to all stations. The A and C bits can be set to one of two logical states, 0 and 1. When the AM generates the frame, the A and C bits in the FS field are set to a 0 state.

- The first active SM that receives the AMP MAC frame resets the A and C bits to the 1 state. Next the SM copies the frame into its buffer. It stores the Upstream Neighbors Address (UNA) from the SA field of the AMP frame. It then starts its T(Notification_Response) timer. When the timer expires, the SM transmits a Standby Monitor Present (SMP) MAC frame back on the ring in an all-stations broadcast. The A and C bits in the SMP frame are reset to the 0 state.

- The next active SM on the ring that receives the SMP frame repeats the above process.

- This process continues around the ring until the AM copies the last SMP frame, then sets its internal flag.

This completes the Neighbor Notification process.

Normal Repeat Mode

Every RS has a state called Normal Repeat mode. When it is in this state, the RS can interrogate all the tokens and frames it receives and can properly copy and repeat them.

Ring Purge

The Ring Purge process is the attempted resetting of the ring to Normal Repeat mode. The AM initiates the Ring Purge process, for four possible reasons:

- When the AM detects an error condition on the ring such as a lost token or frames, a disruption on the ring in the active timing between stations, or the improper execution of a Token Ring process

- When the AM detects the M bit set to the 1 state in the Access Control field of a token or frame

- In order to set the ring back to Normal Repeat mode

- When the AM sees the T(Any_Token) timer expire

After the AM generates the frame, it waits to receive the frame back. If the AM receives the frame back, it assumes that the ring is stabilized, and it resets all Token Ring protocol timers. Next the AM initiates the Neighbor Notification process to restart and put the ring back into Normal Repeat mode.

If for some reason the AM does not receive the frame back, it enters the Claim Token Transmit mode.

Beaconing

Beaconing is the Token Ring process that occurs when an RS generates a warning signal onto the ring after it sees a hard error occur with itself or with its NAUN. The warning signal is the Beacon MAC frame. The Beacon MAC frame has three important fields: the Beacon Generating Station Address, the NAUN, and the Beacon type. The Beacon type can help isolate the location of the hard error problem.

The Agent on every NIC can detect soft and hard errors on the ring. When an RS detects a hard error (such as a cable fault or an improper bitstream transmission), that respective station transmits the Beacon MAC frame onto the ring. The frame is addressed to all stations.

Note that if an REM is present on the ring, it is the key responder to this frame. The REM will generate an Alert warning to the LAN Manager and will record the error in a statistical log.

The station that transmits the Beacon MAC frame is not necessarily the faulty station. The main suspect is usually the NAUN of the station that generates the frame, because every RS is in a listen/receive mode at Normal Repeat mode. But it is also possible that the failure area is either the beaconing station, the NAUN, or even the medium (cable) between the two stations. This logical area is defined by the Token Ring architecture as the fault domain (see fig. 2.19).

FIGURE 2.19
A fault domain
is the logical area
of a hard error
fault in
the Token Ring
network.

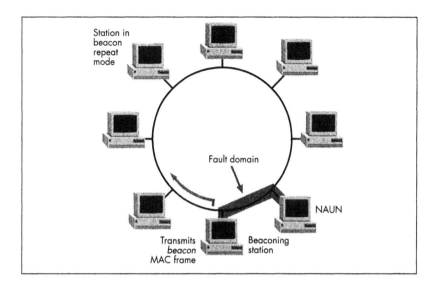

Fault Domain

The fault domain is the logical area of a hard error fault as determined by the Token Ring architecture. The architecture uses the beaconing process to isolate a failure to a fault domain.

The logical area includes three subcomponents:

- The RS transmitting the Beacon MAC frame

- The beaconing station's NAUN

- The connection medium (cable) between the beaconing station and its respective NAUN

You can see how the fault domain concept is a key factor in pinpointing the true location of the cause of failure.

To locate the exact true point of failure within the fault domain, the Token Ring architecture uses the statistics it intercepts from the beaconing process to enter a testing phase called either attempted auto-recovery or auto-reconfiguration. During attempted auto-recovery:

- An RS encounters a hard error and transmits a Beacon MAC frame to an all-stations broadcast. The frame identifies the address of the beaconing station's NAUN.

- Every RS on the ring enters the Beacon Repeat mode, which means they will copy and repeat the frame around the ring.

- The Token Ring architecture locates the fault domain.

- After the beaconing station's NAUN copies the Beacon MAC frame eight times, it removes itself from the ring and goes through a series of self tests. These tests include the Lobe Media and the Duplicate Address tests used in the Ring Insertion process.

- If the NAUN station fails any of the self tests, it removes itself from the ring. The beaconing station then receives the Beacon MAC frame back, and it retransmits a token frame back onto the ring. At this point the ring will have auto-recovered.

- However, if the NAUN station passes all the self tests, it reinserts itself back onto the ring without going through the full Ring Insertion process. Then the beaconing station assumes that its NAUN test has passed, and it takes itself off the ring and goes through the same series of self tests.

- If a beaconing station fails any of the self tests it will remove itself from the ring. The AM will initiate a ring recovery by issuing a Ring Purge and will restart the Token Claiming process.

- If the beaconing station does not fail any of the self tests, it also reinserts itself back onto the ring without going through the full Ring Insertion process. If this occurs and there is still a beaconing condition, the problem requires manual trouble-shooting. The ring is unable to auto-recover and all Token Ring operations are impaired. At this point it's very probable that the problem is with the cabling medium.

To summarize, the concepts of beaconing and fault domains allow for a hard error to be automatically located and eliminated with minimal effect on normal ring operations. These functions add to the fault-tolerance claims of the Token Ring architecture.

Soft Error Counting

Soft errors are less-serious errors that can occur on the ring. They are classified as intermittent and do not necessarily indicate the presence of a serious failure on the ring. When the ring encounters soft errors the normal mode of operation is only temporarily disrupted.

When a soft error occurs the Token Ring architecture attempts to go through a recovery process to log the soft error and to stabilize the ring. Every RS maintains a group of counters to gauge the level of soft errors that it may encounter.

The following steps occur after a soft error:

- If an RS encounters a soft error, the RS's internal counter increments its soft error counter and starts a Token Ring protocol timer T(Soft_Error_Report)

- When the timer is expired the RS generates onto the ring a Report Soft Error MAC frame addressed to the REM functional address

- After the RS transmits the Report_Soft_Error MAC frame it resets its soft error counter and enters the normal mode of operation

The Report Soft Error MAC frame includes the number of soft errors that occur, the RS transmitting station, its NAUN, and the classification type of the soft error.

Some of the errors that occur cause ring performance degradation, which can be measured by the number of ring recoveries that occur. Ring recovery is the process of the ring resetting itself back into a normal mode of operation. Ring recoveries are one of the statistics that can be recorded through protocol analysis.

Ring reconfiguration is the logical process that occurs during Neighbor Notification when certain active RSes enter or leave the ring.

Chapter 6 discusses ring recoveries, ring reconfiguration, and soft errors.

One last note on soft error counting. If the transmitting RS T(Soft_Error_Report) timer expires and does not transmit a Report Soft Error MAC frame, the AM detects the condition and transmits the Report Soft Error MAC frame onto the ring, addressed to the REM.

Hard Error Counting

Hard errors are more serious errors that can occur on the ring. A hard error is an actual solid failure. When an RS detects a hard error it enters the beaconing/fault domain processes to attempt Ring Recovery.

Note that the Ring Recovery process for hard errors is different from its soft error equivalent. When an RS encounters a soft error the Ring Recovery process is usually successful in restoring the ring to normal operation. But with hard errors the actual locating and resolving of hard failures may require an RS be removed, or the repair of the cabling medium.

When hard errors occur, the REM works in conjunction with the LAN Manager console to provide an overall error-management strategy. This strategy effectively provides alert notification and statistical logging of errors that occur on the ring.

Finite State Machines

The Token Ring architecture defines the different modes of relationship between the Token Ring processes as finite state machines. As the Token Ring protocols interrelate on the ring, they are constantly changing states, meaning that the ring itself is always undergoing transitions in its actual mode of operation. This is analogous to the human brain as it constantly enters different states of thought which cause us to take a certain action. The Token Ring architecture also undergoes constant changes in state, causing certain events on the ring that affect the status of the ring. The process is extremely dynamic.

There are many finite state machines on the ring. We cannot cover all the different states here; see reference 1 in Appendix A for further information.

Token Ring Protocol Timers

The Token Ring architecture includes a set of clock utilities called the Token Ring protocol timers. The architecture uses these timers to synchronize the protocols that interrelate on the ring. The architecture also uses the timers to reference proper communication, and it enters certain finite states depending on the protocol-related action.

Timer characteristics break down into the following categories:

- The activation point of the timer
- The action of the timer
- The condition that cancels the timer
- The timing value or duration of the timer

The following descriptions detail each timer's specific role in the Token Ring architecture.

T(Attach). The T(Attach) timer is used to set how long a station can stay in the Ring Insertion process. It is activated when a station enters Phase 1 (Monitor Check) of the Ring Insertion process. T(Attach) will time out after an 18-second period if the Ring Insertion process encounters any problems and is not completed. The timer can be canceled earlier if the process completes before the 18-second period.

T(Claim_Token). The T(Claim_Token) timer sets the length of time that an RS can wait for an AM to win the Token Claiming process while in the Claim Token Repeat mode or the Claim Token Transmit mode. The timer starts when an RS enters either of the two modes. The timer can time out after one second if an AM is not selected. If the Token Claiming process is completed, this timer can be canceled.

T(Any_Token). The T(Any_Token) timer sets the amount of time an AM can wait before it detects a starting delimiter sequence from a token or frame. The timer starts when the AM transmits its first token. The timer will time out after 10 milliseconds if it does not detect a starting delimiter.

T(Physical_Trailer). The T(Physical_Trailer) timer helps to detect improperly transmitted frames. The timer starts when a station transmits a frame. When the station receives the frame back, it attempts to strip the frame's ending delimiter. If the frame is not returned or is not properly copied in 4.1 seconds, the timer will time out and will increment a lost-frame counter. It next attempts to enter Normal Repeat mode. A soft error may be counted and the ring may possibly be purged by the AM.

T(Good_Token). The T(Good_Token) timer helps monitor the ring for problems related to failure of the AM function. It starts at the beginning of the SM function and is reactivated when it detects a proper token/frame sequence on the ring. The timer detects loss of the AM and frame or bitstreaming, which is the (unintentional) continuous transmission of data. The timer will time out in 2.6

seconds if it detects a failure, and the RS will enter the Claim Token Transmit mode.

T(Response). The T(Response) timer monitors the length of time an RS must wait before receiving a proper response to a transmitted frame. The timer starts when an RS transmits a frame that requires a response. The timer will time out in 2.5 seconds if the RS does not see the response frame return, but it will be stopped if the response frame is returned and properly copied. If the timer does time out, the station usually reattempts transmission.

T(Soft_Error_Report). The T(Soft_Error_Report) timer is used to balance the length of time during which an RS can transmit a Report Soft Error MAC Frame. This balance allows the soft error counter to accrue multiple error counts without constantly transmitting the errors and congesting the ring. The timer starts when a ring station soft error counter is incremented. It will time out in 2 seconds and a Report Soft Error MAC Frame will be generated.

T(Transmit_Pacing). The T(Transmit_Pacing) timer helps monitor how long an RS must wait before transmitting Beacon and Claim Token MAC frames. The timer starts when an RS transmits a Beacon or Claim Token MAC frame. The timer will time out in 20 milliseconds if the RS improperly transmits one of the frames. When the timer times out, the RS attempts to retransmit the appropriate frame.

T(Beacon_Transmit). The T(Beacon_Transmit) timer helps to monitor the length of time an RS can transmit Beacon MAC frames before it removes itself from the ring to run a self test. The timer starts when an RS transmits a Beacon MAC frame. If the RS detects Ring Recovery, the timer stops; if it does not detect recovery after 16 seconds, the timer expires and the RS removes itself and runs the self tests.

T(Escape). The T(Escape) timer is used to monitor the length of time an RS can stay in the Beacon Repeat mode before it enters the Claim Token Transmit mode. The timer starts when an RS receives a Beacon MAC frame. Every RS can stay in the Beacon Repeat mode for 200 milliseconds without copying another Beacon MAC frame. If it does not within 200 milliseconds, the timer expires and the RS also enters the Claim Token Transmit mode.

T(Ring_Purge). The T(Ring_Purge) timer monitors the length of time the AM can stay in the Ring Purge process before it stops and enters the Claim Token Transmit mode. The timer length is

1 second, starting at the beginning of the ring-purge process. When it times out, the AM enters the Claim Token Transmit mode.

T(Neighbor_Notification). The T(Neighbor_Notification) timer is used to monitor the Neighbor Notification process. The timer starts when the AM transmits an Active Monitor Present MAC frame. The timer runs for 7 seconds. If it does not copy a Standby Monitor Present MAC frame in that time, the AM retransmits an Active Monitor Present MAC frame and attempts to restart the Neighbor Notification process.

T(Notification_Response). The T(Notification_Response) timer is used to balance the delay between the time in which an RS receives either a Standby Monitor Present or an Active Monitor Present MAC frame and attempts to transmit another Standby Monitor Present MAC frame back out onto the ring. The timer starts when an RS receives an Active Monitor Present or a Standby Monitor Present MAC frame. The timer runs for 20 milliseconds before transmitting a Standby Monitor Present MAC frame.

T(Receive_Notification). SMs use the T(Receive_Notification) timer to verify that the Neighbor Notification process occurs in a timely and proper manner on the ring. The timer starts at the beginning of the SM function. Its duration is 15 seconds, during which it expects to receive an Active Monitor Present MAC frame. If T(Receive_Notification) times out, the SM enters the Claim Token Transmit mode.

802.5 IEEE STANDARD FRAME FORMAT

The three different frame types are the token frame, the data frame, and the abort sequence. The following paragraphs describe the three frame types at the sequence field level.

Token Frame

The token frame is a three-byte frame. It is the actual control signal for the ring. Figure 2.20 shows its format.

Field 1 - Starting Delimiter field. The Starting Delimiter field signals the start of a token frame, a data frame, and the abort sequence. The field is one byte and is formatted as shown in figure 2.21.

FIGURE 2.20
The format of the
three-byte token
frame.

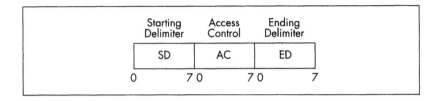

Bits 0 to 7 are always represented exactly as shown in the figure. The J and K bits are code violation symbols. They represent intentional improper transitions against the clock signal in the Differential Manchester Code. This combination is derived to uniquely exhibit the frame sequence as delimiter.

FIGURE 2.21
The starting
delimiter field.

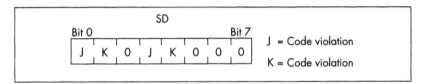

Field 2 - Access Control field. The Access Control field is a status byte that shows the current access level of a frame or token. The field is one byte and is formatted as shown in figure 2.22.

FIGURE 2.22
The one-byte-long
access control
field of the token
frame.

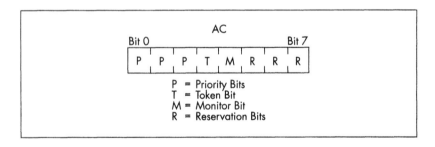

Bits 1, 2, and 3 are the priority bits. They indicate the current priority of the token or frame. The priority bits range from 111 (the highest priority) to 000 (the lowest).

The fourth bit is the token bit, which distinguishes the frame as either a token frame or a data frame. If the bit is set to 1, the frame is a data frame; if the bit is a 0, it is a token frame.

The fifth bit is the monitor bit. The AM monitors this bit to prevent a frame or token from continuously circling the ring. The monitor bit can be set to either a 0 or 1 state. The AM always checks the status of this bit to ensure that it is in a 0 state.

Bits 6, 7, and 8 are reservation bits. An RS sets these bits to request a required priority for gaining access to the ring. The reservation bits range from 111 (highest priority) to 000 (the lowest).

Field 3 - Ending Delimiter field. The Ending Delimiter field signals the end of a token frame, a data frame, and the abort sequence. The field is one byte and is formatted as shown in figure 2.23.

FIGURE 2.23
The one-byte ending delimiter field of a token frame.

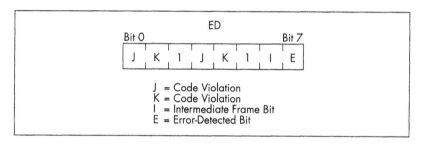

Bits 0 to 5 are always represented exactly as shown in the figure. They represent intentional violations in the Differential Manchester Code, just as with the starting delimiter.

Bit 6 is the intermediate bit and signals that a frame is either the first frame or an intermediate frame of a multiple-frame transmission. The bit state may be either 0 or 1, depending on the frame transmission state.

Bit 7 is the error-detected bit; it flags a frame that contains possible errors in the frame check sequence. The status should be 0 at normal state.

Data Frame

The data frame is a variable-length frame, because it contains either ring control or data information. The frame includes 10 main frame sequences.

The frame will carry a designation as either a MAC frame or an LLC frame. There are 25 MAC frame types, which are discussed later in this section. The LLC frames carry the protocol data unit (PDU) which envelopes the actual high-level user-data information transmitted on the ring. The PDU is also detailed later in this section.

A data frame has multiple frame sequences, including addressing, control, and data information (see fig. 2.24).

FIGURE 2.24
The data frame is a variable-length frame designated MAC or LLC.

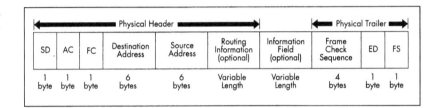

Field 1. This first byte is a standard Starting Delimiter, as discussed above in the token frame description.

Field 2. This second byte is a standard Access Control field as discussed in the token frame description.

Field 3. This third byte is the Frame Control field, which defines whether a frame is a MAC or an LLC data frame. The field is one byte and is formatted as shown in figure 2.25.

FIGURE 2.25
The one-byte frame control field designates a data frame as MAC or LLC.

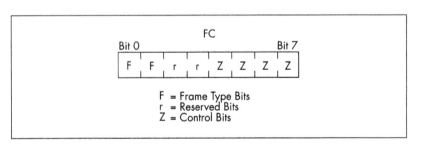

Bits 0 and 1 designate the frame type. The breakdown is Status (00) = MAC frame; Status (01) = LLC frame; Status (10) and (11) = undefined frames.

Bits 2 and 3 are reserved for future IBM designations.

Bit 4 to 7 are called control bits. If the frame is designated as an LLC frame, the bits are reserved for future IBM designations.

If the frame is a MAC frame, the control bits designate how the frame is supposed to be copied into the destination station's input buffers. Each station has normal input buffers and express buffers. If the bits' value equals zero (0000), they are copied into the normal buffer. If the bits have a higher value, the frame is tagged as an express buffer frame, is copied into the express buffer, and is processed at the MAC layer immediately. A frame is usually only tagged "express" if the destination address' normal buffers are full.

Field 4. The next six bytes are the identifiers of the Destination Address. This is the address or addresses of the RS or group of stations that are supposed to receive the frame. The destination address identifier always occupies six bytes and is formatted as shown in figure 2.26.

FIGURE 2.26
A data-frame destination address identifier.

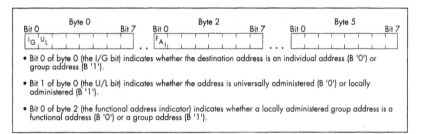

- Bit 0 of byte 0 (the I/G bit) indicates whether the destination address is an individual address (B '0') or group address (B '1').

- Bit 1 of byte 0 (the U/L bit) indicates whether the address is universally administered (B '0') or locally administered (B '1').

- Bit 0 of byte 2 (the functional address indicator) indicates whether a locally administered group address is a functional address (B '0') or a group address (B '1').

Field 5. The next six bytes identify the Source Address. This is the address of the RS that generated the frame (also called the originating station). The source address identifier always occupies six bytes and is formatted as shown in figure 2.27.

FIGURE 2.27
The six-byte source address identifier of a data frame.

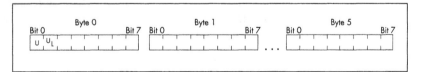

Field 6. This field is called the Routing Information field and contains routing information if the frame is addressed to an RS on a ring other than the source ring in a multiple-ring environment. A bridge or router will interrogate this field. The field is variable length from two to 18 bytes long and is formatted as shown in figure 2.28.

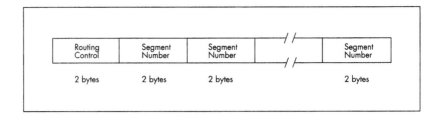

Field 7. This field is the Information field that carries MAC or LLC information.

If the frame is designated as a MAC frame, this field starts with a two-byte sequence called a length identifier (LL). The LL marks the length of the information field.

The next two bytes are the major vector ID (MVID). The MVID indicates the main function and class of the MAC-frame information that follows next.

The next sequence is a variable-length sequence called the MAC subvector, which is the MAC control information data and is formatted as shown in figure 2.29.

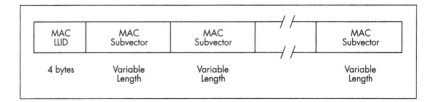

If the frame is an LLC frame, this field is called an LLC protocol data unit (PDU), because it carries data and the necessary protocol information to exchange the data.

The LLC PDU is broken down as follows: The first sequence is a one-byte sequence called the destination service access point (DSAP). The DSAP labels the service access point for the following data.

The next byte is the source service access point (SSAP). The SSAP identifies the service access point that originated the data. The DSAP and SSAP are used locally by the path control layer in the Token Ring network protocol model. They are mainly referenced for addressing in an SNA environment.

The next field is called the Control field and is either one or two bytes long. It designates the type of data as being normal user data, supervisory, or unnumbered. The supervisory destination means that the data is control data for exchanging PDUs. The unnumbered destination means that the data is in unsequenced format.

The next field is a variable-length field containing the actual data information and is formatted as shown in figure 2.30.

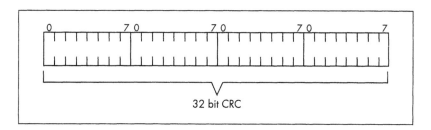

Field 8. This field is called the Frame Check Sequence and is a 32-bit cyclic redundancy check (CRC). The CRC is an error-checking method that involves a calculation of the bit transmission at the sending and receiving ends of each RS. The CRC can detect errors in transmission by bit-calculation errors. The field is four bytes long and is formatted as shown in figure 2.31.

Field 9. This one-byte sequence is a standard Ending Delimiter, as discussed above in the token frame description.

Field 10. This field is called the Frame Status field and is a one-byte field that contains the current status of the data frame. It is formatted as shown in figure 2.32.

FIGURE 2.32
The format of the
frame status field,
field 10 of the
data frame.

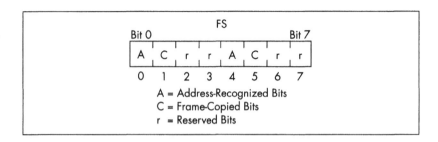

Bits 0 and 4 are the addressed recognized bits (A bits) used by the Neighbor Notification process to verify if the frame is currently recognized by the last station source address (SA).

Bits 1 and 5 are the frame copied bits (C bits). The Neighbor Notification process looks at the C bits to see if the SA copied the frame successfully.

Bits 2, 3, 6, and 7 are reserved for future IBM designations.

Abort Sequence Frame

The Abort Sequence frame is a two-byte frame used to clear the ring when there is a problem with a frame. It is composed of a standard starting and ending delimiter. Figure 2.33 shows its format.

FIGURE 2.33
The format of the
two-byte-long
abort sequence
frame.

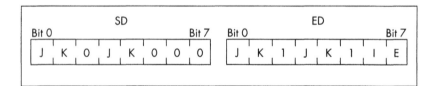

DLC.LAN and DLC.MGR

The Data Link layer of Token Ring is called the DLC.LAN. The DLC.LAN is the layer that encodes, decodes, and routes MAC and LLC information.

The DLC.LAN encompasses a manager function called the DLC.MGR. The DLC.MGR is responsible for managing the control of information between both the LLC and the MAC layers at the Data Link level. It is also critical as a routing manager between the Data Link level and the other layers of the Token Ring network protocol model. Both the Physical layer and the upper layers interact with the DLC.MGR for routing management. The SNA structure protocol model also interacts heavily with the DLC.MGR. Figure 2.34 depicts where the DLC.MGR resides.

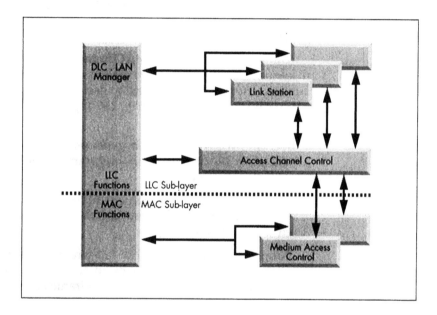

MAC Frame Types

The 25 MAC frames are the communication-protocol tools for the Token Ring architecture. They interact with all the Token Ring processes that occur on the medium. The following paragraphs detail the 25 MAC frame types.

Standby Monitor Present MAC frame. This frame is mainly used during the Neighbor Notification process. An RS generates it to notify the Nearest Active Downstream Neighbor of its address.

Active Monitor Present MAC frame. This frame notifies all SMs that an AM is functioning properly on the ring. The AM typically generates this frame to initiate the Neighbor Notification process.

Ring Station Initialization MAC frame. An RS transmits this frame to the RPS to announce that it is a new RS and is ready to receive any special ring parameters.

Initialize Ring Station MAC frame. This frame is generated by the RPS to respond to an RS's Ring Station Initialization MAC frame. The frame will set any special ring parameters.

Lobe Test MAC frame. An RS generates this frame to test for a bit-error rate with its loopback path to the MAU port. The frame is generated before the actual attachment to the ring, or during the beaconing process.

Duplicate Address Test MAC frame. An RS generates this frame to ensure there are no other stations on the ring with the same address. The frame is addressed to itself. The frame is also generated before the actual attachment to the ring or during the beaconing process.

Beacon MAC frame. An RS generates this frame when it detects a hard error on the ring. It is important in identifying the fault domain, as discussed earlier.

Claim Token MAC frame. An RS that wants to enter into the contention for the AM role generates this frame. It is used during the Token Claiming process.

Ring Purge MAC frame. The AM transmits this frame to all RSes to clear the ring and set it back to Normal Repeat mode. It is generated in the event of an error. This frame is also used at the end of the Token Claiming process.

Report Neighbor Notification Incomplete MAC frame. An RS transmits this frame during the Neighbor Notification process if it does not receive notification from its NAUN before its T(Neighbor_Notification) timer expires. The frame is transmitted to the REM functional address.

Transmit Forward MAC frame. The LAN Manager console or the CRS transmits this frame to an RS to initiate testing of the communication path on the ring.

Report Transmit Forward MAC frame. An RS transmits this frame to the LAN Manager console or the CRS to respond to a Transmit Forward MAC frame, confirming that the communication path is okay.

Report Active Monitor Error MAC frame. The AM generates this frame when it detects an error with its process. This frame is transmitted frequently during the Token Claiming process. It is transmitted to the REM functional address.

Report Soft Error MAC frame. An RS generates this frame when its T(Soft_Error_Report) timer has expired and the RS has accumulated errors in its counter. The frame is transmitted to the REM functional address.

Change Parameters MAC frame. The CRS transmits this frame to an RS that needs to have special operating parameters set.

Remove Ring Station MAC frame. The CRS transmits this frame to an RS that must be removed from the ring.

Request Ring Station State MAC frame. The CRS transmits this frame to an RS to request the operational status of the NIC in that RS.

Report Ring Station State MAC frame. An RS transmits this frame to the CRS to properly respond to a Request Ring Station State MAC frame.

Request Ring Station Attachments MAC frame. The CRS transmits this frame to an RS to interrogate the RS for the Token Ring functions that it has operational.

Report Ring Station Attachments MAC frame. An RS transmits this frame to the CRS to properly respond to a Request Ring Station Attachments MAC frame.

Request Ring Station Address MAC frame. The CRS transmits this frame to an RS to request address information.

Report Ring Station Address MAC frame. An RS transmits this frame to the CRS to properly respond to a Request Ring Station Address MAC frame.

Report NAUN Change MAC frame. An RS transmits this frame to the CRS to announce that it has received a change in its internally stored NAUN address. This usually occurs when an RS receives a new NAUN during the Neighbor Notification process.

Report New Active Monitor MAC frame. An RS transmits this frame to the CRS to notify the CRS that it has become the new AM.

Response MAC frame. An RS transmits this frame to another RS to announce the receipt of a Response MAC frame from an originating station. It is also used to communicate syntax errors in received frames from a respective station.

TOKEN RING AND NETBIOS

NetBIOS Theory

The Network Basic Input/Output System (NetBIOS) is a connection-oriented communication protocol jointly developed by Sytek Inc. and IBM for operation on IBM's PC Broadband LAN.

Originally the NetBIOS code was provided on the NIC itself within a ROM. Today on 4Mbps and 16Mbps Token Ring networks the NetBIOS is loaded with the Token Ring device drivers via the IBM LAN Support Program disk.

NetBIOS became popular very quickly, and many PC and host applications were developed upon the protocol and rely on it.

NetBIOS operates at the Session layer within the Token Ring network protocol model. It communicates by establishing a logical connection between two NetBIOS-defined names. NetBIOS sets up a logical channel for higher-level protocols to use for communication. The actual NetBIOS information is encapsulated within the information section of an LLC data frame (see figure 2.35).

FIGURE 2.35
The NetBIOS information is contained in the information field of an LLC data frame.

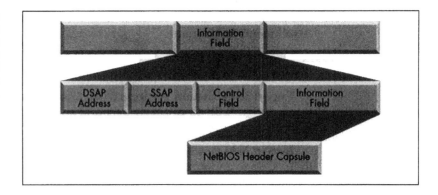

Another important protocol is the Server Message Block (SMB) protocol. Many IBM-oriented LAN operating systems (such as IBM PCLAN and IBM LAN Server) use SMB to communicate at the Application layer of the Token Ring protocol model. SMB relies on the NetBIOS protocol for communication on the ring.

You'll often cross paths with NetBIOS when monitoring and troubleshooting the Token Ring network topology. An in-depth discussion of NetBIOS and SMB is beyond the scope of this book; the following list contains the commands that NetBIOS uses to communicate.

SESSION_INITIALIZE	Sets up a session
SESSION_CONFIRM	Notifies receipt of SESSION_INITIALIZE
SESSION_ALIVE	Checks if session is active
SESSION_END	Terminates the session
DATAGRAM	A datagram transmitted by an application
DATAGRAM_BROADCAST	A broadcast datagram
DATA_ACK	Data-only acknowledgement
DATA_FIRST_MIDDLE	Data is first or middle in frame
DATA_ONLY_LAST	Data is last in frame
NAME_QUERY	Requests a name on the network
NAME_RECOGNIZED	Recognizes a name
NAME_IN_CONFLICT	Detects a duplicate name
ADD_NAME_QUERY	Checks for a duplicate name
ADD_GROUP_NAME_QUERY	Checks for a duplicate group name
ADD_NAME_RESPONSE	Detects a duplicate name after query
STATUS_QUERY	Requests status of a remote name
STATUS_RESPONSE	Reply to STATUS_QUERY
TERMINATE_TRACE	Terminates trace on local/remote names
RECEIVE_CONTINUE	Waiting for outstanding receive
RECEIVE_OUTSTANDING	Retransmit last data

chapter **3**

DEVICE TYPES AND SPECIFICATIONS

In troubleshooting LAN problems, you need a good understanding of the devices on the LAN, their specifications, and how they were designed to meet those specifications. Then you need a solid understanding of the technical guidelines for the particular topology. This is critical for isolating a particular area of the network as the point of failure. One of the trigger points will be whether particular hardware or software entities are operating within their standard specifications.

This chapter provides an overview of some of the industry-standard Token Ring devices and their specifications, and of various Token Ring products that are widely used in the industry. Many manufacturers have excellent products for the Token Ring environment; all of them cannot be detailed here. This chapter presents some of the most commonly used products in the LAN marketplace.

CABLES

The Token Ring standard has seven recognized cabling types, which are often referred to as the IBM cabling system. Many vendors manufacture cabling for the Token Ring community, and most of them try to comply with the IBM specifications for cabling design.

All seven cabling types have design specifications, along with length guidelines for use and installation. The seven IBM cabling types are listed below by their design and use specification. Figure 3.1 displays each cable type. Later in the section the way in which the lengths relate to installation is discussed.

FIGURE 3.1
The seven IBM
cabling types:
(a) shielded
twisted pair,
(b) unshielded
twisted pair, and
(c) fiber optic.

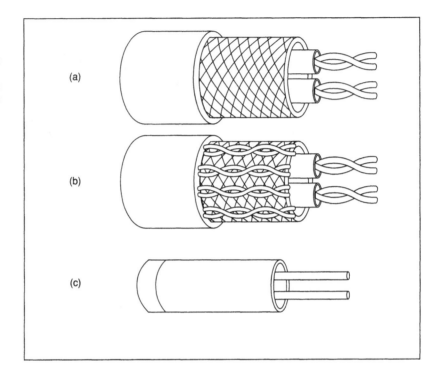

Type 1. Type 1 cable has two wire shielded twisted pairs. It is data-grade solid wire: 22 AWG (American Wire Gauge). It is the most widely used cable type and is considered the most reliable. It is not very susceptible to interference from electrical and high frequencies. This cabling type supports both 4Mbps and 16Mbps transmission.

Type 2. Type 2 cable is close to the Type 1 specification. It also has two wire shielded twisted pairs, but adds four twisted pairs of 26 AWG stranded wire between the shield and the cabling insulation. It is used frequently for cutting the expense of running extra cable in areas that need more than just a Token Ring connection.

Type 3. Type 3 cable is unshielded twisted pair. It is telephone-grade wire: 22 or 24 AWG. The number of pairs is usually two but can vary depending on the manufacturer. Given that this cable type is unshielded and is not considered data grade, type 3 is more susceptible to crosstalk and electrical interference from power cables, radio frequencies, HVAC, and so on. But with the introduction of new hubbing technologies, twisted pair is fast becoming the new standard for LAN cabling.

Among the strongest points of type 3 cable are that it is easy to install and that many buildings are already cabled with (unused) telephone wire.

Type 5. Type 5 has two solid fiber conductors. It is data grade: 100/140 micron fiber cable. Type 5 is an excellent choice for a large variety of installations. Type 5 cable offers extremely high quality transmission over increased distances. Fiber cabling is expensive and today is still mainly used in main ring path and backbone cabling applications. (Backbone cabling is a common cabling path that connects primary LANs.)

Type 5 cabling is considered unsusceptible to virtually all interference. It is used frequently in repeater configurations at both 4Mbps and 16Mbps transmission.

Type 6. Type 6 cable has two wire shielded twisted pairs. It is data-grade stranded wire: 26 AWG. Due to distance limitations, Type 6 is only used for patch and jumper cable applications. (Patch cables are used between a ring station (RS) and a wall plate. Jumper cables are usually used at a patch panel.)

Type 8. Type 8 cable has two wires with plastic ramp insulation. It is data-grade solid wire: 26 AWG. With its parallel design it is used for under-carpet installations.

Type 9. Type 9 cable has two wire shielded twisted pairs. It is data-grade solid or stranded wire: 26 AWG. Its lower cost makes type 9 a frequent alternative to type 1 when distance requirements are not as critical.

Cable Lengths

There are two types of ring-wiring schemes, the main ring path and the lobe. For designing a Token Ring network layout, the distance can be critical to proper functioning of the network. The cables listed in the preceding section have distance specifications that must be used as guidelines for designing the actual lengths of a LAN layout.

The main ring path length is variable and depends on the number of wiring closets, MAUs, and repeaters in the configuration. These factors determine an adjusted ring length (ARL). (This book does not cover ARL calculations. See references 3, 6, and 7 in Appendix A.)

The rough mean distance for the main ring path is approximately 1200 feet for one wiring closet and one or two MAUs. Again, this will change depending on the number and types of hardware technologies used in the layout. Later in this chapter is a discussion about new hubbing technologies and how they allow exceeding standard distances.

The lobe distance also varies depending on the technology used, but each cable type has defined specifications for lobe installation length. Again, with new technologies these specifications are being exceeded. The standard lobe lengths are listed below by cabling type.

Type 1. Maximum lobe length is 330 feet (100m). This cabling type supports up to 260 nodes.

Type 2. Maximum lobe length is 330 feet (100m) for the 22 AWG pairs and approximately 220 feet (66m) for the 26 AWG pairs. The 26 AWG cable limits the type 2 distance and node capacity to about two-thirds that of type 1 cabling.

Type 3. Maximum lobe length is 150 feet (45m). This cabling type supports up to 72 nodes. Type 3 cabling requires type 3 media filters at the termination point to convert to the standard IBM data connector, and to filter any interference encountered on the medium. Type 3 cabling usually uses a standard RJ11 or RJ45 phone plug for termination.

Type 5. Type 5 cable is typically used for the main ring path and for backbones. If fiber is used in the main ring path, the rough mean distance increases from 1200 feet to approximately 2.5 miles. There are no currently defined hard lobe lengths for type 5 cabling.

Type 6. Again the 26 AWG cable aspect of type 6 limits its distance and node capacity to about two-thirds that of type 1 cabling. Maximum lobe length is approximately 220 feet (66m).

Type 8. Maximum lobe length is approximately 165 feet (50m). The type 8 design limits its distance and node capacity to about one-half that of type 1 cabling.

Type 9. Type 9 is also 26 AWG cable and thus is limited to about two-thirds of type 1 cabling's distance and node capacity. The maximum lobe length for type 9 is approximately 220 feet (66m).

Cabling Connectors

The Token Ring network cabling scheme uses two main types of connectors: the IBM data connector and the male/female DB9 connector.

The IBM data connector is a self-shorting connector, which means that when disconnected it self-shorts and loops the internal twisted pairs. This is important for fault redundancy, as discussed in the Design and Layout section of Chapter 2.

The data connector is made to connect with another identical data connector (see fig. 3.2). Most type 6 patch cables use this connector on at least one end to terminate. This allows type 6 patch cables to connect to patch panels, wall faceplates, and MAUs, all of which use this connector as a standard internal connector.

The male DB9 connector is usually used on the other end of type 6 patch cables to connect to a Token Ring network interface card (NIC). Figure 3.3 shows the pin layout of the male DB9 connector as it relates to the patch cable, with the associated Token Ring conductor color codes and polarities. The NIC uses the female DB9 connector for its own external port.

With new technology in the type 3 unshielded twisted pair (UTP), many Token Ring NICs and MAUs today use RJ45 phone-type connectors for termination.

Figure 3.4 shows how the standard Token Ring connectors mate to create an RS-to-MAU link.

FIGURE 3.2
The IBM data connector connects to another, identical data connector.

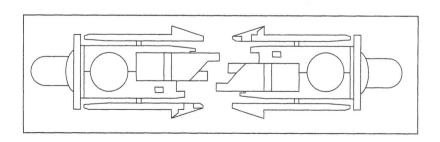

FIGURE 3.3
A DB9 male
connector, at the
end of a type 6
patch cable,
attaches to a
Token Ring NIC.

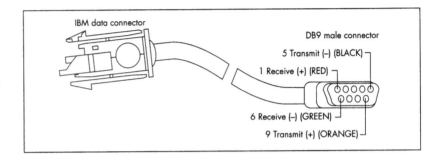

Multistation Access Units and Wiring Hubs

In Chapter 2 we discussed the standard IBM 8228 MAU. When the 8228 MAU was introduced it was considered state of the art. Today the menu of wiring hubs offers many more choices for configuring a Token Ring LAN. There is an excellent selection of new Token Ring hubbing technology. This new technology can have a significant effect on how a Token Ring LAN operates and performs.

A lot of the hubs on the LAN marketplace still parallel the original 8228 design. But many of the hubs are being designed with intelligence built-in. Hubs are available with LED diagnostic ports and diagnostic software to test the hub independent of the network operating system.

One of the most popular new hub product lines is UTP-based intelligent hubs, such as those of SynOptics and Cabletron. UTP cabling systems are cost-effective and easy to maintain. In some cases they offer increased cabling distances. Some of them can mix topologies for internetworking. A large segment of the LAN marketplace is quickly shifting over to UTP.

IBM Standard 8228 MAU (IBM P/N6091014)

The IBM 8228 MAU has an excellent track record for reliability. It uses passive ports, and the MAU itself does not use an external power source. The ports have a relay, which is actuated by the phantom DC current from the NIC. These ports may need to be charged at installation or at certain intervals to open the relay. A charger that is usually shipped with the 8228 is used for this purpose (see fig. 3.5). Before troubleshooting, a suspected bad port should always be charged by inserting the charger into the port.

Other MAUs on the market use external power and have more complex logic than the 8228. Another noteworthy point is that the IBM 8228 MAU is modular in relation to its size and port capacity, which makes it cost-effective for small LAN configurations. Again, because of its reliability and cost-effectiveness, the IBM 8228 is still the most commonly used MAU.

FIGURE 3.4
The cable (type 6, in this example) and data connectors work together to connect a ring station to the MAU.

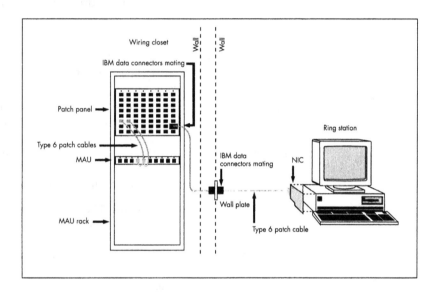

IBM 8230 Controlled Access Unit (CAU)

The IBM 8230 CAU is IBM's latest introduction to the hubing market. The 8230 CAU is a highly intelligent concentrator. It is configured as an attachment center for lobe attachment modules (LAMs) that allow 20 RS connections. Using a maximum of four daisy-chained LAMs, the 8230 unit can handle up to 80 RS connections. LAMs can come configured with either IBM data connector ports or with type 3 RJ45 phone plugs so UTP cabling can be connected directly to the ports on the LAM.

FIGURE 3.5
Having no external power source, the IBM 8228 MAU requires a charger.

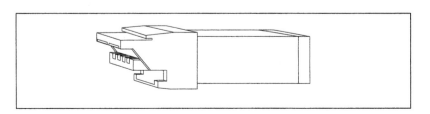

The CAU unit allows LAMs to be switchable between 4Mbps and 16Mbps. The 8230 also can be configured with optical fiber converter modules for implementing a fiber backbone. The unit also has bidirectional internal repeaters and will often allow for increased lobe lengths over the 8228 MAU. The design of the 8230 makes it an excellent component in the IBM LAN Management scheme. I would expect that IBM will interface to the unit for ring management (see fig. 3.6).

Proteon Series 70 Wiring Centers

The Series 70 Wiring Centers by Proteon are an intelligent alternative to the IBM 8228 MAUs. The Proteon Wiring Centers are highly intelligent MAUs that use an external power source. They have the same port capacity as the IBM 8228 MAUs, which also makes them modular and cost effective. They are available in various models that support STP, UTP, and fiber. All models support both 4Mbps and 16Mbps. Proteon has its own 10Mbps proprietary transmission for Token Ring LANs called ProNET-10.

The Proteon units have a solid track record for reliability. Their mean time to repair (MTTR) is low, due to their inherent diagnostic capability. Each port has a diagnostic status LED which shows activity on the port. The Ring In (RI) and Ring Out (RO) ports also have status LEDs to show loop status. Every port has slide switches to disable and enable the port. The RI and RO ports have loop switches for manual looping. These features are extremely helpful when troubleshooting the ring. Isolating a possible bad port is much easier with the technology that Proteon offers.

Proteon also has a comprehensive Token Ring LAN management approach that uses the Proteon Series 70 Wiring Centers along with management software called TokenVIEW Plus and TokenVIEW Manager. These software packages interface with the Series 70 Wiring Centers to provide a fault-tolerant management system.

TokenVIEW Plus monitors status on individual rings, while TokenVIEW Manager works with multiple TokenVIEW Plus stations to create an overall distributed management system that brings all statistics to a centralized management console. The software takes advantage of the 802.5 standard management roles and collects data that is transmitted to the REM, CRS, and RPS (see fig. 3.7).

FIGURE 3.6
An IBM 8230
Controlled Access
Unit (CAU) serves
as an attachment
center for lobe
attachment
modules (LAMs).

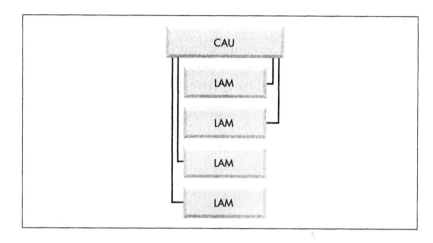

SynOptics LattisNet

SynOptics LattisNet hubs were designed primarily for the EtherNet topology, but today the product line has had significant improvements in the Token Ring environment. The LattisNet system is mainly targeted for UTP cabling environments.

SynOptics has an excellent hub system that supports multitopology configurations. The newest series, LattisNet 3000, supports Token Ring 4/16Mbps and EtherNet over a variety of cabling types, including STP, UTP, and fiber.

Recent Token Ring additions to the LattisNet 3000 include multicable host modules that allow Token Ring connections to the 3000. The 3505 UTP Host Module allows 12 stations to connect at 4Mbps or 16Mbps via a phone-type connector. These modules can be combined to allow up to 144 RSes on a type 3 cabling system, versus the 72-station standard. The 3502A STP/UTP allows connection of both type 1 and type 3 cabling. The 3552 Token Ring In/Ring Out module allows connection to an additional 3000 hubs and other manufacturers' MAUs.

The 3000 hub currently supports external bridging for multiple Token Ring LANs, for either 4Mbps-to-4Mbps or 4Mbps-to-16Mbps configurations. SynOptics says it will introduce a bridging module that will support internal bridging.

SynOptics also has a line of repeater modules that allow other Token Ring repeaters to connect to the 3000. Fiber repeating can be accomplished through the 3534-ST Token Ring Fiber Repeater module, which allows a Token Ring LAN to be extended to two kilometers on a fiber link.

One of the advantages of the SynOptics 3000 system is the LattisNet network management software. The system captures real-time data on the network and allows for automatic reconfiguration of certain operational parameters. The software views the LattisNet system at the physical board module level. Operators can monitor, log, and analyze all areas of network activity, which is extremely important for both managing and troubleshooting a LAN.

FIGURE 3.7
Proteon's p7302 Series 70 Workgroup Wire Centers with power provided by a p7202 Intelligent Wire Center.

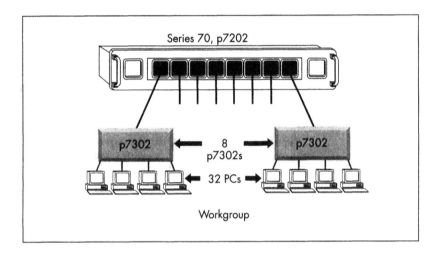

SynOptics also recently introduced Simple Network Management Protocol (SNMP) agents into the LattisNet Network Management System. SNMP is a popular network management protocol that is fast becoming an industry standard.

One other note on the LattisNet 3000 and Token Ring. SynOptics has developed a software product called NETMAP which allows the IBM SNA NetView system to interface to the LattisNet 3000 system. This allows operators in the IBM SNA environment to monitor a LAN connected with LattisNet from an SNA central location (see fig. 3.8).

Cabletron Multi Media Access Center (MMAC)

Like SynOptic's LattisNet, the Cabletron MMAC was originally designed for the EtherNet 10BASE-T environment. Cabletron recently introduced its Token Ring additions to the MMAC product line.

Cabletron MMAC supports FDDI in addition to Token Ring and EtherNet. Cabletron has developed an internal bus backplane structure called the Flexible Network Bus (FNB), which allows multiple topologies to coexist on the bus. This innovative design makes the MMAC extremely flexible for internetworking. The MMAC supports full internal bridging and repeating.

Cabletron calls its complete integration system of hardware and software products Integrated Network Architecture (INA). INA incorporates an excellent management software package platform with two main components, LANVIEW and SPECTRUM.

LANVIEW interfaces with the architecture to provide real-time data at the Physical layer. SPECTRUM is a sophisticated management platform for the internetworking environment that includes SNMP agent communication capabilities. Cabletron also has an IBM NetView product called NetView Gateway.

FIGURE 3.8
The SynOptics LattisNet hubs support a variety of Token Ring topologies and cabling types.

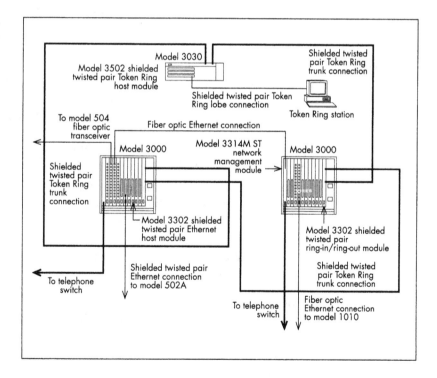

The MMAC main Token Ring components consist of Token Ring Media Interface Modules (TRMIM), Token Ring Management Modules (TRMM), Token Ring Management Bridging Modules (TRMBM), and Intelligent Repeater Modules (IRM). The TRMIMs are available for both STP and UTP cabling types. Cabletron's UTP TRMIMs have not yet exceeded the 72-node connection standard. All the TRMIMs can be configured to run at 4Mbps or 16Mbps. There is also a TRMIM that is just used for Ring In and Ring Out connections to other MMACs and to other manufacturers' MAUs.

Cabletron also has a Token Ring NIC product line and a passive eight-port MAU (TRC-800) that works interactively with their MMAC system.

The Cabletron TRMM collects statistics that are transmitted to certain Token Ring management roles, including the REM, the CRS, and the RPS. The TRMM and the LANVIEW/SPECTRUM/NetView Gateway packages work together to provide an excellent Token Ring LAN management solution (see fig. 3.9).

BRIDGES

A bridge is a device that connects a LAN to another LAN at the Data Link level of OSI. Bridges are mainly used to segment traffic when the need is to have the internetwork still look like one large network, so the individual LANs seem transparent to the user. Typically in the Token Ring environment, bridging is done for ring load balancing and to segment 4Mbps and 16Mbps rings.

Because bridges communicate at the Data Link level, they are protocol-independent. This means they can forward frames that contain high-level protocols such as SMB and SNA.

Some bridges are labeled MAC-layer bridges, meaning that they communicate at the MAC level; in this case both LANs must be similar. For instance, if a Token Ring LAN is bridged to another Token Ring it can communicate fully on a MAC-layer bridge. But if a Token Ring LAN is bridged to an EtherNet LAN, the LANs are dissimilar and cannot communicate at the MAC layer. In this case an LLC-layer bridge is used.

The LAN environment includes several bridging techniques. The Token Ring topology relies heavily on a bridging methodology called source routing (SR).

IBM developed SR to allow Token Ring frames to cross a multiple-ring environment. SR differs considerably from the bridging technique used most by EtherNet, transparent bridging (TB), which depends on a bridge being intelligent. TB expects a bridge to decide which frames are to be forwarded and where frames are to be forwarded, and to build tables for routing.

FIGURE 3.9
Cabletron's Token Ring hubs can be configured to run at both 4Mbps and 16Mbps.

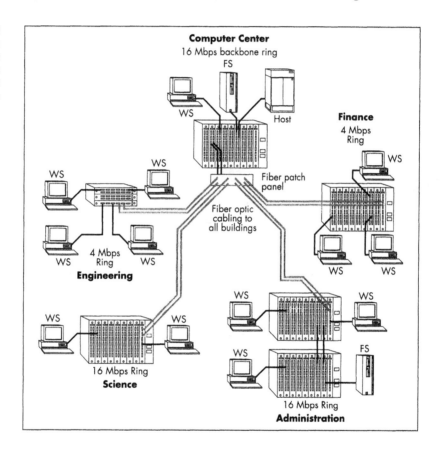

(Some bridge manufacturers and organizations are working to develop a standard that will combine the two techniques to form a new standard called source routing/transparent bridging. Some bridges today in fact employ this technique for internetworking.)

The SR method is designed to have the originating RS determine the actual route and to forward the frame. SR uses the Routing

Information (RI) field in the data frame to accomplish the task. The originating RS sets certain bits within the RI field and transmits a query frame onto the ring to locate the most efficient path to the destination station. Once the destination station receives the frame, it copies it and transmits the frame back to the source station.

On the return trip the frame appends to itself identification information about the ring and bridges it passes through on the way home. When the originating station receives the frame back, it interrogates the RI field for the newly established route to the destination station. Now the originating station has a selected route for transmission, and it builds an internal routing table for its destinations.

In large ring configurations there may be many routes from an originating ring to a destination ring. You need a method to select the best possible path for transmission.

Token Ring's most commonly used method is the spanning tree algorithm (STA). The STA method has two important impacts on bridging. First, it ensures that the best possible path is being used; second, it inherently stops looping, which is when a frame arrives on a ring from two different paths.

The STA method determines the best possible path by first selecting the highest priority bridge within the WAN as a root bridge. Next, every other bridge identifies the port that is logically the closest to the root bridge as a root port. The selection process follows as the individual LANs next pick the closest bridge to the root bridge as their designated bridge.

When the election of the main bridge components is complete, the main logical route, or tree-branching scheme, is considered defined. The algorithm will look for redundant paths (multiple paths to one ring) and it will lock the root ports on those designated bridges. This establishes a nonlooping multiple ring path.

Source-routing bridges use two routing methods to forward frames, a single-route broadcast and an all-routes broadcast. A single-route broadcast sends a query frame so that it passes through every individual ring only once. An originating station employing the single-route broadcast method uses the STA method to communicate with all other bridges on the internetwork.

An all-routes broadcast sends the query frame on all possible paths and then determines the best path. While a single-route broadcast actually reduces the amount of overhead traffic on the ring, an all-routes broadcast increases the amount of overhead traffic on the ring. The only real advantage of an all-routes broadcast is that it dynamically balances the traffic among all bridges.

Source-routing bridges have an inherent feature called the hop count limit (HCL). The HCL's purpose is to stop frames from continuously circling a Token Ring internetwork. The HCL limits the number of bridges a frame may travel, or "hop," through. IBM source-routing bridges allow frames up to seven hops. Some other manufacturers have designed bridges that can increase the hop limit above seven hops.

Bridges in a multiple-ring configuration work together by communicating through a message protocol called Hello Bridge Protocol Data Units (BPDU). The frame transmission has its own format which is based on an LLC type-1 connection. This book does not discuss BPDU frames; for further information see reference 1 in Appendix A.

For Token Ring, the source-routing method works with the STA method to allow stations to determine the best possible method for transmission over a multiple Token Ring configuration.

Some bridges (nicknamed "kit bridges") are composed of a software/hardware kit which must be configured in a workstation or a file server. A kit bridge configured in a file server is called an internal bridge by some network operating system and bridge manufacturers. Kit bridges configured in workstations are called external bridges.

The next looks at various types of Token Ring bridges. Not all vendor bridging products talk to Token Ring through straight SR method technology; some use the TB method and communicate to source routing.

The IBM Token Ring Bridge Program v2.2 (P/N 53F7724)

IBM offers a bridging solution based on its original PC Network Bridge program. The IBM Token Ring Bridge v2.2 program source-routing bridge can operate at 4Mbps or 4/16Mbps. The bridge can be configured as either a local or a remote unit. It can interactively communicate bridge statistics to the IBM LAN Manager v2.0.

The IBM local bridge configuration requires a dedicated PC and two Token Ring NICs. The first step in setting up an IBM bridge is configuring and testing the hardware. Next the IBM Token Ring Bridge Program is loaded and configured.

The IBM remote bridge configuration requires a dedicated PC and one Token Ring NIC, along with one of IBM's remote adapters. The first step again is configuring and testing the hardware, then loading and configuring the IBM Token Ring Bridge Program. The remote bridge can operate at remote speeds from 9.6Kbps to 1.344Mbps. Installation and configuration of both units is simple.

The IBM Token Ring Bridge Program solution is still a popular one, but it requires a dedicated PC (see fig. 3.10.). Other technology offers standalone units with even more bridging capabilities.

The IBM 8209 Token Ring Bridge (P/N 8209001)

IBM recently introduced a new bridge, the 8209. The IBM 8209 is a standalone unit with two internal slots for internal bridging modules. It is a local bridge that uses source routing and can operate at 4Mbps or 4/16Mbps. It has its own management capabilities and can communicate with the IBM LAN Manager v2.0.

The 8209 entry is unique for IBM in that it can be configured with two Token Ring Feature modules (P/N 74F8628) or it can communicate with EtherNet with the installation of an EtherNet Feature module (P/N 55F4781) that plugs in to one of the two slots. IBM calls this module an Etherand Module.

When the Etherand Module is plugged into one side of the bridge, it uses the TB method but appears as source routing. The internal design of the 8209 allows this, as well as communication to the other Token Ring module, which is using the SR method. The EtherNet Feature is also available with enhanced management capabilities (P/N 74F5156) that allows the LAN Manager to monitor its statistics.

The 8209's open design gives it capabilities to forward non-IBM protocols such as TCP/IP. The LAN industry considers the 8209 to be a positive move by IBM for internetworking with other topologies (see fig. 3.11).

FIGURE 3.10
The IBM Token
Ring Bridge
Program v2.2
configuration
includes a
dedicated PC.

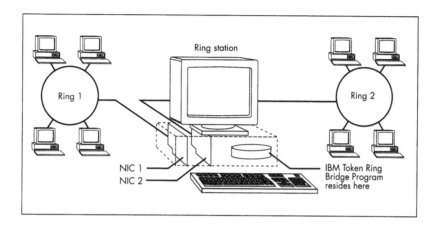

Andrew Bridgeport Source-Routing Token Ring Bridges

The Andrew 7000 series source-routing bridges are highly efficient, as they are designed to work directly with the 802.5 SR method. The bridges are completely compatible with all major aspects of the Token Ring topology.

The 7000 series bridges have the unique capability to fully communicate with IBM LAN Manager and NetView consoles. Andrew bridges can emulate all the main management server functions of the Token Ring model: the LRM, the LBS, the RPS, the CRS, and the REM. This creative approach has made Andrew bridges an excellent choice for bridging components in the Token Ring environment.

This approach is further enhanced by Andrew's Bridgeport 7010 Bridge Manager Program, which offers a central-point management station capability. The Bridge Manager allows overall status viewing and automatic reconfiguration through a process called Netscan. The program also offers diagnostic and security features.

The 7000 series is offered in both local and remote Token Ring configurations. The 7404 model is a local 4Mbps bridge that can connect to both 4Mbps and 16Mbps bridges. It forwards frames at 850 packets a second. The 7606 bridge is switchable to either 4Mbps or 16Mbps. It can forward frames at 1600 packets a second. The 7404 can be easily be upgraded to a 7606.

The Bridgeport 7412 remote bridges can communicate remotely at either 4Mbps or 16Mbps by being connected to an RS232 or a V.35

FIGURE 3.11
The IBM 8209
Token Ring bridge
can be configured
for either two
Token Ring
networks or an
EtherNet LAN.

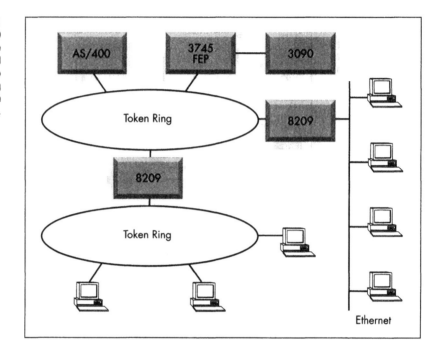

interface. They also can communicate through a Data Service Unit/Channel Service Unit (DSU/CSU) configuration. The remote 7412 transmission speed ranges from 9.6Kbps to 2.048Mbps.

Andrew has an excellent selection of Token Ring products. They also offer a full complement of products including MAUs, NICs, repeaters, and media filters. Their products are fully compatible with the IBM environment (see fig. 3.12).

Netronix TokenMaster 100 and 400 Token Ring Bridges

The TokenMaster 100 and 400 series bridges are full source-routing bridges. The TokenMaster bridges are MAC-layer compliant and are available in both 4Mbps and 4/16Mbps versions. Netronix has designed its bridging products to be 100 percent compatible with the IBM platform. The TokenMaster can communicate with IBM NetView in both DOS and OS/2 environments. If the environment does not involve SNA, the Netronix Bridge Support Program offers a full-status view of the bridging environment. It is complete with alarm notification and full diagnostic capabilities, as well as overall bridge management control.

The TokenMaster 100 is a local bridge that can support both 4Mbps and 4/16Mbps. It is fully compliant with the SR standard. It can forward frames at 1650 packets a second.

The TokenMaster 400 is a remote 4Mbps or 4/16Mbps bridge that communicates at 9.6Kbps to 2.048Mbps. It supports RS232, V.35, RS422, RS449, and RS530 interfaces. It is fully compatible with T1 and fractional T1. It also forwards frames at 1650 packets a second (see fig. 3.13).

The TokenMaster bridge product line employs data compression techniques, optimizing the data transfer rate by using a compression algorithm that reduces the size of the bit stream being transmitted across the bridge.

ROUTERS

A router differs from a bridge in that it connects a LAN to another LAN at the OSI Network level rather than the Data Link level. Routers are used to connect LANs that need to share the same protocols. They are protocol-dependent devices that must understand the protocol they are forwarding. They are most commonly used in larger internetworks where there is a need to logically separate LANs.

A router still segments traffic, but at the same time it can be selective on what protocols are being passed through to the next LAN. This can be very important; for a large internetwork running multiple protocols, a router allows boundaries to be defined and allows for administrative control over what protocols are running on each LAN.

Most Token Ring routers support source routing and the spanning tree algorithm. A router is highly intelligent, and maintains internal routing tables that contain what protocols it can pass through, along with statistical data on other routers in the internetwork.

Some routers do allow logical loops so that redundant paths are available on the internetwork. This is not a problem because they can selectively filter by protocol, which means that unwanted packets do not have to arrive on certain networks.

Installation of a router is usually more complex than that of a bridge, because setting up the protocol configurations requires a good understanding of the protocols being used. Some routers are slower on packet throughput because they are doing more processing at the protocol level than bridges do.

FIGURE 3.12
The Bridgeport 7606 bridge is configurable for 4Mbps or 16Mbps operation; the 7404 provides 4Mbps connections for 4Mbps and 16Mbps networks.

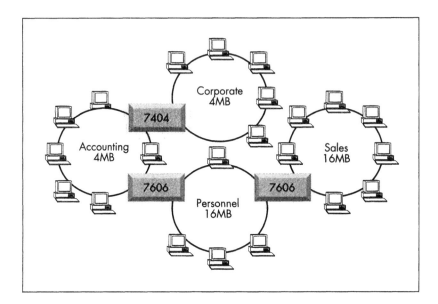

FIGURE 3.13
Netronix TokenMaster 100 bridges can support both 4Mbps and 4/16Mbps Token Ring networks.

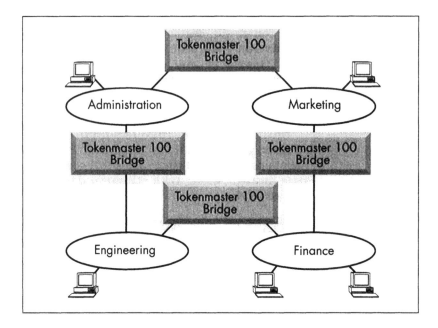

Today there is also a category called brouters, which are a hybrid between a bridge and a router: They combine the Data Link layer and the Network layer forwarding capabilities. Brouters can be selective of protocols or not. A brouter is sometimes called a bridging router.

The next section details a few of the most popular Token Ring routers available.

The Proteon 4100+ Bridging Router

Proteon has the first router that can handle multiple protocols at 16Mbps with source-routing capabilities coupled with STA. The 4100 is an excellent choice for a large Token Ring WAN running multiple protocols. The 16Mbps backbone feature allows easy access to the IBM host environment.

The 4100 has flexibility to handle connections to multiple medium types, such as fiber optics, STP, and UTP. The 4100 Bridging Router can handle topology connections from Token Ring to EtherNet, ProNET-10, and Apollo Token Ring. Remote connection configurations are available at speeds up to 2.048Mbps, along with an X.25 option.

One of the advantages of the 4100 is its capability to handle multiple- protocol routing in the Token Ring environment. It can route IBM protocols such as SMB and SNA, along with non-IBM protocols, specifically TCP/IP, NetWare IPX, DECnet, XNS, OSI, Apollo DOMAIN, and AppleTalk. This palette of protocols is broad for the Token Ring topology. More and more protocols other than the standard IBM suites are running on Token Ring.

Another Proteon unit, the CNX 500 Bridging Router, is the first RISC-based router and supports an assortment of protocols, along with FDDI connectivity. It is an extremely high-end product that is excellent for the IBM SNA arena.

For the Token Ring topology, Proteon is consistently on the leading edge with products that not only meet 802.5 specifications but also provide new avenues for interoperability with the Token Ring topology (see fig. 3.14).

The Cisco Systems MGS Router

Cisco Systems is a pioneer in network routing research. They realize that today's LANs have many protocols running across multiple platforms, and that sophisticated routers are going to be the cornerstone of modern networks. Cisco's routing products allow the design and implementation of some of the largest internetworks to date.

Cisco has formed strategic relationships with both IBM and Madge Networks to enhance the performance of their Token Ring products. The alignment with Madge involves an agreement to use Madge's FastMAC NIC microcode on the Cisco Token Ring interfaces.

Cisco Systems has an array of products for various topologies. Here we look at one of their routers commonly used in the Token Ring environment.

The Cisco MGS Router is a multiprotocol, multimedia router that exceeds normal ranges of performance. The unit can handle up to 11 network and serial segments. It is completely flexible for the internetworking environment by providing protocol support for almost every vendor. The unit can be configured for most standard remote types of connection; it supports everything from X.25 to SDLC. The MGS can handle all the major routing protocols in the LAN arena. And it can be configured to work with most vendors' management schemes.

The MGS is based with a four-slot card cage. The core router manager is the main CPU card, which is a Cisco System Processor Card CSC/3 that uses a Motorola 68020 30MHz processor and 4MB of RAM. Its built-in system bus runs at 160Mbps. It also has serial console capability. The other remaining slots can be configured with combinations of Token Ring, EtherNet, and Serial Synchronous interface cards.

The MGS fits into the Token Ring environment comfortably with the capability to support full source routing both in local and remote configurations. The auxiliary slots can be loaded with a combination of two different Token Ring interfaces.

The Token Ring Interface CSC-R is a one-ring 4Mbps interface attachment, and the Token Ring Interface CSC-R16 is a one-ring interface attachment that is switchable between 4Mbps and 16Mbps transmission speeds. Both controllers use RISC 16MIPS onboard processors that allow for extremely high performance.

With the addition of Cisco's Serial-Port Communication Interface (SCI) cards, the MGS unit can handle a variety of remote Token Ring connections.

FIGURE 3.14
Proteon's p4100+
Bridging Routers
can work with
multiple media
types and multiple
protocols.

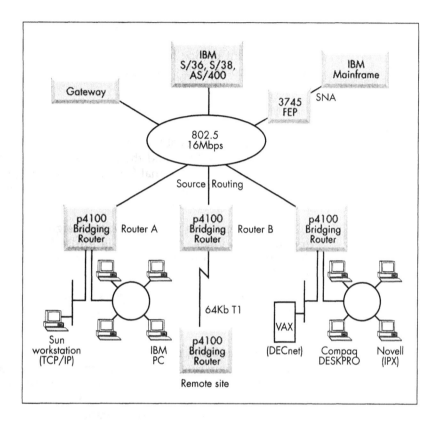

Cisco also uses the Token Ring interfaces in another unit, the AGS+ Router. It fully supports FDDI to serve as an excellent backbone router. It also supports remote connections up to T3 transmissions speeds.

IBM host integration is a pleasure with the Cisco routers, which are designed with full IBM SNA routing communication capabilities. Cisco routers look like a physical unit to the IBM SNA environment. Chapter 2 discusses how an LU-LU session takes place across an SNA internetwork. Cisco routers allow this because they fully support peer-to-peer communication through IBM's Advanced Program-to- Program Communication (APPC).

Cisco routers can interface to both the IBM LAN Manager and the SNA NetView management schemes.

One of Cisco's strongest points is that full support is available to route all major protocols on the Token Ring topology. Cisco Systems is an excellent choice for a large internetwork that incorporates Token Ring connectivity (see fig. 3.15).

REPEATERS

A repeater operates at the Physical layer, the lowest layer of OSI. Repeaters electrically extend the physical lengths of a LAN cabling segment. They take the signal from one cabling segment, regenerate it, then pass it on to another cabling segment. The repeater actually boosts the strength of the signal.

Because repeaters just regenerate a signal, they are protocol-dependent devices. A repeater is limited to passing the same protocols that are present, and they must be connected to the same type of topology.

Repeaters do not do the high-level processing of bridges and routers. Thus repeaters usually have the highest throughput capability.

With Token Ring, repeaters are mainly used to regenerate the signal on the main ring path, but in some cases a repeater is installed to extend a lobe for a critical RS. You often see repeaters in large buildings where standard cable lengths will not allow a ring to function standalone without regeneration. Repeaters were originally available for only standard STP, but today they can accommodate the new fiber and UTP backbone configurations.

The IBM 8218, 8219, and 8220 Repeaters

When Token Ring was just gaining a presence, IBM introduced a series of copper and fiber repeaters.

The IBM 8218 Repeater (P/N 63395320) was the first to make its mark. It is still frequently used and like most IBM products is considered very reliable. The 8218 unit regenerates signals on the main ring path up to 2500 feet. The 8218 Repeaters must be installed in pairs if both the main ring path and the backup path are being extended. This is recommended with the 8218 because the fault redundancy of the IBM cabling scheme relies on the backup path. Distances longer than 2500 feet are possible with multiple units installed. The 8218 must be installed with STP and only operates at 4Mbps transmission speed.

The IBM 8219 Repeater (P/N 8219001) is an optical fiber repeater that can extend a main ring path up to 6600 feet. The 8219 Repeaters take a signal on main ring path STP cabling media and regenerate the signal as well as matching the STP to the fiber media. At least two 8219 units are required on the main ring path: the first to

FIGURE 3.15
With full IBM SNA routing communication capabilities, Cisco routers can interface with both IBM LAN Manager and NetView.

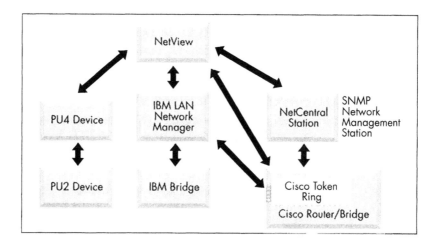

convert from STP to fiber, and the second to convert from fiber back to STP.

The 8219 Repeaters must also be installed in pairs if both the main ring path and the backup path are to be extended. Multiple units can be installed to achieve longer lengths. The 8219s only operate at 4Mbps transmission speed.

The IBM 8220 Optical Fiber Converter Repeaters (P/N 96X5810) are a more-intelligent solution from IBM. They have all the features of the 8219 Repeaters but with the ability to communicate with the IBM LAN Manager console. Automatic monitoring is built in for the main and backup ring paths, and the 8220 can initiate backup path operation on the fly if a loss of signal is detected on the main ring path. The 8220 can operate at either 4Mbps or 16Mbps transmission speed (see fig. 3.16).

The Andrew 8200 Series Repeaters

Another significant Andrew contribution to the Token Ring community is the 8200 Repeater series, which offers substantial feature additions over other repeaters in the marketplace. They offer longer distances than standard repeaters, along with multimedia capabilities. Diagnostic LEDs are available for monitoring the presence of a signal and for the repeater's configuration. One advantage of the Andrew repeaters over standard IBM repeaters is that they need not be installed in pairs to maintain fault redundancy. They automatically handle both pairs.

The Andrew TRR 8218L-DC Repeater is available in two versions. The 8218L-DC can use type 1 or type 2 cable and can extend distances on the main ring path and lobes up to 2400 feet. The unit only operates at 4Mbps transmission speed. It uses phase lock loop circuitry to retime incoming signal and filter noise.

The 8218L uses type 3 UTP cabling and can extend distances on the main ring path and lobes up to 1000 feet. The unit operates at only 4Mbps transmission speed and also uses phase lock loop circuitry.

Andrew also has a fiber optic repeater, the TRR 8219. Like the IBM repeaters, the Andrew 8219 converts from STP to fiber and then fiber back to STP. They can also be set up in succession for longer distances. The Andrew 8219 can extend distances on the main ring path and lobes up to 10,000 feet. This unit also only operates at 4Mbps transmission speed (see fig. 3.17).

FIGURE 3.16
The IBM 8218, 8219, and 8220 Token Ring Network Repeaters include models for both copper and fiber optic media.

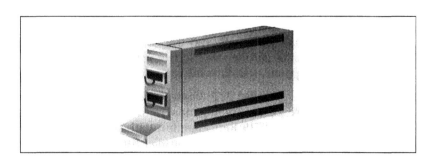

NETWORK INTERFACE CARDS (NICS)

It seems that new technology emerges daily from vendors' development galleries. Recent significant events include 32-bit EISA boards running at 16Mbps speeds. Improvements in UTP hubing technology have brought a wealth of new designs for Token Ring UTP NICs.

Vendors for Token Ring NICs have been busy working on new Token Ring drivers for their cards to enhance performance. Some of the drivers allow 16Mbps NICs to take maximum advantage of the new, full 18000-byte bandwidth.

Most Token Ring NICs are also available with remote program load (RPL) capability, which allows a diskless RS to attach to a server via a PROM on the Token Ring NIC. The PROM contains the firmware code to go out on the ring, access the file server, and download the necessary shell code from a network operating system.

The following section details some of the most popular Token Ring NICs available in the marketplace today.

IBM Standard 4Mbps and 4/16Mbps Token Ring NICs

Just like IBM MAUs, the IBM Token Ring NIC product line has long been an industry standard. IBM has provided high-quality NICs since the inception of the Token Ring LAN design.

The following five standard IBM card types are available:

IBM Token Ring Network Adapter II (P/N 25F9858). This 4Mbps adapter is intended for the IBM PC/XT/AT and IBM PS/2 Models 25 and 30. The adapter is frequently installed because it is an AT machine-type NIC, and most PC manufacturers besides IBM have standardized on the AT bus design.

IBM Token Ring Network Adapter II/A (P/N 69X8138). This 4Mbps adapter is intended for use in IBM PS/2 Models 50 through 95. It is designed for IBM Micro Channel Architecture (MCA) machines. (MCA is a proprietary CPU bus architecture designed by IBM.)

IBM Token Ring Network PS/2 P70 386 Adapter /A (P/N 39F9598). This 4Mbps adapter is used in the IBM PS/2 Portable Model P70 386. This adapter is a half-slot-size adapter.

IBM Token Ring Network 16/4 Adapter (P/N 25F7367). This 4/16Mbps switchable adapter is for the IBM PC/XT/AT and IBM PS/2 Models 25 and 30. This adapter has early token release (ETR) capability. It is easily switchable from 4Mbps to 16Mbps to allow for larger frame sizes.

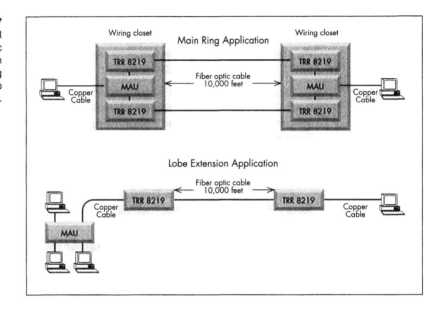

FIGURE 3.17
The Andrew TRR
8219 fiber optic
repeaters can
extend main ring
and lobe paths up
to 10,000 feet.

IBM Token Ring Network 16/4 Adapter (P/N 16F1133). This adapter is also a 4/16Mbps switchable adapter used in the PS/2 Models 50 through 95. It also has ETR capability.

ProNET 4/16Mbps UTP/STP Token Ring NICs

Proteon is an innovative leader in the Token Ring industry. Their products are reliable and offer high performance and great flexibility. They were the first to support 16Mbps over UTP with onboard transceivers. Proteon has also developed support for Extended Industry Standard Architecture (EISA), which is the industry's 32-bit bus architecture rival to IBM's MCA bus. The ProNET NIC family is extensively tested for IBM compatibility.

The ProNET NICs use their unique software drivers that optimize the adapter for a highly efficient data transfer rate. They are also compatible with all major LAN operating systems.

Proteon has three main Token Ring NICs available:

ProNET p1390 4/16 PC AT NIC. This adapter is a 16-bit-bus NIC that is also compatible with an eight-bit I/O bus in the XT models. It is switchable between 4Mbps and 16Mbps speeds. It provides 128K of buffer space onboard to handle larger frame sizes, helping to eliminate congestion-type bottlenecks. Congestion errors, as we'll see later, are a frequent cause of Token Ring soft errors. The p1390 comes with both DB9 STP and RJ45 UTP onboard connectors.

ProNET p1990 4/16 EISA NIC. This adapter features a full 32-bit burst-mode direct memory access (DMA) bus. It is an extremely high-performance adapter that provides maximum advantage for an EISA-architecture-based PC. It provides 128K of buffer space onboard to handle larger frame sizes and is also switchable between 4Mbps and 16Mbps speeds. The p1990 also comes with both DB9 STP and RJ45 UTP onboard connectors.

ProNET p1890 4/16 MCA NIC. This adapter is Proteon's answer to IBM's Micro Channel Architecture. It uses a 16-bit bus interface but is completely compatible with the IBM Personal System/2 MCA product line. The NIC features DMA and provides excellent throughput. The adapter supports PS/2-like software-selectable options called Programmable Option Select (POS), options that include I/O address, interrupt, and DMA arbitration settings. The p1890 also provides 128K of buffer space onboard and is switchable between 4Mbps and 16Mbps speeds. The p1890 only comes with a DB9 STP connector onboard, but the Proteon p2906 UTP Type 3 Media Filter can be used as a transceiver.

Madge Smart Ringnode NICs

Madge Networks is one of the pioneers in the development of Token Ring products, which are their specialty. Their leadership is clear in some of their innovative designs.

Madge is deeply involved in Token Ring protocol software and hardware design, giving them an advantage in the quality and performance of their products. For instance, Madge recently announced development of new driver microcode for the TI chipset called FastMAC. When the drivers were released, TI responded with TurboMAC drivers as an upgrade from the BasicMAC drivers which are standard for their chipset. Madge designs still outperform the TI drivers.

Madge offers a full menu of Token Ring NICs for all CPU bus platforms, with 4Mbps and 4/16Mbps speeds for STP and UTP connections. They also have an MAU line called Ringhubs and network management software called Ring Manager II.

The six Madge Ringnode NICs are as follows:

Smart ISA Ringnode NIC. This Ringnode adapter runs at 4Mbps and is compatible with an eight-bit and 16-bit I/O bus. It has 128K of buffer space and comes with a standard STP DB9 connector onboard.

Smart AT Ringnode NIC. This full 16-bit adapter runs at 4Mbps. It also has 128K of buffer space. It is equipped with both STP DB9 and UTP RJ45 connectors onboard.

Smart MC Ringnode NIC. This full 32-bit IBM MCA-compatible adapter runs at 4Mbps. The MC Ringnode has burst mode DMA and exceptional throughput. It has 128K of buffer space. It only comes with an STP DB9 connector.

Smart 16/4 AT Ringnode NIC. This 4/16Mbps switchable high-throughput adapter is compatible with an eight-bit and 16-bit I/O bus. It also has 128K of buffer space and is equipped with both STP DB9 and UTP RJ45 connectors onboard.

Smart 16/4 MC Ringnode NIC. The 16/4 Ringnode is an IBM MCA-compatible adapter that is switchable between 4Mbps and 16Mbps. It has 128K of buffer space. It has both STP DB9 and UTP RJ45 connectors onboard.

Smart 16/4 EISA Ringnode NIC. The EISA Ringnode adapter provides a full 32-bit bus capable of a full 33Mbps EISA bus burst speed. It operates at maximum bandwidth performance. It has 128K of buffer space onboard and is also switchable between 4Mbps and 16Mbps speeds. The EISA Ringnode only comes with a DB9 STP onboard connector.

chapter 4 TEST EQUIPMENT

This chapter acquaints you with some LAN-industry test equipment and explains how you use the equipment to troubleshoot a LAN problem. This chapter starts with an overview of protocol analysis and performance tuning methodology. You also look at basic use of a protocol analyzer and Token Ring cable testers. Next, you learn some of the industry-standard Token Ring protocol analysis and cable testing devices. Many manufacturers have designed superb test instruments for the Token Ring environment. Because all these instruments are too numerous to be detailed in this book, this chapter discusses the most familiar to the industry.

PROTOCOL ANALYSIS AND PERFORMANCE TUNING METHODOLOGY

To use these test tools efficiently, you must develop skills in *protocol analysis* and *performance tuning*. You'll see these two terms repeatedly throughout this chapter.

Protocol analysis is the process of capturing, viewing, and then analyzing how a communication protocol is operating in a particular network architecture.

Performance tuning is using the statistics gathered in a protocol analysis session and making modifications to the software or hardware components of a LAN to improve its operational performance.

Before you can tune your Token Ring LAN, you must initiate a protocol analysis session. Then you can study your LAN statistics and decide what action to take.

Protocol analysis and performance tuning are both arts. The art of protocol analysis is an expression of a troubleshooter's initial approach to capturing and then the attached logical process of deciphering the protocol that is being viewed.

The art of performance tuning is the process of closely focusing on detailed data to reshape a LAN for optimal performance.

To develop your artistic abilities in protocol analysis and performance tuning, you should take a methodical approach to learning both. The proper way to do this is to have a defined methodology; the next sections introduce the methodology used for both these arts.

Protocol Analysis Methodology

You follow six logical steps in a protocol analysis session. Consider these steps to be an actual methodology. (Chapter 6 discusses each of these steps in further detail.) The six basic steps of protocol analysis methodology are as follows:

- **Capture.** Start capturing data for all layers of your Token Ring protocol model.

- **View.** Examine the data at each layer, starting with the MAC layer and working up to the Application layer.

- **Analyze.** Observe and scrutinize the data at each layer for the proper fluent communication processes.

- **Check Errors.** View and note any soft errors transmitted to the REM functional address.

- **Benchmark Performance.** Monitor the network bandwidth utilization at an overall baseline view and at individual ring station levels.

- **Focus.** Further analyze any potential problems by focusing on the particular component through filtering, triggers, time setting marks, and other categorizing techniques.

As figure 4.1 shows, when you start a protocol analysis session at step 1 of the methodology, your scope of vision is wide and your detail of focus on the LAN is narrow. By step 6 your scope of vision is narrow, because your detail of focus on the LAN is wide.

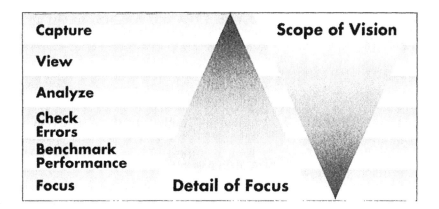

This approach increases your scope of vision on your LAN's overall technicalities. You should now be able to get an initial feeling for the health of your Token Ring network, and if any problems do exist, you should be able to focus more directly on them.

Performance Tuning Methodology

Again, performance tuning is an art; it can be developed, but it requires extensive experience in LAN design. After you gather your conclusions from a protocol analysis, you must take the necessary actions to increase the performance of the LAN. This action requires an understanding of both the network software and hardware intricacies and their synergies.

The next section details the methodology to use for performance tuning, but do not make modifications until you feel confident of your LAN design skills.

The details of the following steps are not covered because the scope of this book is not LAN design. But again, you can develop dexterity for performance tuning by following a defined methodology. Use the following eight basic steps for performance tuning:

1. **Review.** Study all gathered statistics for layer communication from the protocol analysis session.

2. **Target.** Pinpoint specific trends in network bandwidth utilization.

3. **Isolate.** Segregate any captured errors to specific network components.

4. **Allocate.** Designate resources to test any problem areas for a closer benchmark.

5. **Define.** Specify any network improvements that are needed in the software and hardware components. Look at all alternatives. Assess all LAN environmental impacts.

6. **Implement.** Implement the changes to a network component one at a time. For network integrity, it is extremely important to make changes one at a time, and then retest.

7. **Retest.** Next, rerun a protocol analysis session focused on that particular component. If there are no improvements in the test results, you may need to redefine and reimplement the changes.

8. **Document.** Record all your findings. Sometimes you should publish the results to let other technical people and management understand the scope of what has occurred and its impact on the LAN.

Figure 4.2 depicts the relational flow of LAN performance tuning methodology.

FIGURE 4.2
Proceeding through the eight steps of the Token Ring LAN performance tuning methodology.

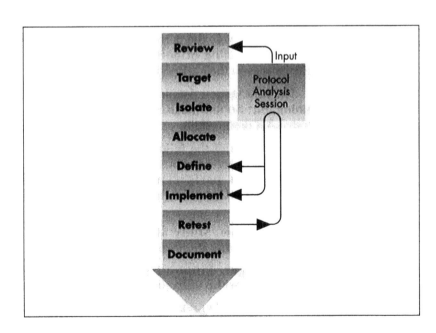

OPERATING A PROTOCOL ANALYZER

To use a protocol analyzer effectively, you must have a good overall perception of the following combination of domains:

- Knowledge of the involved LAN architecture
- Consciousness of a protocol analysis methodology
- Understanding of the basic operational modes of the particular protocol analyzer used

You already understand the Token Ring LAN architecture and protocol analysis methodology. The next section overviews the basic components of a generic protocol analyzer and its operational modes.

Basic Components of a Protocol Analyzer

Protocol analyzer—the phrase sounds like a futuristic physiologist, but it actually is a hardware/software device that can peek into the cabling medium of your LAN.

A protocol analyzer physically connects to a network and captures data traveling on the network cabling medium for the purpose of decoding the specific data for analysis.

Most protocol analyzers consist of a PC configured with the specific LAN topology NIC and network analysis software that is loaded onto the disk drive in the PC.

The protocol analyzer is then connected to the LAN via the NIC, just like a regular network node. The difference between the protocol analyzer node and a regular node is that the analyzer copies all the frames that pass through its NIC. A regular node only copies frames addressed to its own specific network address.

Most Token Ring protocol analyzers operate within this mode. The Token Ring NICs that are used for analyzer applications usually have a special chipset modification that allows the NIC to be indiscriminate as to frame addressing. These types of Token Ring NICs are nicknamed *promiscuous* mode NICs.

The network analysis software that is loaded onto the disk drive is a layered model. This model is composed of a base operating code that handles the actual control and decoding of the particular data that is captured. Above the base operating code is the topology-specific code that enables the protocol analyzer to interrelate with the particular topology. The next layer above the topology code is the protocol suite decodes that allow deciphering of the protocols being analyzed. Figure 4.3 shows a representation of this model.

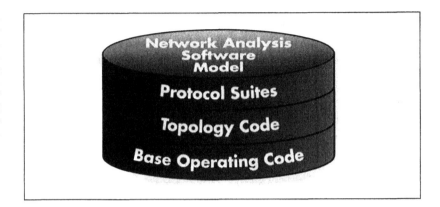

Basic Operational Modes of a Protocol Analyzer

The main operational modes of a protocol analyzer are capturing, decoding, and displaying network protocol data. Three techniques built in to the protocol analyzer allow the standard operating mode parameters to be modified: triggering, filtering, and display options.

With the triggering and filter techniques, you can select which part of the network data you want to capture or display and when to capture or display.

With filtering, captured data can be displayed and a particular frame can be filtered to display only certain data on the protocol analyzer. Capturing a frame from a PCLAN transmission is a good example. Suppose that you just want to see the SMB protocol. You can filter out the MAC, DLC, and NetBIOS protocols. The only protocol left to view and analyze is SMB.

Triggering enables you to capture and display only if certain events occur. For example, if you set the protocol analyzer to trigger on an SMB read file command, the analyzer should start capturing or displaying network data only after an SMB read event occurs.

The display options usually allow for displaying data in numerical and graphical formats. Most protocol analyzers allow for certain time-relationship options. Most of the display options correlate with a protocol analyzer's capabilities to print and access disks so that almost anything you can display to the analyzer screen, you can print and log to disk.

In summary, the guide for using a protocol analyzer is to follow the methodology—*capture, view, analyze, check errors, benchmark performance*—and then to *focus* closely on a puzzling area by using the filtering, triggering, and display options techniques.

Figure 4.4 depicts the relational flow of the way you can use a protocol analyzer's operational features and techniques.

One of the most important things to remember as you use a protocol analyzer is to take the time to thoroughly learn its features and capabilities. If you have a strong understanding of its operation, you can analyze your data in a more timely and effective manner.

FIGURE 4.4
The operational features of protocol analyzers provide the tools for protocol analysis and the subsequent performance-tuning session.

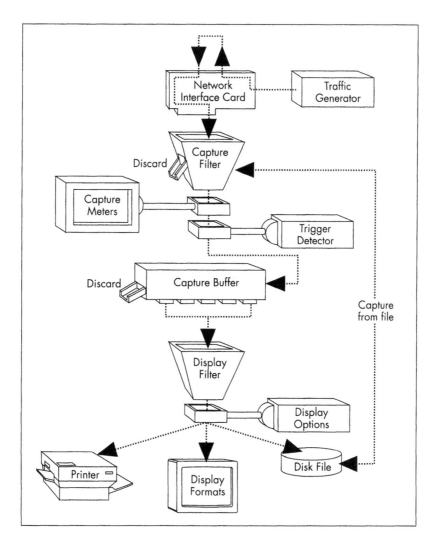

PROTOCOL ANALYZERS AND NETWORK MONITORING TOOLS

The Token Ring environment has an excellent assortment of protocol analyzers, with many types of protocol analyzers offered now, and new technology emerging daily. Many protocol analyzers parallel each other's operational modes and features. But new protocol analyzers are being designed with innovative techniques and features. As the different types of protocol analyzers are introduced, concentrate on their respective features for monitoring and analyzing the Token Ring topology.

The following section is an overview of some of the industry-standard Token Ring protocol analyzers and their specifications.

Network General Sniffer Analyzer

Network General has a strong presence in the LAN/WAN analyzer marketplace. Founded in 1986, the company has experienced phenomenal growth. They currently are the industry leader in high-level protocol analyzers. The Sniffer Analyzer product line has a superb reputation for quality and performance. Network General has set its sights beyond the frontier of simple LANs and has developed products that span today's complex environment of multiple networking topologies and protocols.

The Sniffer Analyzer product family has a full menu of protocol analyzer configurations. It offers both standard standalone analyzers and complex Distributed Sniffer configurations. The standalone product is offered in two ways (see fig. 4.5): a preconfigured PC analyzer packaged in either a Compaq or Toshiba portable, and a NIC/software package so that you can configure it in your own PC.

The Distributed Sniffer System (DSS) is a new Network General product that allows the same analysis functions as the standalone product, but its main focus is to monitor LANs that are dispersed across intricate geographical layouts from one central point. The DSS product line will be discussed in detail later in this section.

The Sniffer Analyzer products are designed across a full range of topologies, including Token Ring (4Mbps and 16Mbps), IBM PC Network, EtherNet, ARCnet, StarLAN, LocalTalk, and WAN Synchronous Links.

The protocol suites the Sniffer supports are IBM SNA, NetBIOS, OS/2 IBMNM, SMB, Novell, XNS:MSNET, TCP:IP:SNMP, DECnet, Banyan Vines, AppleTalk, XNS, SUN:NFS, ISO, X Windows, X.25, SDLC, and HDLC.

The Sniffer Analyzer implements the basic modes of operation and added features through a creative menu system. Figure 4.6 shows the main menu. From the main menu you can vector to submenus to further configure the features for a specific analysis session.

The Sniffer Analyzer enables you to filter network data when capturing and displaying by protocol, data pattern matches, addresses, and time relationships. You can trigger when capturing and displaying by external and internal pattern matching.

The Display features display data in both numerical and graphical formats. You can set up multiple viewing windows to view the summary of frames, frame detail, and hex representation on the same screen. A display option presents network bandwidth utilization by frame. All statistics can be viewed in multiple time relationships. The Sniffer Analyzer also is capable of symbolic naming of specific addresses, which is helpful when viewing traces of data for easy identification of nodes.

FIGURE 4.6
The main menu of
the Sniffer Analyzer
provides access to
the operational
modes for a Token
Ring protocol
analysis session.

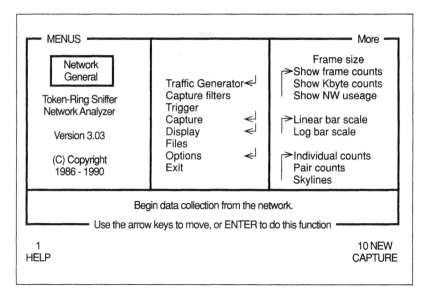

The main menu options also include a traffic-generation feature and a cable tester. The traffic-generation feature enables you to load the network with traffic to check its flexibility of load. The cable tester operates as a time domain reflectometer (TDR). (TDRs are discussed later in this chapter.)

The Sniffer Analyzer offers excellent report-generating features. Almost all the statistics you can view can be printed in various formats and fed in to most major PC applications for management reports.

One of the overall strengths of the Sniffer Analyzer for Token Ring is its Advanced Monitoring for Token Ring. Advanced Monitoring for Token Ring was originally developed as the Network General Watchdog product; now it comes bundled with the basic analyzer. It functions as a separate software module from the main Sniffer protocol analyzer software. Its main mission is to monitor and display vital Token Ring network statistics. The main menu is shown in figure 4.7.

The major statistics gathered by Advanced Monitoring for Token Ring are Global Statistics (see fig. 4.8), Station Statistics, Token Transmit Timing, Error Statistics (including hard and soft errors), Protocol Statistics, Frame Size Statistics, Traffic History, Ring Routing Information, Report Writer, and Alarms.

Figure 4.9 is a screen shot of one of the many useful features, called the Routing Path. This display shows the location and percentage of frames that are routed through a multiple-ring environment, in relation to each ring.

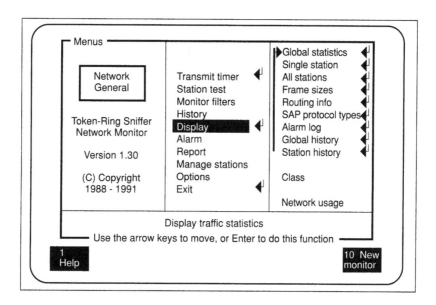

FIGURE 4.7
The Network General Sniffer includes an Advanced Monitoring for Token Ring feature, which provides vital network statistics.

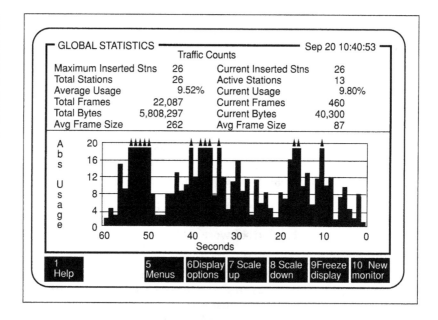

FIGURE 4.8
The Global Statistics screen of the Sniffer's Advanced Monitoring for Token Ring includes numeric and graphical representations.

Another notable feature is the Network General Telesniffer. This feature also functions as a separate software module from the main

FIGURE 4.9
The Sniffer's
Routing Path
screen depicts the
location and
percentage of
frames routed
through a
multiple-ring
environment.

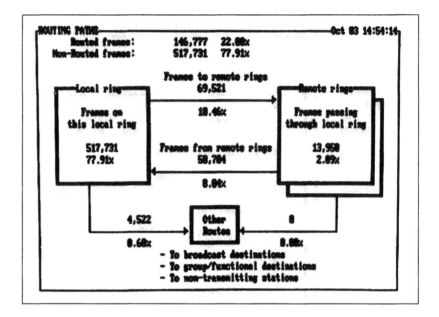

Sniffer protocol analyzer software. Using a modem link and remote communication software, it provides remote access and control of the Sniffer analyzer.

The Distributed Sniffer System (DSS) is an innovative approach to protocol analysis. Rather than running out and physically connecting a stand alone unit to a LAN, the DSS integrates protocol analysis devices and a LAN. The DSS is ideal for multiple-ring environments.

The DSS method is to implement monitoring devices on individual rings, then have those units capture, analyze, and communicate network data to a master monitoring console. This method provides a web effect, permitting protocol analysis on multiple rings to be monitored dynamically from one central point.

Network General's DSS product line has three main components: the SniffMaster Consoles, the Sniffer Servers, and the DSS application software.

The Sniffer Servers are placed on each ring as slaves, and continuously monitor the statistics for that ring. They communicate across rings to the SniffMaster Console via bridges and routers. The Sniffmaster Console acts as a client to the server and gathers the statistics from the Sniffer Servers. The DSS application software provides all the main Sniffer functions, with the addition of multiple-ring statistics.

Because the actual analysis processing is done at each Sniffer Server, minimal data traffic is being transmitted across the LAN to the SniffMaster Console. Figure 4.10 depicts a Token Ring application for the DSS system.

The Sniffer analyzer's strengths are its full range of support for major multiple topologies and extensive protocol suite support.

FIGURE 4.10
The Distributed Sniffer System allows monitoring geographically dispersed networks from a central point.

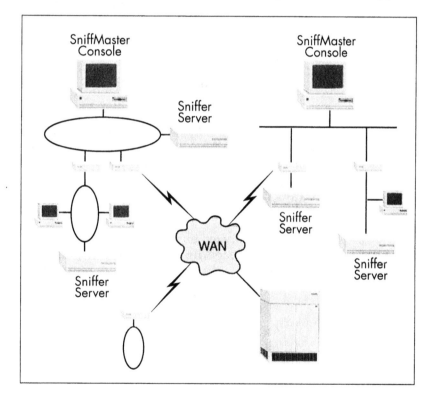

Also, the DSS approach is significant because it creates a new niche in network protocol analysis by allowing protocols on internetworks to be analyzed from a central point.

Note that Network General is currently working on new product developments that include expert system technology and an FDDI analyzer.

ProTools Protolyzer

Founded in 1990, ProTools is a new and emerging company in the LAN/WAN analyzer marketplace. In 1990 ProTools introduced the Protolyzer, a unique product in the LAN analysis domain because it is designed to run on OS/2. It uses the Presentation Manager user interface, giving that warm Windows feeling. The full operation is based on icons and pulldown menus.

The Protolyzer is a software-only product that must run on an OS/2 platform. ProTools recommends a 386 25MHz PC with the following configuration:

- 8M memory

- 100M of disk storage

- OS/2 v1.2 or greater or OS/2 EE

- ProTools-supported topology-specific NIC

The topologies supported by the Protolyzer include Token Ring (4Mbps and 16Mbps) and EtherNet. (For Token Ring the Protolyzer must run on a promiscuous-mode NIC.)

The protocol suites supported are IBM LAN Server, Microsoft LAN Manager, NetBIOS, SMB, Novell, 3Com, TCP:IP, Banyan Vines, and XNS.

The Protolyzer implements the basic modes of operation—capturing, decoding, and displaying—but terms them input, process, and output. Twelve icons represent all the mode and feature choices:

- Acquire

- Display

- Playback

- Zoom

- Title

- Switch

- File

- Transmit

- Sentinel

- DDE

- Statistics
- Filter

Figure 4.11 shows the creative main icon window.

FIGURE 4.11
Fourteen icons in
the main window
of the ProTools
Protolyzer provide
access to the
basic operational
modes.

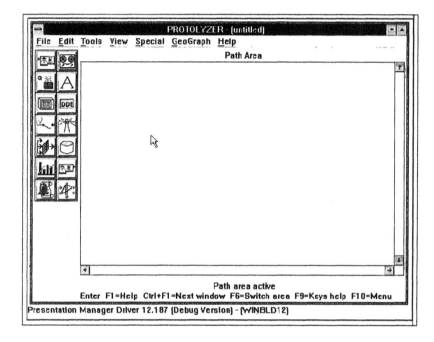

The Protolyzer has all the key filtering, triggering, and displaying features. From the main window you can click on the main icons to construct OS/2 path strands. The path strand relationship represents analysis session modes, as figure 4.12 shows.

Network data can be displayed in numerical and graphical formats. You can organize multiple viewing windows on the Presentation Manager desktop. Frames can be viewed in summary, detail, and hex modes. You can also display a full range of statistics on network bandwidth utilization. The Transmit icon allows traffic generation. The Protolyzer also supports symbolic naming of specific addresses.

Report generation is a snap with the Statistics icon, for generating graphical charts, and the Dynamic Data Exchange (DDE) icon, which allows communication with most major PC applications.

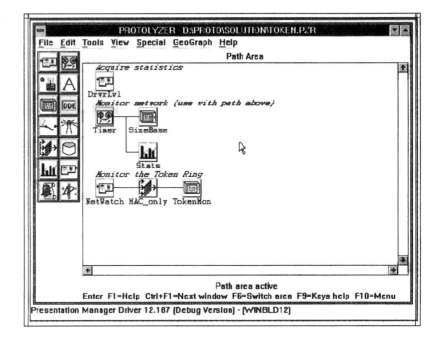

The Protolyzer provides error statistics for the Token Ring environment. One of the neat features of the Protolyzer is the Mapper, which shows a real-time graphical depiction of dynamic data transfer between stations on a ring. The Mapper screen is shown in figure 4.13. ProTools is due to release a Mapper update that will display a multiple-ring environment.

One of the overall strengths of the Protolyzer is its Validation Routine Language (VRL), which is based on the C language and which allows for development of custom modes and features. For Token Ring, ProTools is expected soon to introduce many new advanced monitoring modes, such as source-routing statistics.

Overall the Protolyzer is powerful, flexible, and easy to use. The OS/2 Presentation Manager base helps to make the Protolyzer a strong solution for integrating protocol analysis capabilities directly into basic LAN operations.

IBM LAN Manager with Trace and Performance

IBM's contribution to the LAN analysis arena is really a composite of two IBM programs: the LAN Manager program and the Trace and Performance program.

FIGURE 4.13
The Mapper is a
Protolyzer feature
that graphically
depicts the
dynamic data
transfer between
Token Ring
stations.

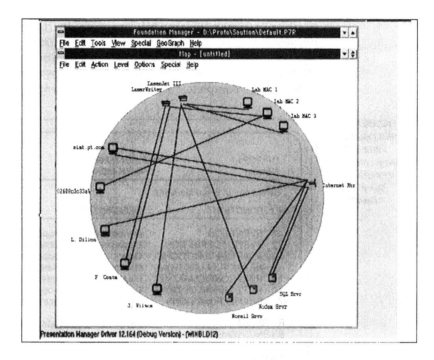

The LAN Manager is a software program that enables you to monitor a multiple Token Ring network. It can gather a variety of network statistics and log them to a disk and a printer. The program has full Token Ring error-logging capabilities.

The Trace and Performance program comprises two utilities: the Trace facility and the Performance facility. The Trace and Performance program is a software-and-hardware package that includes the software package and an IBM Token Ring Trace and Performance Adapter.

The Trace facility is used for capturing, decoding, and displaying network data. The only protocol suites supported are Token Ring MAC and LLC, NetBIOS, and IBM SNA.

The Performance Facility collects Token Ring statistics on network bandwidth utilization and allows for displaying, printing, or disk logging of the gathered data.

Figure 4.14 depicts the IBM LAN Manager main menu. It has full Token Ring event-logging capabilities. A ring configuration can be captured and viewed. Individual ring station statistics can be gathered down to the NIC microcode level. The program implements full Token Ring hard and soft error monitoring and logging features. As Chapter 2 discusses, the program interacts with all ring management servers to collect, analyze, and log statistical data about a complete Token Ring environment.

FIGURE 4.14
The main menu of IBM's LAN Manager product for monitoring Token Ring networks.

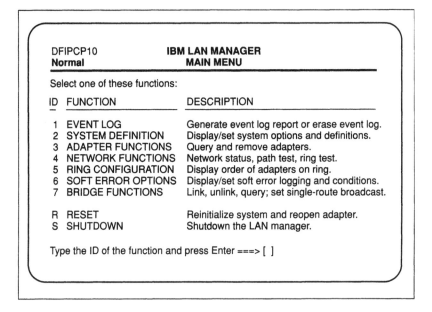

```
DFIPCP10              IBM LAN MANAGER
Normal                MAIN MENU

Select one of these functions:

ID  FUNCTION                  DESCRIPTION

 1  EVENT LOG                 Generate event log report or erase event log.
 2  SYSTEM DEFINITION         Display/set system options and definitions.
 3  ADAPTER FUNCTIONS         Query and remove adapters.
 4  NETWORK FUNCTIONS         Network status, path test, ring test.
 5  RING CONFIGURATION        Display order of adapters on ring.
 6  SOFT ERROR OPTIONS        Display/set soft error logging and conditions.
 7  BRIDGE FUNCTIONS          Link, unlink, query; set single-route broadcast.

 R  RESET                     Reinitialize system and reopen adapter.
 S  SHUTDOWN                  Shutdown the LAN manager.

Type the ID of the function and press Enter ===> [ ]
```

The Trace and Performance program can display breakdown decodes of network data in total frames, MAC frame format, or LLC format. The program has some limited filtering and triggering features.

The only topology supported by both programs is Token Ring (4Mbps and 16Mbps). Obviously both of these programs are Token Ring-only solutions. But by combining both programs on the same PC, you can assemble a good protocol analyzer for a pure IBM-based Token Ring environment.

Spider Systems SpiderAnalyzer

Spider Systems Inc. is owned by Spider Systems Ltd., a European company that markets protocol analysis products worldwide. The company was founded in 1983 and has a respectable presence in the analyzer marketplace.

The SpiderAnalyzer product line offers a comprehensive solution to implement preventive measures to ensure that network faults are identified quickly and resolved. The SpiderAnalyzer product family has a full palette of protocol analyzer configurations, including standard stand alone analyzers and complex multi-network configurations through their SpiderProbes.

The stand alone product is offered in several ways. The SpiderAnalyzer P320 is a preconfigured PC analyzer packaged in a Compaq portable PC. The SpiderAnalyzer K320 is a NIC-and-software kit for configuring the analyzer in your own PC. The P320 and K320 are stand alone units (slaves) for single network configurations. Both the P320 and K320 can be configured as P325 or K325 analyzers, described next.

The P325 and K325 analyzers can be automatically configured to act as slave analyzers or as master analyzers, which can gather statistics in multiple network environments. The 325 analyzers can work with the 320 slaves or with SpiderProbes to capture, analyze, and communicate network data.

The SpiderProbes are non-PC, self-contained units that can act as slaves. The SpiderProbes have full slave capture and analysis capabilities. They are designed as a cost-effective solution for the wide-range implementation of protocol analysis on an internetwork. Figure 4.15 shows a P320 with a SpiderProbe.

The SpiderAnalyzer products support Token Ring (4Mbps and 16Mbps) and EtherNet topologies. The protocol suites supported are:

- IBM SNA
- NetBIOS
- SMB
- Novell
- TCP:IP
- DECnet
- Banyan Vines
- AppleTalk
- XNS
- ISO

The SpiderAnalyzer uses the basic modes of operation. Figure 4.16 shows the main menu. The Alarm mode allows the SpiderAnalyzer to send alarms to an alarm log when specific events occur. The Development mode is where you set and view the main capturing, decoding, filtering, and triggering features in multiple windows. The Performance mode monitors network bandwidth utilization by multiple time-relationship modes. The Statistics mode can monitor individual ring station statistics in an overall mode by frames (see fig. 4.17) and by detailed ring error breakdowns.

The Summary mode maintains a chronological ring activity history for peak and average usage. The Test mode has a built-in TDR along with individual station testing capabilities. You can simulate network load effects with the Traffic Generator. Every mode has custom setup parameters in its submenu.

The SpiderAnalyzer includes a system setup screen for setting up the main operating environmental and logging parameters. You can select the system softkey from the main menu. From this menu you set the base screen display mode along with the main logging route. You can choose either a disk or a printer. The SpiderAnalyzer also supports symbolic naming of specific addresses.

The SpiderAnalyzer has overall multitasking capabilities. Thus you can be gathering statistics in one mode and then switch to another operational mode. You can also run SpiderAnalyzer modes

FIGURE 4.16
The main menu of the Spider Systems SpiderAnalyzer.

```
MODE SCREEN              16 Aug 1991        15:55:23
                      ─── local ───

SpiderAnalyzer

Available modes:

        Alarms                 - Display alarm conditions
        Development            - Capture and decode packets
       │Performance           │- Display current network activity
        Statistics             - Display station statistics
        Summary                - Display network activity history
        Test                   - Test media and stations
        Traffic Generation     - Generate network load
        Open                   - Open on to the ring
        Errors                 - Display error log
        Exit                   - Press RUN or <cr> to exit

Current mode is │Performance│ on │local│ probe

 F1    F2     F3     F4    F5     F6   F7    F8     F9    F10
MODE  ADDR  SET-UP  RUN  SYSTEM              ENVDIR  NEXT  PREV
```

FIGURE 4.17
The SpiderAnalyzer's Statistics mode provides a detailed breakdown of Token Ring error statistics.

```
MODE SCREEN              16 Aug 1991        15:55:23
                      ─── local ───

SpiderAnalyzer

Available modes:

        Alarms                 - Display alarm conditions
        Development            - Capture and decode packets
       │Performance           │- Display current network activity
        Statistics             - Display station statistics
        Summary                - Display network activity history
        Test                   - Test media and stations
        Traffic Generation     - Generate network load
        Open                   - Open on to the ring
        Errors                 - Display error log
        Exit                   - Press RUN or <cr> to exit

Current mode is │Performance│ on │local│ probe

 F1    F2     F3     F4    F5     F6   F7    F8     F9    F10
MODE  ADDR  SET-UP  RUN  SYSTEM              ENVDIR  NEXT  PREV
```

and at the same time enter DOS. They have even built in a custom utility called "tmake123" which can convert SpiderAnalyzer files to Lotus 1-2-3.

The SpiderAnalyzer has some security features. You can set up the Development and Traffic Generation modes with password protection.

One of the SpiderAnalyzer Token Ring strengths is its excellent MAC Error Log, which keeps a chronological log of beacon frames, Neighbor Notification frames, Active Monitor frames, all soft errors, and ring recoveries.

Spider Systems has a fine reputation for providing high-quality products. The multinetwork approach using the master/slave relationship with the 325 Master SpiderAnalyzers and SpiderProbes addresses the new demand for achieving protocol analysis from one central point.

FTP Software LANWatch Network Analyzer

FTP Inc. is a Massachusetts-based company founded in 1986. They are known for developing reliable, sophisticated PC networking software for extremely cost-effective prices. They are also dedicated to supporting open architectures for the LAN marketplace. FTP Software has a slew of excellent products. This review concentrates on an FTP LAN analyzer product called LANWatch.

The LANWatch Network Analyzer is a software-only product that relies on the user having a specific type of hardware. The software package requires a PC with an FTP-supported, topology-specific NIC.

The LANWatch Network Analyzer supports the following topologies: Token Ring 4Mbps (FTP is working on support for 16Mbps), Proteon's ProNET-10, and EtherNet.

The protocol suites supported are:

- Novell
- TCP:IP
- UDP
- ICMP
- DECnet

- NFS
- Banyan Vines
- AppleTalk
- XNS
- CHAOSNET
- ISO
- X.25

The LANWatch Network Analyzer has two basic modes of operation, Real Time Display and Examine.

The Real Time Display mode captures and displays a chronological listing of network frames dynamically as they are captured. Multiple display modes are available for all seven OSI layers.

The Examine mode allows the network frames that are captured during the Real Time Display mode to be decoded and examined. Captured data can be displayed in two modes, Short and Long. The Short mode gives an overall listing of packets received. The Long mode shows detailed information for a selected frame. Figure 4.18 shows LANWatch's Examine Long mode screen.

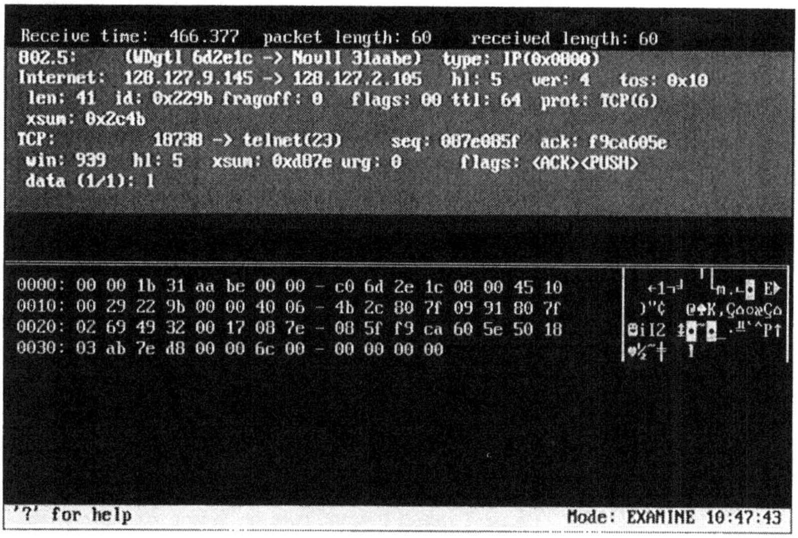

FIGURE 4.18
The LANWatch analyzer includes an Examine Long mode screen, which gives detailed information on an individual captured frame.

```
Receive time:  466.377   packet length: 60    received length: 60
802.5:    (WDgtl 6d2e1c -> Novll 31aabe)  type: IP(0x0800)
Internet:  128.127.9.145 -> 128.127.2.105   hl: 5   ver: 4   tos: 0x10
  len: 41  id: 0x229b fragoff: 0   flags: 00 ttl: 64  prot: TCP(6)
  xsum: 0x2c4b
TCP:         18738 -> telnet(23)      seq: 007e005f  ack: f9ca605e
  win: 939  hl: 5  xsum: 0xd07e urg: 0      flags: <ACK><PUSH>
  data (1/1): 1


0000:  00 00 1b 31 aa be 00 00 - c0 6d 2e 1c 08 00 45 10
0010:  00 29 22 9b 00 00 40 06 - 4b 2c 80 7f 09 91 80 7f
0020:  02 69 49 32 00 17 08 7e - 08 5f f9 ca 60 5e 50 18
0030:  03 ab 7e d8 00 00 6c 00 - 00 00 00 00

'?' for help                                    Mode: EXAMINE 10:47:43
```

The LANWatch Network Analyzer has a good set of filtering, triggering, and alarm features that will allow you to modify the Real Time Display and Examine modes for optimal viewing and decoding. By keying a **?** at any of the main modes, you can enter the LANWatch Help main menu, which will guide you through most of the custom setup features that you will need.

LANWatch has a histogram feature to capture, display, and record frames captured and general network traffic statistics. The package also includes statistic gathering for most network errors, including Token Ring MAC soft errors.

FTP offers a programmer's aid that will allow you to develop custom protocol decodes, filters, printing routines, and report generators.

FTP is working on some new developments such as auto-print report generation and network bandwidth monitoring. Currently the LANWatch Network Analyzer's main focus is to provide capture and decode capabilities for most major protocols and major topologies. The complete protocol analysis capabilities of LANWatch and its cost-effectiveness give the LAN analysis marketplace a good reason to consider using this product.

Triticom TokenVision Monitor

Founded in 1989, Triticom is based in St. Paul, Minnesota. The company designs and markets high-quality LAN monitoring, management, and modeling products. They have a number of good LAN monitoring products available, including TokenVision, EtherVision, and ArcVision. Triticom also has a software-only protocol analyzer product line called the LANdecoder series. This product line currently supports Token Ring and EtherNet.

The TokenVision Monitor is precisely that: a Token Ring network monitoring tool. Designed specifically for the Token Ring topology, it monitors and displays all major Token Ring environmental statistics.

TokenVision is a software product for which the user must have specific types of hardware, including a 286 or 386 PC with a Triticom-supported Token Ring NIC. TokenVision will run on most promiscuous Token Ring NICs.

TokenVision is a Token Ring monitoring tool; it does not function as a protocol analyzer, so it does not identify and display high-level protocol suites. Only certain pertinent MAC types are identified.

The TokenVision Monitor has an extremely user friendly menuing system; figure 4.19 shows its main menu.

FIGURE 4.19
The main menu
of Triticom's
TokenVision
Monitor.

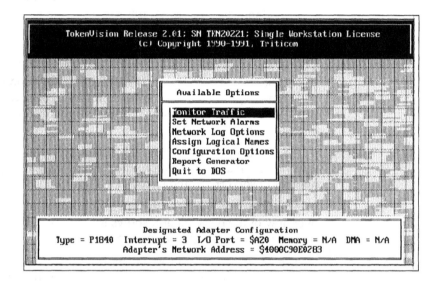

The TokenVision Monitor uses one main operational mode, the Monitor Traffic Mode, which is the first choice on the main menu. The other menu choices are:

- Set Network Alarms

- Network Log Options

- Assign Logical Names

- Configuration Options

- Report Generator

These choices are for configuring the main operating environment. The Monitor Traffic Mode is based on four Real Time Display Modes for viewing the traffic being captured:

- **Statistic Mode**. Shows an extensive view of all Token Ring statistics.

- **Skyline Mode**. Displays a skyline graphical view of network bandwidth utilization or frame count statistics.

- **Station Mode**. Traces frames sent from individual stations.

- **MAC Mode**. Displays an overall information screen about captured MAC frames.

Once you enter the Monitor Traffic Mode you can vector into any of the Real Time Display Modes for viewing the network traffic.

All the Real Time Display Modes interrelate to show a synergistic and chronological listing of network frames dynamically, as they are captured. Multiple display modes are available by frame and individual stations.

The Station Mode shows the full variety of station-to-frame statistics, such as total frame count, total Kbytes, average frame size, number of soft errors, and so on.

The Statistic Mode is a real plus in that it displays a total overview of the network and shows important Token Ring statistics, such as source-routing information.

The MAC mode is an excellent Token Ring feature. It displays critical Token Ring information such as Active Monitor MAC frames, Ring Recovery frames, and a full detailed Token Ring Soft Error MAC frame report. Figure 4.20 shows the MAC Mode screen.

FIGURE 4.20
The TokenVision
Monitor MAC
mode includes
information on
Active Monitor,
Ring Recovery,
and Soft Error
MAC frames.

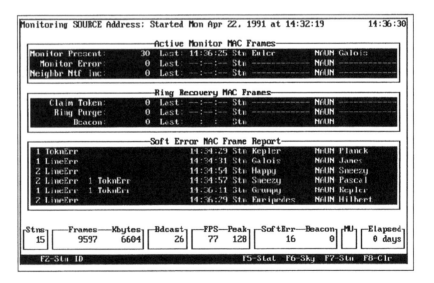

The Set Network Alarm feature permits the TokenVision monitor to dispatch alarms when specific Token Ring events happen.

A great troubleshooting aid is the Network Log Options feature, which maintains an event log of major network events such as monitor traffic mode ON and OFF, Token Ring errors, alarms, and peak network utilization. You can set up this log to be sent dynamically to disk file or a printer. The important part of this feature is that you can set up your network testing environment and then let the testing statistics be automatically saved.

The Assign Logical Names feature allows you to assign specific Token Ring addresses with symbolic names. The Configuration Options feature is for setting up additional alarm features.

A new feature added by Triticom is the Report Generator, which has excellent report-generating features for the Token Ring environment. Some of the statistics that can be generated are Frame Distribution, Global Network Summaries, Network Utilization, Individual Station Statistics, Station Bandwidth, and Logical Name Assignments. You can print most of the viewable statistics in various formats and can feed them into several popular PC report applications.

Triticom has a superb monitoring tool for the Token Ring topology. Its key functions are extremely easy to use, and the screen displays are easy to understand. This product is cost-effective, informative, and a pleasure to use.

Novell

The LANalyzer was originally designed by Excelan in 1984. In 1989 Novell acquired Excelan and then in 1990 formed a separate internal division called the LANalyzer Products Division, which develops and markets network monitoring and management products.

Besides the LANalyzer, the LANalyzer Products Division markets the LANtern Network Monitor product line, which focuses on remote monitoring and management of multiple LANs from a central point. The LANtern product line currently integrates with the LANalyzer only through remote communication software applications that allow remote gathering of statistics captured by the LANalyzer (such as Norton-Lambert's Close-Up LAN). Novell still considers the LANalyzer's main role to be as a portable protocol analyzer and has not yet implemented the product into a distributed monitoring approach for LAN environments.

The LANalyzer itself is a full-blown high-performance protocol analyzer. The product offers full decoding for most major protocol suites and can interface with most topologies.

You can buy the LANalyzer product from Novell in a NIC-and-software kit package and configure it in your own PC. Some Novell resellers offer the LANalyzer kit preconfigured in selected portable PCs.

The LANalyzer supports the following topologies:

- Token Ring (4Mbps and 16Mbps)
- EtherNet
- StarLAN

The protocol suites supported are:

- IBM SNA
- NetBIOS
- SMB
- Novell (including decodes for v3.11)
- TCP:IP
- DECnet
- Banyan Vines
- AppleTalk
- XNS
- SUN:NFS
- ISO

The LANalyzer executes all the basic modes of operation, with an extremely user-friendly menu system. From the main menu you can maneuver to other submenus. Figure 4.21 shows the main menu.

The Application menu is the main entry point for setting up the LANalyzer capturing mode, concerning all selections for protocol suites, filters, triggers, alarms, and so on. From the Application menu you can either choose and configure custom applications test suites, or you can pick one of the predefined Token Ring application test suites.

FIGURE 4.21
The main menu of the LANalyzer provides access to the application suites for analysis of various protocols.

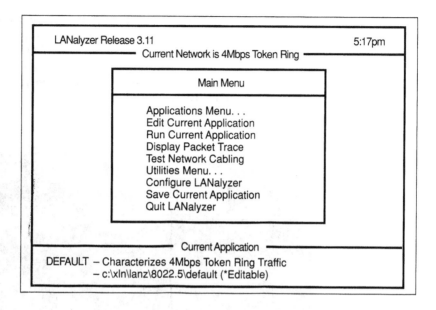

The LANalyzer is designed so you can activate a particular application test suite that has predefined triggers, filters, and other custom setup parameters. One of the innovative features in the LANalyzer setup parameters is that you can define up to nine custom receive channels. Receive channels are the actual filter channels for what you want to capture during a protocol analysis session. LANalyzer also has six custom transmit channels. These transmit channels allow you to generate six selective traffic patterns onto the network.

The Edit Current Application menu pick allows you to dynamically modify the original parameters for the current application test suite that is running. From its submenu you can specify certain data collection parameters, such as the main statistics disk-logging file and printing options. The LANalyzer does not offer any custom report-generation features, but statistic files can be imported into various PC applications.

The Run Current Application menu pick simply activates the current application test suite that was selected in the main Application menu. Once it is activated you are subvectored to the main network monitoring display modes. There are four main modes for displaying the network environment that can be selected:

- **Global display mode.** The Global mode gives you an overall, detailed screen that displays overall network utilization statistics in a blended graphical and numerical format. This screen also displays vital Token Ring statistics such as Ring Recoveries and Token Rotation Time. Figure 4.22 shows the Global mode display.

FIGURE 4.22
The LANalyzer's Global Display mode depicts overall network statistics in both graphic and numeric formats.

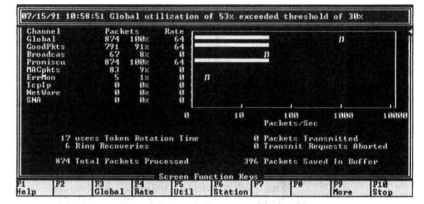

- **Rate display mode.** This mode displays statistical information about the individual packets received through the receive channels.

- **Utilization display mode.** This display mode gives a universal depiction of the network bandwidth being used by any active channels.

- **Station display mode.** This displays statistics on an individual station's interaction with the active channels being monitored.

The Display Packet Trace menu is where you view captured frames in an overall chronological frame list or in detailed frame view. From this mode you can load previously captured traces from disk or can view the current captured trace. You can also save a current trace to disk. The Display Packet Trace mode has individual setup parameters for most decoding needs.

The Test Network Cabling menu pick allows you to perform a series of network tests, including a basic cable test, LANalyzer connection status, and ring condition status tests to detect failures such as beaconing.

The Utilities menu pick activates a submenu that includes four LANalyzer utilities for performing certain tasks to further customize how you use a particular application test suite. The four utilities are:

- **Name utility.** This utility allows you to assign names to specific Token Ring addresses.

- **Genname utility.** This is a Novell-related feature that can automatically generate a name file for a set of specific node addresses on a network.

- **Stats utility.** This utility allows you to view a previously saved file from an application test in the main display modes.

- **Template utility.** With the Template utility you can further customize how the main transmit and receive channels are configured.

The Configure LANalyzer menu pick is where you can configure the main operating environment for the LANalyzer. This feature allows you to configure the network topology type, file buffer options, disk-logging routes, and alarm parameters.

The LANalyzer has some good Token Ring strengths. There is an Automatic Mapping feature (MAP) that dynamically generates all the Token Ring network nodes in chronological order. Novell has designed a special application test suite called "ERRMON" which will configure each of the receive channels to capture a specific Token Ring error. There is also another application test suite called "SEGMENTS" that dynamically monitors Token Ring bridge traffic.

One of the LANalyzer's main advantages is the custom application test suites shown in Figure 4.23. Novell has packaged in some excellent predefined application test suites designed specifically for the Token Ring architecture. With some ingenuity you can even customize special, unique tests for the Token Ring environment. Another point for the LANalyzer is its ability to dynamically handle routing of multiple transmit and receive channels.

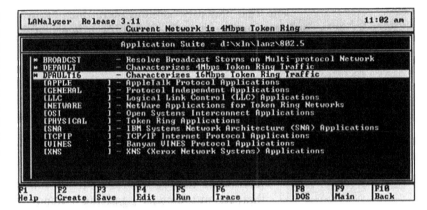

FIGURE 4.23

The main menu of the LANalyzer application test suites provides the ability to predefine specific testing for various Token Ring network problems.

Novell has made the LANalyzer extremely cost-effective by including most of the major protocol suites at no additional cost. Overall this product has power-packed performance, along with excellent statistic-gathering features. The menuing system is well designed and is simple to operate.

For the record, Novell is currently developing a series of network management products that will enhance the overall capabilities of the LANalyzer.

Digilog LANVista

Digilog Inc. is a subsidiary of the CXR Corp., which develops communication and test equipment with creative high-technology characteristics and high quality. Digilog was formed in 1989 and specializes in communication test equipment and network management products. Recently Digilog has been a leader in the test equipment arena with its introduction of the LANVista protocol analysis product line.

The LANVista analyzer product family has a full array of protocol analyzer configurations. It includes both standard standalone analyzers and complex distributed systems. The standalone product is offered in two ways: a NIC/software package for configuring within your own PC, and preconfigured in a Dolch 386 or Compaq portable PC.

Digilog markets the LANVista systems in a 100 and 200 series. The 200 series is the same as the 100 series, except that it is designed with a higher-performance platform. If you implement additional memory and certain design features, the 200 series can accomplish advanced precapture filtering and can support multiple protocol suites simultaneously.

The distributed LANVista system's core mission is to monitor from one principal point LANs that are dispersed across complex LAN layout patterns. Obviously another manufacturer has caught on to the need for observing LANs from a central point.

Digilog implements its distributed system via a master/slave design scheme. Their slave units are self-contained units with full capture and analysis capabilities. The master unit is a PC with a Master Interface Card (MIC) and software designed to continuously gather and decode statistics from the slaves and then to provide a real-time overview of the internetwork environment.

The slave units can communicate with a master unit via two different methods: by the internetwork itself, or by RS232 links. The RS232 links allow for a fault-redundant backup path between the master and slave units in the event of a LAN segment failure. (The 100 series LANVista cannot support remote access to slave units via RS232.)

Currently the LANVista analyzer products are designed for the Token Ring (4Mbps and 16Mbps) and EtherNet topologies.

The current protocol suites supported are:
- IBM SNA
- SMB
- NetBIOS
- Novell
- TCP:IP (DOD)
- XNS:MSNET
- Banyan Vines
- AppleTalk
- XNS

The basic modes of operation for the LANVista analyzer are listed on the main menu shown in figure 4.24. They include:
- Configure
- Monitor Segment
- Network Management
- Simulate Traffic

- Test LAN Cable
- Examine Frames
- Run Diagnostics
- Modify Password

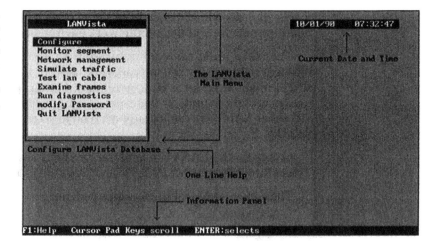

FIGURE 4.24
The basic protocol-analyzer modes of operation are accessible from the main menu of the LANVista analyzer.

The Configure mode allows you to set the analysis operating environment. With this feature you can set up the network type, the protocols to decode, filtering, the capture buffers, and all the custom configurations for the distributed system, if it is being implemented.

The Monitor Segment mode allows you to initiate capturing and decoding of network data for protocol analysis. Also in this mode you can configure triggering, alarms, additional filtering, and disk or printer logging routes. Most of the statistics that you can capture can be printed in various forms.

The Network Management mode allows you to view statistical information on the performance of the LANs being monitored. Statistics are available for Token Ring functional addresses, individual nodes, bridge utilization, protocols, and frames.

Generating traffic onto the LAN for troubleshooting purposes can be done through the Simulate Traffic mode. The Test LAN Cable mode includes some of the basic TDR functions. The Examine Frames mode allows you to view captured frames in a frame list format or in detailed frame breakdown mode. From this mode you can view the protocols at all layers.

In a distributed system, the slaves can be tested with the Run Diagnostic mode. The diagnostics allow you to test the RAM and LAN NICs in the slave units.

The LANVista analyzer has some excellent security features built-in to the core operations, including enhanced security features in the LANVista analyzer. First, there are three basic modes for entering the main menu: Administrative (Admin), Secure, and User.

The Admin mode allows for overall LANVista operations, including the initial designing of the master/slave configurations for a distributed system. The Secure mode allows for all operations except setting up master/slave parameters. The User mode allows most LANVista operations, but does not allow the user to enter the Examine mode or the Simulate Traffic mode, or to modify any master/slave setup parameters. Through the Modify Password mode you can update the Administrative and Secure mode passwords.

The LANVista analyzer has excellent Token Ring monitoring features. Digilog has included a Token Ring Statistics Screen (TRSTATS) monitoring screen from which you can view vital Token Ring statistics, such as beacon frames, Ring Purge frames, MAC and non-MAC frame breakdowns, errors, and network utilization bandwidth for local and multiple-ring environments. The TRSTATS screen is shown in figure 4.25.

FIGURE 4.25
The LANVista Token Ring Statistics screen displays vital Token Ring network statistics.

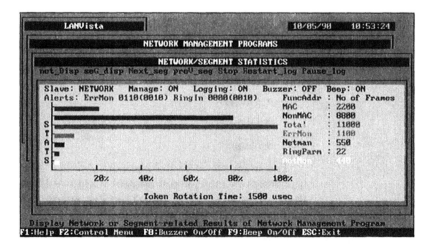

Another important feature is that all LANVista screens are fully compatible with Microsoft Windows. This is an excellent feature for integrating with a distributed system when you need to view multiple rings from a master console.

Because of its thorough approach to protocol analysis features and its distributed system capabilities, the LANVista product is an excellent analysis product for both basic and extensive Token Ring installations. One of its overall best features is the security attributes available. These security features can play a key role when you're implementing a distributed system in a multiple-ring environment.

Hewlett-Packard Network Advisor

Hewlett-Packard has long been a leader in the test equipment arena. So it's no surprise that they have also entered the LAN protocol analyzer market with the recent introduction of their Network Advisor protocol analyzer.

The Network Advisor has a unique feature called the "Finder Expert System." This innovative artificial intelligence system analyzes captured data from a protocol analysis session and gives logical suggestions as to a general analysis of the network communication processes. It also can identify possible failure causes for any network errors encountered during an analyzer session.

The HP Network Advisor is a self-contained standalone unit based on RISC architecture. Currently the Network Advisor product is designed for the Token Ring (4Mbps and 16Mbps) and EtherNet topologies.

The current protocol suites supported are:

- IBM SNA
- SMB
- NetBIOS
- Novell
- TCP:IP
- DECnet
- 3Com

The main menu of the Network Advisor has graphical displays of a series of main menu control windows from which you access the Control, Config, and Display setup menu windows for configuring the testing environment.

The Network Advisor has some excellent Token Ring features. The unit can display vital Token Ring statistics with unique gauge-type displays that show network measurements that are dynamically occurring, such as statistics about ring purges, the claim token process, and both soft and hard errors. Figure 4.26 shows the "Token-Ring MAC Protocol" screen.

FIGURE 4.26
Hewlett-Packard's Network Advisor analyzer provides some excellent Token Ring-specific information.

You can also plot testing results in graphical algorithmic bar and line charts. Figure 4.27 shows the "Token-Ring Detail" screen.

The HP Network Advisor's RISC-based hardware architecture allows for high-performance gathering and decoding of network data, with the added touch of being extremely dynamic.

The Finder Expert System gives you the option of focusing on the network symptoms that occur rather than spending time analyzing the data captured during a protocol analysis session. You can still view and decode the captured data from a protocol analysis session, but with the Finder Expert System you can often locate the cause of a failure more quickly and efficiently.

The overall advantage of this product is that it gives you all the basic protocol analyzer features, along with an expert system to help you decode and make logical analysis assessments and troubleshooting conclusions on the causes of network failures.

FIGURE 4.27
The Token-Ring
Detail screen of
the Network
Advisor includes
graphical
depictions of
analysis-session
statistics.

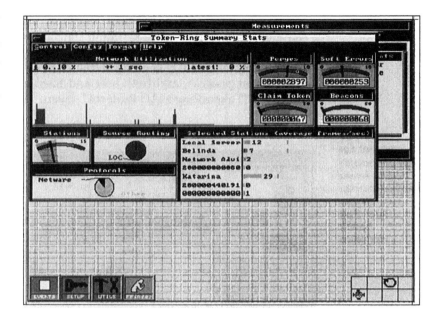

FIGURE 4.27
The Token-Ring
Detail screen of
the Network
Advisor includes
graphical
depictions of
analysis-session
statistics.

TIME DOMAIN REFLECTOMETER (TDR) THEORY

Cable problems cause a very high percentage of failure symptoms in today's networks. Years ago, troubleshooting a possible bad cable was a chore. But today there is a variety of test equipment on the market that makes the task a lot easier. The new TDRs that have hit the marketplace are innovative, fast, and effective.

A TDR is a device that generates and transmits a specific signal down a cable and monitors the cable for a signal reflection. This process is sometimes nicknamed "cable radar," because it acts somewhat like normal radar.

The signal sent out by a TDR has predefined amplitude and time span. The TDR next eavesdrops on the cable to sample and then measure any signal reflection that occurs. If there are no problems with the cable and it is properly terminated, a signal reflection should not occur. But any problems will cause a signal reflection.

A cable can have a number of different problems:

- Open cables (physically broken)

- Shorted cables (two or more internal conductors crossed)

- Crimped cables

- Bad cable termination (improper or no termination)

- Other miscellaneous problems (cable kinks, bends, and so on)

Depending on the type of problem, a problem-type-specific signal reflection will occur. This unique reflection is sometimes called cable signal fault signature (CSFS). Today, TDRs are designed to capture and interpret most of the different CSFS-type problems that can occur on a cable. Most of the units analyze the polarity and amplitude of the CSFS to determine the probable cable fault type. Some of the units actually tell you the probable fault type and fault distance, to the approximate foot, from the test point.

Optical TDRs are available for testing fiber cable. They operate in the same manner, except they use a laser for a light source to generate optical pulse signals, and they use an optical receiver. OTDRs contain a microprocessor that converts the received optical signal to a digital signal. The digital signal results are typically decoded by custom data-acquisition software.

Fiber testing employs different terminology for problem causes and measurements. OTDRs measure signal losses as Rayleigh Backscattered Signals. Opens, bends, kinks, and splices are usually measured as Fresnel Reflections or splice losses. OTDRs also measure fiber signal signature spikes as ghosts.

For the Token Ring environment there are TDRs that also address some of the Token Ring topology error conditions, such as beaconing. TDR manufacturers have been coming out with some imaginative gear for testing a ring, including TDRs with actual network bandwidth monitoring features.

Using a Time Domain Reflectometer

The first step before testing any cable is to make sure that the section of cable that is suspect is isolated from the rest of the LAN. Some PCs, hubs, repeaters, and bridges may respond with return signals in response to a TDR signal test. The best way to avoid this is to unplug these devices and test each cable section separately.

It is also important to make sure that the section of cable that is being tested is properly terminated. Most TDRs come with terminators for the type of cable they can test. A good way to be sure is to use one of the TDR terminators.

When first using a TDR you should select the switch for the type of cable you are going to test. Next, generate a general signal test. If there are any problems, the TDR should tell you. It's that easy!

With a fairly sophisticated TDR, you can receive a full complement of information. If there are no cable problems, you should receive some sort of cable OK message. If there are problems, most TDRs will tell you the probable type of cable fault and the distance to the fault.

Some TDRs have separate tests for cable resistance, DB loss (signal loss), continuity (opens and shorts), and cable noise. Other units collate the tests in different ways. It is always best to first generate a general signal test to get a cable quality benchmark, then to perform any specific categorized testing. Some innovative units allow you to save and print the test results. This is a great feature for documenting your test results.

Next, some of the industry-standard cable testing equipment is presented.

CABLE-TESTING EQUIPMENT

For the Token Ring topology, there is a good selection of cable-testing equipment. LAN cable test gear has been available for many years, but today the LAN marketplace features many new innovative types of instruments.

The following section gives an overview of some of the cable-testing equipment standard to the Token Ring industry. Most of the products here have been designed with specific features for testing and monitoring the Token Ring topology cabling medium.

Microtest Ring Scanner and Pair Scanner

Microtest has been developing high-technology testing gear since 1984. They have a reputation for excellent products that provide innovative leadership in the LAN test equipment arena.

In 1988 Microtest introduced their Cable Scanner, which was one of the marketplace's first cost-effective handheld cable-testing tools. Their more recent introduction of the Ring Scanner is what this section will focus on, as it is designed specifically for the Token Ring topology. The Pair Scanner will also be discussed, because Microtest has designed an interface with the Ring Scanner to offer extended Token Ring monitoring features.

Let's first discuss the Pair Scanner and its features. The Pair Scanner is a highly advanced TDR that has leading-edge network-monitoring features. Figure 4.28 shows the Pair Scanner. It includes all the basic functions, TDR signal testing, DB Loss, continuity testing, noise testing, and resistance testing, along with UTP-specific testing.

FIGURE 4.28
The Microtest Pair Scanner is a time domain reflectometer, which checks for cable and termination problems.

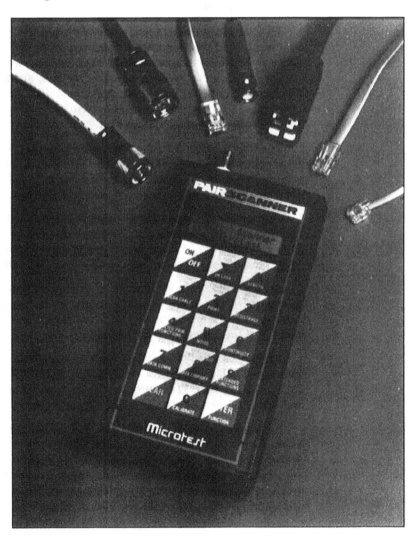

The Pair Scanner can test the following cable types:

- Token Ring
- Thick and thin EtherNet
- ARCnet and RX-Net
- PVC
- Full twisted pair support, including 10BASE-T
- Additional support for testing IBM cable types 1, 2, 3, 6, and 9

The Pair Scanner also has a slew of extended features. Microtest included a set of data communication tests that allows the Pair Scanner to function as an RS232 data line monitor. There is a full choice of advanced twisted-pair-specific tests, such as Activating a Twisted Pair Hub, Checking for Crosstalk, Office Locator for checking cable drops, Conductor Wiring Checks, and a complete overall Twisted Pair Cable Scan Test.

The Pair Scanner interfaces with the Microtest 10BASE-T injector to accomplish some of these tests. The Pair Scanner is also fully compatible with the Microtest Cable Tracer II to detect cables that may be hard to locate in walls, floors, and ceilings.

One of the foremost advanced features is that the Pair Scanner can produce printed reports for all its testing functions. The unit has a Print Data Store Library buffer and can print serially at 300 to 38,400 baud from its data communication printer interface port.

Another nice feature is the Pair Scanner Management software that allows the Scanner's data communication port to also be interfaced to PC COM ports 1 or 2, so the reports can be saved to a text file for future viewing and printing.

The unit can fully interface with an oscilloscope to view all the generated TDR signals and their respective CSFSes. Microtest has also included an alarm mode which can monitor the cabling medium and trigger an alarm when certain events occur.

In association with testing the Token Ring topology, the key domain for the Pair Scanner is the Network Monitoring Buffer feature, which allows the Pair Scanner to capture data transmitted on a cabling medium and to display and print the relative network traffic. Interfaced with the Ring Scanner, the Token Ring bandwidth utilization can be measured and also displayed and printed.

Next we discuss the Microtest Ring Scanner and how it interfaces with the Pair Scanner.

The Ring Scanner is the newest member of the Microtest scanner family. This unit does not include TDR capabilities, but it interacts with the Microtest Pair Scanner for TDR testing and monitoring. It was specifically designed for testing only the Token Ring topology cabling medium. It can quickly test and isolate bad Token Ring cabling sections and defective MAU ports. The unit tests both 4Mbps and 16Mbps rings.

The Ring Scanner functions logically divide into two categories:

- **Token Ring cable tests for IBM cable types 1, 2, 3, 6, and 9,** which include specific testing for general loopback testing and unshorted tests.

- **Network tests,** which include data rate detection, ring status indication, fault simulation capability, and data traffic monitoring.

Let's overview the Token Ring cabling tests. There are two modes for testing Token Ring cable sections.

Mode 1 allows you to test a specific Token Ring cable section, such as a lobe, to determine if the shorting pins in the cable connector are working properly. This test can be performed with the standard IBM data connector and a type-3 RJ45 connector (with RJ45 female coupler).

If the shorting pins are correctly looping back the internal transmit and receive pairs, the green OK LED will illuminate. If any of the four individual conductor LEDs (red, orange, green, black) illuminate red, there is a problem. The Microtest manual will guide you to the exact probable problem and solution.

Mode 2 is for testing a specific Token Ring cable section with its cable connector shorting pins open. This allows you to detect cable problems that cannot be found when the shorting pins are internally looping back. This test is different, because without the cable connector internal pins shorting, data should be able to fully flow in and out of the data connector. By using a special loopback connector and the "Activate Cable Test" button, you can perform an actual data loop test.

This test also tests for proper shielding in all cabling types except for type 3. The green OK LED will illuminate if there are no test failures. If there are any problems detected, a combination of the four individual conductor LEDs will illuminate red. Again, the Microtest manual will guide you to the probable problem and solution.

There is also a LAMP test mode which will verify proper operation of all the Cable Test LEDs. By putting the Ring Scanner in the LAMP test mode and pressing the "Activate Cable Test" button, you can test all the LEDs.

Next let's look at the Network Monitoring Tests. The Ring Scanner includes an automatic Data Rate Detection feature. The ring speed can be dynamically identified as either 4Mbps or 16Mbps.

The Ring Status Indication feature allows you to test the capability of passing data completely around the ring. By using the "Activate Ring Test" button you can generate a data pattern onto the ring. If the data makes a complete trip around the ring, the "Ring Status" LED will light green. The LED will light red if it does not receive the transmitted data. This is simply a ring path integrity test and is excellent for verifying MAU port relays.

The Fault Simulation feature allows you to introduce a simulated fault onto your Token Ring network. This type of feature can be a good aid for troubleshooting, in conjunction with other network monitoring tools such as protocol analyzers and LAN management/diagnostic packages.

During this test the Ring Scanner enters the ring as a node but does not generate any data. This is a simulation of an actual failed ring station. I advise extreme caution in performing this test, as it will cause your ring to go through Ring Recovery. Make sure that your ring users are not active and there are no open files on the file server. Overall this is a good test to benchmark other testing gear.

There is a Data Traffic Monitoring function built in to the Ring Scanner. It is a dynamic function that allows you to monitor data traffic on the ring. Every time data travels around the ring, the Ring Scanner "Data Traffic" LED will illuminate.

The Data Traffic Monitoring and the Data Rate Detection features work together to provide the necessary data for the bandwidth utilization testing via the Pair Scanner, as discussed earlier. The Ring Scanner interfaces to the Pair Scanner via an RJ45 connector (To Scanner Port).

What actually occurs is that the Ring Scanner collects the Token Ring-specific data rate and transmit frequencies and passes them to the Pair Scanner. The Pair Scanner then uses its Network Monitoring Buffer feature to display and print the Token Ring bandwidth utilization. Figure 4.29 shows a sample Network Monitor Report printout from a Ring Scanner/Pair Scanner test.

Note that the Ring Scanner only monitors data frames and not tokens. Also note that two other Microtest units, the Cable Scanner and the Quick Scanner, include most of the same Network Monitoring Buffer features to work with the Ring Scanner.

Overall, Microtest has shown a dedication to the cable-testing environment. Microtest is due to release a TDR called the Next Scanner that will include some built-in artificial intelligence, for determining which tests should be run and dynamically measuring the specific cable type.

FIGURE 4.29
Microtest's
Pair Scanner
processes data
from the Ring
Scanner for
display or printing.

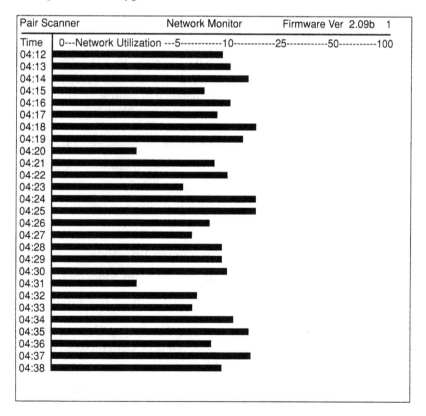

All their testing instruments are well-documented and a pleasure to use. The Ring Scanner and its interoperability with the Pair Scanner's TDR and monitoring capabilities provide a superb testing approach for the Token Ring topology.

Bytex RingOut Cable Tester

Bytex Inc. is a Massachusetts-based company that specializes in high-technology LAN products. In 1990 Bytex introduced the RingOut Cable Tester, which is a cable tester designed specifically for the Token Ring topology.

Bytex's approach to testing the Token Ring cabling medium is unique. The RingOut Cable Tester does not function as a TDR, but it can interface with an oscilloscope to perform signal trace testing. The Bytex philosophy is that the Token Ring cabling system can be troubleshot more effectively by Token Ring-specific tests, rather than by using a TDR. It is true that certain Token Ring cable sections may pass a TDR signal test and yet not properly carry Token Ring frames on the medium.

The sell is as follows: With the Token Ring topology, if you only troubleshoot a section of cable at a time, there is really no need to know how far the distance of failure is. This is a different approach, and it is effective if your troubleshooting methods follow along. It will work if you test a cable by first unplugging each section, terminate it, and then test that cable section separately.

The RingOut Cable Tester includes four main testing modes:

- Cable Test mode
- Ring Test mode
- DC Continuity Test mode
- Signal Degradation Test mode

Figure 4.30 displays the Bytex RingOut Cable Tester.

Before using any of the main test modes you must preset the RingOut Tester operation parameters switches. The parameters switch choices are (1) either STP or UTP cabling, (2) either 4Mbps or 16Mbps, and (3) either Data or Cont modes. (Cont mode is only set for DC Continuity Test mode.)

The Cable Test mode allows an intelligent loopback test. Once you set the parameter switches and connect the unit to a cabling medium section or MAU port, all you have to do is turn the unit on and it will initiate a cable loopback test. The RingOut Tester acts intelligently by monitoring the cable for network traffic before activating a cable loopback test.

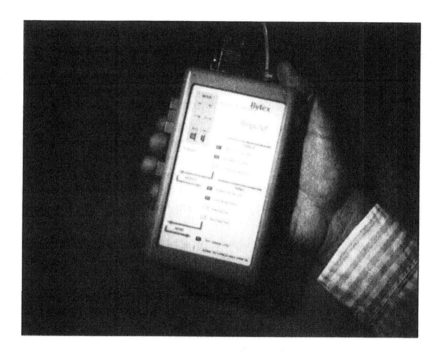

The unit indicates no cable problems by illuminating the green LOOPBACK/CABLE OK LED. If there are any problems, the RingOut Tester will either illuminate the red MAU PORT FAILURE LED (indicates bad loopback in MAU port) or the red NO CABLE LOOPBACK LED (indicates bad cable or bad loopback in the shorting pins of the cable connector).

The Ring Test mode includes two subtests: the Insertion Test and the Send Test.

To activate an Insertion Test, you need only push an "Insert" button on the RingOut Tester. During the Insertion Test the RingOut Tester activates an actual ring insertion by asserting DC phantom voltage to the MAU port. There are four possible LED responses from the RingOut Tester:

- The yellow RING INACTIVE LED (indicating either no traffic on the ring, a data transmission rate mismatch, or a signal degradation)

- The green RING ACTIVE/DROP OK LED (indicating successful insertion to a normally functioning ring)

- The red INSERTION FAILURE LED (indicating unsuccessful insertion to ring)

- The red BEACONING LED (indicating presence of a beaconing ring station on the ring)

The RingOut Tester can actually enter a beaconing ring. This feature is extremely helpful when troubleshooting a beaconing ring, because you can remove stations until the beaconing LED goes out.

The Send Test mode follows the Insertion Test mode because you must first be physically inserted into the ring. Once the RingOut Tester is inserted you activate the Send Test by simply pushing the "Send" button on the tester. The Send Test transmits an actual Token Ring test signal onto the ring and then waits to receive the signal back. The RingOut Tester provides two possible LED responses:

- The green SIGNAL RETURNED/DROP OK LED (indicating successful transmission and receive back status)

- The red TEST SIGNAL LOST LED (indicating either an MAU port failure, or a ring signal degradation)

The Signal Degradation Test mode allows you to perform a more-detailed Token Ring signal signature analysis. You can simulate certain tests to receive the data that a normal TDR would provide. These tests can be performed by connecting the RingOut Cable Tester to an oscilloscope, via instructions in the RingOut manual.

The DC Continuity Test identifies specific cable faults such as cable shorts and open cables. To perform the DC Continuity tests you must use the RingOut Tester in conjunction with the Bytex Continuity Tester. The Bytex RingOut manual guides you through testing a specific Token Ring cable section and helps you isolate the exact probable problem and solution.

The tests monitor the cable's internal transmit and receive pairs and illuminate four LEDs with different result combinations. Four individual conductor LEDs (red, orange, green, black) on the Continuity Tester represent the test results.

The overall strength of the Bytex RingOut Tester is that it can generate, capture, and decipher actual Token Ring data patterns. When it enters a ring it does so transparently, without affecting the ring state. Its ability to enter and test a beaconing ring also gives the troubleshooter a conclusive edge.

The RingOut Tester has a well-documented manual that provides you with good instructions for using the Tester to troubleshoot a ring. Bytex has put a lot of careful Token Ring thought and performance into the handheld RingOut Tester.

IBM Cable Tester (IBM P/N 4760500)

IBM introduced the IBM Cable Tester years ago, when Token Ring was first conceived. It was the first cable tester specifically designed for the Token Ring LAN arena. It has most of the features included in basic Token Ring loopback and DC continuity tests. It is a handheld unit that includes data wrap connectors for specific cable-section testing.

The unit also includes four LEDs (red, orange, green, black) to monitor the four individual conductors. It can test the Token Ring cable's internal transmit and receive pairs, and illuminate the LEDs to signify different test conclusions.

The unit is still a good test instrument for basic Token Ring cable medium testing.

Antel Optronics AOC10 OTDR

Antel Optronics was founded in 1985 and is a Canadian company that specializes in the design and manufacture of fiber optic instruments and optelectronic semiconductor components. In 1990 they introduced an innovative product called the AOC10 OTDR, which is a portable PC-based optical time domain reflectometer.

The AOC10 OTDR is offered in both a standard standalone board-and-software package and a preconfigured PC portable configuration. The standalone product is offered as a fiber NIC-and-software package. The PC OTDR is packaged by preconfiguring the fiber NIC/software in a portable PC. Figure 4.31 displays both configurations.

The AOC10 OTDR NIC is the heart of the unit. It has a highly advanced onboard laser light source, receiver, and processor. It works interactively with the Antel data-acquisition software to provide the full OTDR package.

FIGURE 4.31
Antel Optronics'
AOC10 is an
optical time
domain
reflectometer
which includes
both software and
hardware
components.

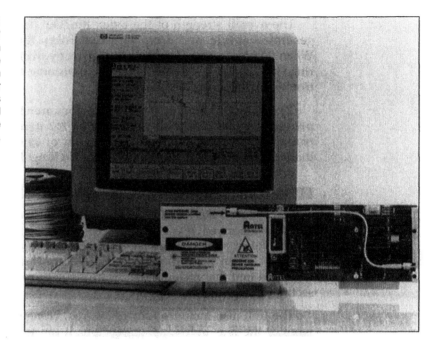

The NIC is switchable between single- and multimode fiber. It is also dynamically switchable between 850/1300 NM and 1310/1550 NM fiber wavelengths.

The AOC10 OTDR includes five main test display modes:

- Parameter Display mode (displays all fiber and OTDR parameters)

- Distance Bar Graph mode (full graphical display of OTDR signal distance ranges)

- Measurement Display mode (marked display of absolute and relative OTDR signal position)

- Splice Loss mode (displays a comprehensive measurement of splice loss in least-squares approximation and two-point methods)

- Dual Waveforms mode (displays two real-time or stored-waveform OTDR signal traces)

The menuing system offers a full set of function keys for displaying and testing, along with custom setup modes for the OTDR environmental parameter settings. There is also a Comment Pad feature that allows you to keep real-time notes on testing results.

Because of its PC-based operation, the Antel AOC10 can forward testing data to disk files or printers.

The AOC10 OTDR is designed specifically for testing a fiber cabling medium and is not restricted to the Token Ring topology. The overall strengths of the portable Antel AOC10 are its full range of fiber testing features, along with its innovative data-testing software, which offers an extremely user-friendly menuing system.

chapter **5** DOCUMENTATION

When problems occur on a local area network, one of the most important safeguards is proper network documentation. Just as file backups are critical to recovering a blown network operating system, network documentation is the critical archive of your Token Ring LAN layout and design. A Token Ring LAN installation is not truly complete until the network documentation is complete.

It is impossible to always detect when a failure is going to occur with your Token Ring LAN, but a proper set of network documentation will allow you to isolate a failure more efficiently and quickly. Almost every time you have a problem with your Token Ring network, you'll reference the network documentation.

The sophistication of the Token Ring topology complicates the art of documenting its layout and design. There are so many components involved, and each must be listed according to its integral configuration within the Token Ring layout. You'll need a methodical approach to documenting the network.

This chapter introduces the documentation most critical to a Token Ring LAN. Some of the documentation discussed here is standard, but each type is a component of a proper Token Ring documentation library.

Next, the main Token Ring network documentation components are discussed. Remember that all the components work together to form a comprehensive library, and you need all of it for an overall, accurate picture of your Token Ring environment.

Chapter 2 covered Token Ring topology theory. Designing a Token Ring network requires a comprehensive set of skills that are mainly gained from years of experience. Maintaining proper network documentation will help you gain these skills.

Early in my career, I wondered what separated the basic field engineer, which I was, from the technical support specialists. One day I asked a local technical support representative that exact question. The answer was, not necessarily remembering every fact or constantly studying, but knowing where to get needed information. The representative told me to look around the office; I did, and all I saw was neatly organized manuals. From that day on I began to organize my technical documentation. Needless to say, it increased my level of effectiveness when troubleshooting. I was the guy who always had the information that was needed when a problem occurred.

The point is that after you read this chapter and learn what documentation you need for your Token Ring network, remember one thing: Keeping it neatly organized, in the proper binders, is the key to finding it when you need it.

NETWORK LAYOUT DOCUMENTS

Certain documents are critical to implementing a Token Ring network design. In my career I have been involved in a slew of Token Ring installations. Most were a success, but some were stressful experiences. There is nothing like getting halfway through an installation and being unable to continue because you do not know where a particular cable is run, or where a certain ring station needs to reside, or where an MAU port is supposed to be connected on the patch panel.

These types of occurrences are real-life stuff, and I have learned that certain network layout documents are critical for LAN implementation and need to be at the installation site. I consider *all* these documents mandatory.

Building Blueprints

When a cabling contractor arrives at a site to design, install, or troubleshoot LAN cabling, the first question that contractor will ask is, "Where are the blueprints?" Before a Token Ring network can be properly designed, you'll need the building blueprints. They are important initially, at design inception, and are also important to maintaining the site, for the following reasons:

- Depending on the building and where ring stations are to be located, the main ring path and lobe cabling lengths must be properly calculated to stay within Token Ring specifications.

- Once the required lengths are defined to physically lay out the network, another important factor is the cabling type. Depending on the length and layout of the cabling paths, you may need certain cabling types.

- Depending on the physical layout of the Token Ring network, you might shift your design from standard STP cabling to UTP cabling.

- Another factor of the layout design is the possible need for repeaters to extend the main ring path or lobe cabling lengths.

- Whenever problems occur, the blueprints will be essential for tracking the main ring path and lobe cabling paths through the building during the troubleshooting process.

Maintaining a copy of the building blueprints will allow for a more accurate design and a smoother path for troubleshooting your Token Ring network.

Figure 5.1 is a sample building blueprint used in a Token Ring layout.

MAU Rack Layouts

This section discusses the location of the multistation access units (MAUs). It is always best to physically place them together in common wiring closets. I have seen sites where the MAUs are placed all over the building, including up in the ceiling and under the floor panels. This is a problem just waiting to happen. For instance, if you encounter a problem that appears to be located in an MAU or the main ring path cabling, your troubleshooting capabilities will be affected. If all the MAUs are located in common wiring closets, you can isolate a problem much faster because you can switch MAUs or cabling paths easily.

When you place the MAUs together in a wiring closet, mount them in some sort of rack. The next logical step is to properly number and physically mark each MAU with some sort of small sticker, or any other effective means. Each port should also be numbered and marked.

FIGURE 5.1
A typical building blueprint used for a Token Ring layout. Maintaining a set of building blueprints aids both network installation and troubleshooting.

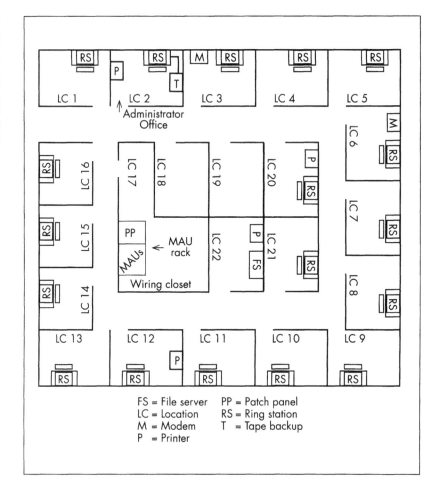

FS = File server   PP = Patch panel
LC = Location   RS = Ring station
M = Modem   T = Tape backup
P = Printer

All lobe cables should run directly from their respective building locations to the common wiring closets. This configuration allows for a physical star layout and provides for solid, logical design. Make sure that each lobe cable is properly labeled on both ends with where it is actually run, for example, a cubical or office number.

Now you have a logical matrix for your wiring and hubing scheme. As you will see, there are some standard industry documents for this procedure. You can choose them or create your own. In either case, there is a methodology to this documentation scheme. Understanding this methodology gives you an edge when it comes to troubleshooting problems.

Patch Panel Layouts

Cable patch panels are becoming standard at most large Token Ring installations. A patch panel is a central point at which the lobe cables on the LAN meet before they are attached to MAUs. The patch panel is usually mounted directly in the rack with the MAUs. Most often it is placed on the top part of the rack and the MAUs are placed underneath. This setup allows for easier changes of lobe cable location-to-MAU port configurations.

In configuring a wiring closet with a patch panel, you should follow a certain method. All the lobe and main ring path cables, incoming and outgoing from the wiring closet, should enter and then attach to the rear of the patch panel. Then use patch cables to attach from the front of the patch panel to the respective MAUs.

To document this arrangement properly, all the patch cables from the patch panel to the MAUs should have the same label designation as the lobe cable to which they attached through the patch panel.

I recommend that you document the patch panel layout and its relation to the MAUs and cabling with a diagram table. Figure 5.2 shows how the logical matrix for patch panels, MAUs, and a cabling scheme correlates with a sample diagram table. The diagram can be based on a grid to show how the lobe cable label correlates with its respective MAU port label.

IBM Token Ring Planning Forms

IBM has assembled a series of forms for planning and maintaining Token Ring network configurations. They are considered an industry standard for Token Ring documentation. Using the IBM documentation forms is an excellent way to keep a handle on your Token Ring network.

IBM has taken into account most of the major areas of the Token Ring topology and has created logical forms to use for documenting those areas. The reference section of this book lists the IBM Token Ring reference guides; throughout most of IBM's documentation (especially the *IBM Cabling System Planning and Installation Guide*) you will find good descriptions for the purpose of their documentation schemes.

The following figures show some of the most frequently used IBM Token Ring planning forms.

FIGURE 5.2
A grid-based
diagram table,
and its correlation
with the patch
panel, MAUs, and
cables.

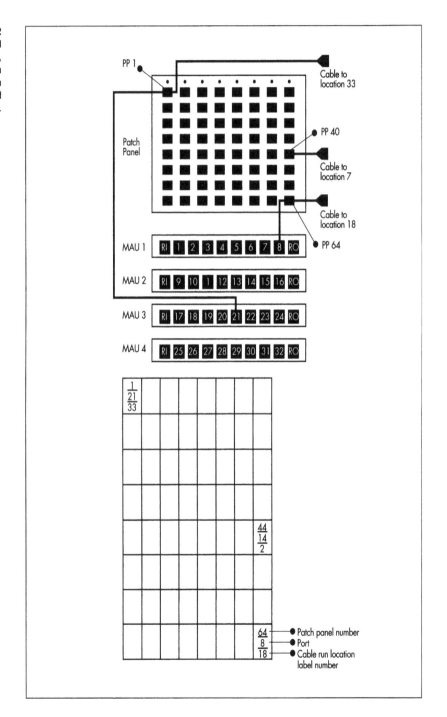

Physical Location to Adapter Address Locator Chart

Physical Location	Adapter Address	Device Identification	Ring Number	IBM 8228 Unit No.

IBM 8228 Cabling Chart

Date _____

Section 1 Identification

| Unit Number _____ | Building _____ Location _____ | Rack-mounted ☐ Wall-mounted ☐ | Ring _____ |

Section 2 Receptacle Connections

Receptacle	1	2	3	4	5	6	7	8
Connect to:								

Device								

Section 3 Ring Connections

A. Connect RI of this 8228 to: _____

B. Connect RO of this 8228 to: _____

FIGURE 5.5
The IBM Ring
Sequence Chart.

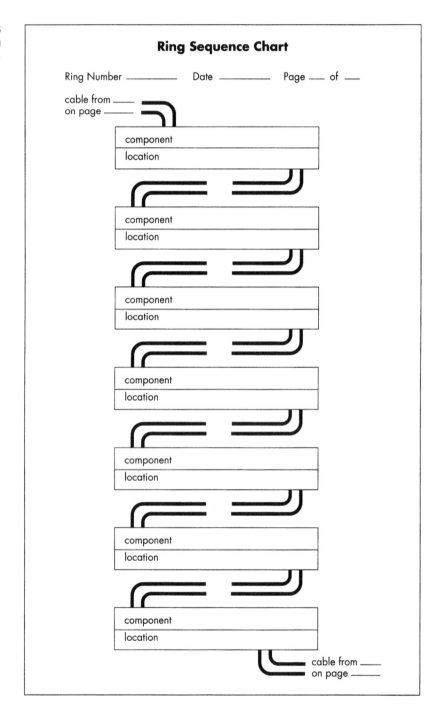

FIGURE 5.6
IBM's 8218
repeater cabling
form.

IBM 8218 Cabling Chart for Telephone Twisted-Pair-Based Rings

Section 1

Date _____

Ring _____

_____ Unit Numbers _____

Building _____

Location _____

Rack-Mounted ☐

Wall-Mounted ☐

Section 2

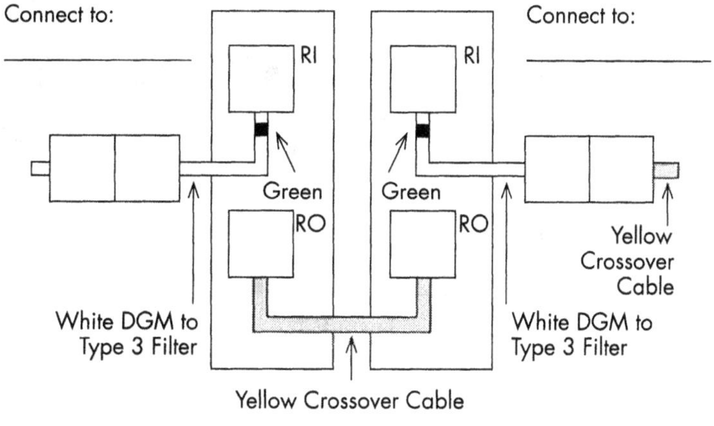

Connect to: _____

RI   RI

Green   Green

RO   RO

Yellow Crossover Cable

White DGM to Type 3 Filter

White DGM to Type 3 Filter

Yellow Crossover Cable

Connect to: _____

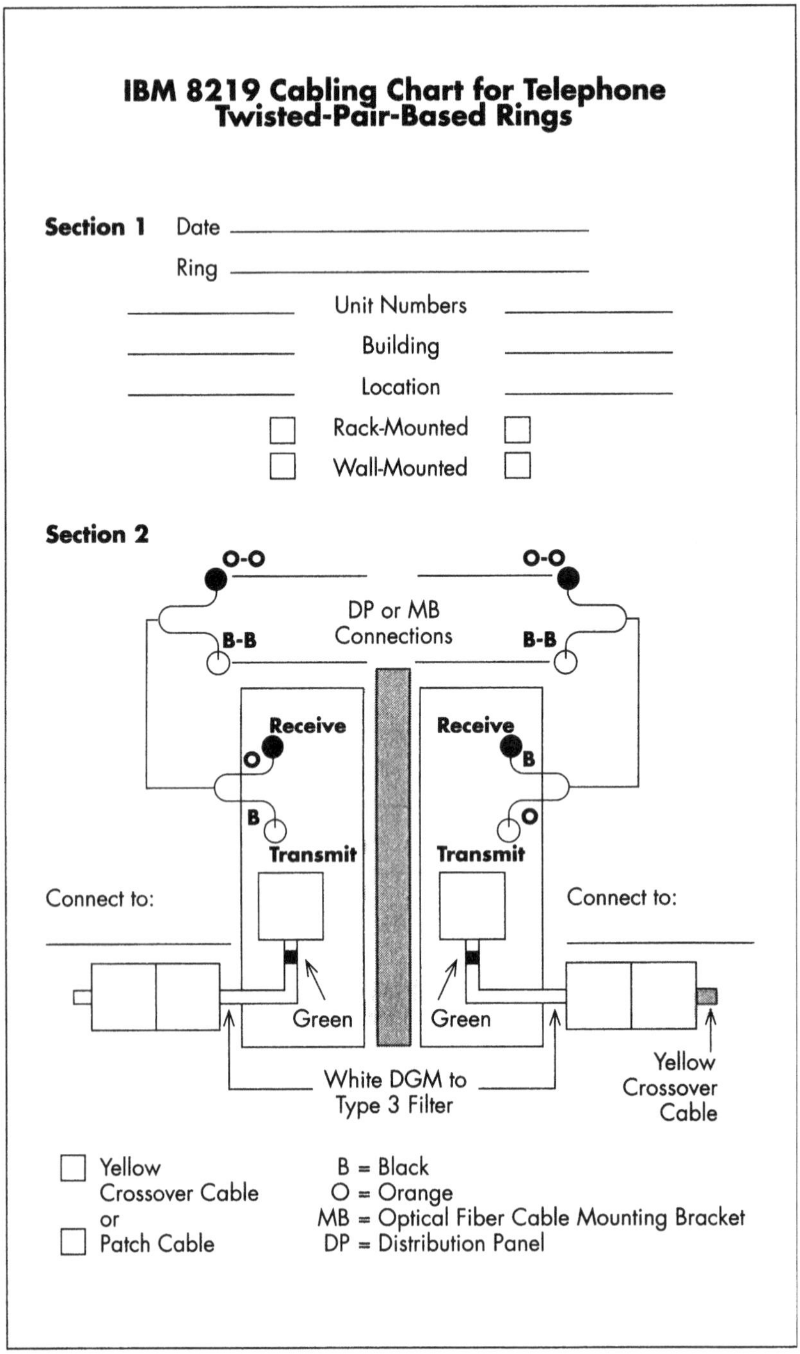

FIGURE 5.7
The IBM 8219
repeater cabling
form.

IBM 8219 Cabling Chart for Telephone Twisted-Pair-Based Rings

Section 1   Date _____

Ring _____

_____ Unit Numbers _____

_____ Building _____

_____ Location _____

☐ Rack-Mounted ☐

☐ Wall-Mounted ☐

Section 2

O-O   O-O

DP or MB
Connections

B-B   B-B

Receive   **Receive**
O   B
B   O

Transmit   **Transmit**

Connect to: Connect to:

Green   Green

Yellow
Crossover
Cable

White DGM to
Type 3 Filter

☐ Yellow   B = Black
  Crossover Cable   O = Orange
  or   MB = Optical Fiber Cable Mounting Bracket
☐ Patch Cable   DP = Distribution Panel

FIGURE 5.8
The IBM Bridge
Planning Chart.

Bridge Planning Chart

Date —————— Bridge Identification ———————————

Check one: Load manually —— Load automatically ——

Section 1 - Bridge Configuration Parameters

Check one: Alter configuration —— Use defaults ——

Bridge number (Default = 1)	
Ring number connected to primary adapter (Default = 001)	
Ring number connected to alternate adapter (Default = 002)	
Frame forwarding active (Default = Y)	
Bridge performance threshold (Default = 10)	
Restart on error (Default = Y)	
Drive for memory dump no error (Default = 0)	
Drive for error log (Default = 0)	

	Primary Adapter	Alternate Adapter
Hop count limit (Default = 7)		
Single-route broadcast (Default = Y)		
Locally administered address (Defaults = 000000000000)		
Ring parameter server (Default = Y)		
Ring error monitor (Default = Y)		
Configuration report server (Default = Y)		

Shared RAM address (Primary adapter default = 0000)	
(Alternate adapter default = 0000)	

	Old	New
Link password 0 (Default = 00000000)		
Link password 1 (Default = 00000000)		
Link password 2 (Default = 00000000)		
Link password 3 (Default = 00000000)		

NETWORK FILE SERVER AND RING STATION DOCUMENTATION

With any type of LAN topology, documenting the file server and the LAN station configurations is extremely important for future reference. This section overviews the components of both the file server (FS) and ring stations (RSes) that are important to document for the Token Ring topology.

The outlined components can be easily documented by building a structured list. Some network operating system (NOS) manufacturers, such as Novell, provide excellent documentation sheets for file server and LAN station configurations. This book calls the list a Station Configuration Sheet. Every file server and ring station should have its own Station Configuration Sheet.

There are four key areas to document for both the FS and the RSes in a Token Ring environment. It's important that you note information in all four areas on the Station Configuration Sheet. The key areas are hardware configuration, software configuration, Token Ring architecture management roles, and cable and MAU port and locations. The parts of these areas that require documentation are as follows:

Hardware Configuration

- CPU type (FS and RS)
- Memory (FS and RS)
- Disk types and capacity (FS and RS)
- All I/O boards (FS and RS)
- NICs (FS and RS)
    - I/O address
    - IRQ
    - DMA
    - Token Ring address
    - STP or UTP cabling connector
    - 32-, 16-, or 8-bit card
    - Microcode level
    - Primary or secondary setting

Software Configuration

- LAN drivers and their configuration (FS and RS)
- Network shell software (RS)
- Network operating system revision, configuration, and drivers (FS)
- CONFIG.SYS (FS and RS)
- AUTOEXEC.BAT (FS and RS)
- Bridge configurations (FS and RS)
- Printing configurations (FS and RS)
- Security (FS and RS)
- Users and groups (FS)
- Directory and file structure (FS and RS)
- Server name (FS)

Token Ring Architecture Management Roles

- Note any Token Ring management roles that are collated with an FS or RS on the Station Configuration Sheet.

Cable and MAU Port and Locations

- Every Station Configuration Sheet should also contain the station's physical location, MAU port, and cable that connect to the respective FS or RS. These notations will provide all the proper documentation to map every FS's and RS's actual lobe path to the physical ring.

NETWORK MAINTENANCE AND SERVICE LOGS

When you have a Token Ring network problem, it's always nice to experience *deja vu*. Certain failures repeat themselves frequently, and if you have seen that type of problem before, it's an advantage from the troubleshooting angle.

When that happens, you can rely on your memory to act as a statistical database for information on how you resolved the problem last time. Or you can check the Maintenance and Service Log.

Maintaining a historical log of all problems that occur in your Token Ring environment will decrease the mean time to repair (MTTR) for your LAN. Most field service outfits track this statistic from their field operations; it's important because, obviously, the goal is to get the customer up and running as quickly as possible.

Keeping a Maintenance and Service Log is simple. First, arrange a binder with the following main Token Ring LAN component sections: File Servers, Ring Stations, Hubs and MAUs, Bridges, Repeaters, Communication Gear, Printers, and so on. Next, separate the sections with labeled inserts.

Now the most important part: Make up a problem entry sheet with the following information :

- Equipment Type
- Serial Number
- Special Notes
- Location
- Network User or Users
- Problem Description or Symptom
- Problem Cause
- Problem Resolution

Next make multiple copies of the sheets and insert several sheets into each of the main Token Ring LAN component sections in the binder. Figure 5.9 shows a sample Maintenance and Service Log problem entry sheet.

FIGURE 5.9
Sample problem
entry sheets in the
Maintenance and
Service Log.

Problem Entry Sheet

1. Equipment type   IBM MOD 55 Ring Station
2. Serial number   9SX52541
3. Special notes   Has IBM 4/16 NIC
   connected by cable-33-to MAU 4/port-28
   through PP.16
4. Location   #33
5. Network users   Tim Ringman
6. Problem symptom   Cannot access ring
7. Problem cause   Damaged Token Ring driver files
8. Problem resolution   Reload new drivers-Tests OK.

Problem Entry Sheet

1. Equipment type   Bridge-IBM-8209
2. Serial number   89XFQRTS
3. Special notes   From ring 3 to ring 4
   -(To access FS-WHITEKNIGHT)
4. Location   #22
5. Network users   All of ring 4 & group
   WPUSERS on ring 3
6. Problem symptom   Intermittent drop in access
   to file server WHITEKNIGHT
7. Problem cause   Bad Token Ring card in slot 2
8. Problem resolution   Replace card-Tests OK.

Now you have a way to track equipment history, and you have a problem reference guide for your Token Ring LAN. You can use this method, or you can get more automated by using a statistical database. The point is, that by recording in an organized manner the history of all problems that occur on your Token Ring network, the odds are that you will be more efficient and effective when it comes to troubleshooting.

NETWORK VENDOR AND PERSONAL RESOURCE TABLES

Just as a Token Ring network has many integral hardware and software components, there are also many people associated with its basic existence. These people usually fall into one of three categories: network product vendors, network support personal, or network users. You should assemble tables for each of the three categories.

For network product vendors, list the following items:

- Company name
- Address
- Phone and fax numbers
- Key marketing and service support people
- Logs of all key conversations and meetings

For internal support people make sure you have the following information:

- Name
- Location
- Phone, beeper, and fax numbers
- Technical involvement with the LAN
- Logs of all key conversations and meetings

Last, make sure that there is a composite list of your LAN user base, with the following categories:

- Name
- Location
- Phone and fax numbers
- LAN hardware and software resources used

Some of this information is a given. But remember that a documented listing of the key people involved with your Token Ring environment might be a lifesaver at a critical time. Let's face it: These people are the society that gives your Token Ring network its smooth heartbeat.

NETWORK DOCUMENTATION SOFTWARE TOOLS

To close this chapter, here are a couple of software approaches that might make the documentation job a little easier.

Most of the information that you record on File Server/Ring Station Configuration Sheets and Network Vendor/Personal Resource Tables can be implemented in a database. There are many innovative ways to design a system that will meet your needs.

Another aid to documenting and keeping up with a growing Token Ring network is a software package that can gather LAN statistics, such as hardware and software configurations. Brightwork Development has an excellent package called LAN Automatic Inventory, or LAI. The LAI package dynamically builds and maintains a database of most hardware and software components in a LAN. What is innovative about LAI is that it actually goes onto the LAN and gathers real-time, critical information from the file servers and workstations.

For Token Ring, LAI can gather the NIC addresses and a full array of internal station components such as CPU type, memory, disk drives, and more. The LAI package will also scan each ring station for assigned network operating system parameters such as shell type and version.

Brightwork's LAI package will allow you to perform quickly a thorough hardware and software inventory that could normally take days or weeks.

Brightwork's LAI follows some of their other creative products for LAN management, such as NETmanager and NETremote. NETmanager allows for controlling and monitoring multiple LAN stations from a central point. NETremote is a dial-up remote access package that performs a lot like NETmanager with a diagnostic theme; you can access a LAN remotely, cutting downtime.

Other hungry software developers are out there working on packages that will do it all for you. Remember, however, that by using the methods outlined in this chapter, you can keep a logical, organized database of all your Token Ring network components and problems.

chapter 6 NETWORK FAULT ISOLATION

This chapter acquaints you with essential troubleshooting techniques you can use when you encounter problems in a Token Ring network. Every logical component of a Token Ring network has distinct failure symptoms, causes, and appropriate troubleshooting methods. You find a detailed discussion of the methods of fault isolation for each network component in this chapter.

Each of the following sections builds on the previous section. Read and study the sections in this chapter consecutively.

Before you can troubleshoot any problems in a Token Ring network, you need a proper troubleshooting *approach*.

THE TROUBLESHOOTING APPROACH

Knowing where to start and where to go after encountering a problem with a local area network is the key to resolving the problem quickly and efficiently. Without the proper troubleshooting approach, you can get lost in a maze of MAUs and cables, which can be quite frustrating.

The first thing to do is to approach the Token Ring network from the symptom. A symptom is a sign of the problem. If a group of network workstations is freezing, the problem is that network workstations are freezing, and the symptom is that a *group* of network workstations is freezing. You need to define the problem that is occurring by a specific symptom.

Next, a troubleshooter needs to step back and look at the complete network from a bird's eye view. Divide the network into three areas: (1) the complete network, (2) a group of network users, and (3) an individual network user or specific network component. You should place the symptom in one of these three groups. The question to ask: Is the symptom occurring with every network user, a group of users, or just one network user or component?

After the symptom and the area of the network that is experiencing the symptom are defined, you must categorize the symptom as a solid problem or an intermittent problem. A *solid* problem is one that can be re-created at will. An *intermittent* problem is one you cannot re-create at will; it may occur at any time.

Your troubleshooting approach should be as follows:

- Define the symptom.
- Place the symptom in a specific network area.
- Define the symptom as solid or intermittent.

FAULT-ISOLATION VECTORING

Fault-isolation vectoring is the art of deciding the correct direction to follow as you troubleshoot a LAN problem.

Troubleshooting any type of problem involves making logical decisions. Depending on the complexity of the problem, the number of decisions will vary. Try to picture yourself lost in a forest and walking down a path. Without a trail map, it will be very difficult to find the proper exit. But if you turn in the correct direction at every cross path, you will find your way out.

Troubleshooting a Token Ring network is a very complex path that can involve many decisions before you find the source of the symptom. But if you make the correct decisions, you will get that much closer to the source of the problem.

The foundation of fault-isolation vectoring is the principle of cause and effect, which is:

Every effect has an associated cause, and the effect is related to the symptom. The goal of troubleshooting the symptom or effect is to find the cause and resolve it.

When making decisions while troubleshooting try to think about what parts of the network could be associated with the symptom the network is experiencing. It will be helpful to think of different parts of the network as *network components*.

For example, think of a disk drive as a component, or a software application as a component. Next, one by one try to logically eliminate the components as the cause. Try to pick the most probable components first. Every time you eliminate a component you will be closer to the cause of the symptom.

Another important troubleshooting approach you'll need is the Problem Reversal Theory. The problem reversal theory involves taking known testing results and reversing the respective troubleshooting procedure by reconnecting the found bad network component to re-create the problem (for problem verification) before finally implementing the newly tested network component into the network. This approach will verify that all the testing results are conclusive.

Let's troubleshoot the following problem together.

The symptom is that one group of network users connected to different MAUs have their stations freeze while running a particular software application on the network. When the group of users logs in, the stations freeze with a message, `Cannot find XYZ.file`. The odd thing is that all the other users on the network use the application, but only this group is having this problem.

Step 1. Define the symptom. A group of network users is having their stations freeze during a common application.

Step 2. Define the network area. The network area is a group of users.

Step 3. Define the symptom as intermittent or solid. The problem can be re-created because it occurs every time they log in. This is a solid problem.

Step 4. Define the first set of possible network components you can associate with the symptom. Component 1 is the application; component 2 is the users' stations.

Step 5. Let's examine the application first. Does the group of users have access rights to all the directories that are needed to load the application into their stations? You can check this easily by comparing their security rights to those of one of the users who can load the application.

The answer is yes, they all do have the necessary rights to access the application. Now this vectors us over to component 2, the users' stations, because there must be something different about their stations.

Step 6. Next let's divide the station into more components. The first component will be the software configurations or requirements, and the second component is the hardware configuration or requirements.

Step 7. Check the manual of the application that the symptom occurs with for the software requirements and configuration. Also compare the setup and requirements of other workstations on the LAN that are not experiencing the problem.

It turns out that the workstations have all the necessary software requirements that the manual calls for, specifically, correct operating versions and the necessary directories/files. And the nonworking units have the same software configuration and requirements as the working stations. So next let's vector to the hardware configuration and requirements.

Step 8. Check the manual of the application that the symptom occurs with for its required hardware configuration and requirements. Recheck the stations to make sure they have the necessary hardware installed and the hardware station configuration is correct, according to the information in the application's manual. Also compare the hardware configuration and requirements with other workstations on the LAN that are not experiencing the problem.

It turns out that the workstations do *not* have all the necessary requirements that the manual calls for. The workstations that exhibit the symptom only have 1.5M of system board memory, while the ones that are working with the application have 2M of system board memory.

Step 9. Test *one* station with a problem fix. Install the extra .5M of needed memory into the system board of one workstation that has the symptom and test run the application in that workstation. It works!

During this example we took the following steps:

• We defined the network symptom.

• We put the symptom into a network area—this was vector 1.

- We defined the problem as solid.

- We broke the associated area into two preliminary network components: the application and the stations.

- We eliminated the application—this was vector 2.

- We broke the network stations into two more network components, the station's software and hardware portions.

- Next we eliminated the software portion—this was vector 3.

- The symptom was now isolated to the station's hardware portion.

- We defined the cause of the symptom to be the lack of needed memory to run the application.

- We verified this was the fix by installing the memory in a nonworking station and loading the application, and it worked.

Good troubleshooting, Tex!

Developing the art of fault-isolation vectoring will take time. The troubleshooting flow guides in Chapter 7 will help you to develop this skill.

TROUBLESHOOTING FAULT DOMAINS AND LOBE AREAS

Sometimes a network symptom will lead you directly to a specific network component, while other times network symptoms will lead you to specific network areas, such as a fault domain or a lobe area. The first step in troubleshooting a fault domain is to isolate the failure to a specific lobe area. Once the failure is identified to a lobe area, you must isolate the failure to a specific network component within that lobe area. (I next overview the proper approach.)

Troubleshooting a Fault Domain

If a ring station (RS) beacons, and both the station and its NAUN pass all the self tests performed during the beaconing process, they will both reinsert back onto the ring. When this occurs, there is a solid beaconing condition on the ring and you'll need to troubleshoot the problem manually.

One of the best ways to start troubleshooting a fault domain is by examining the Beacon MAC frame through a protocol analysis session. The Beacon Type field in the Beacon MAC frame helps to isolate the exact location of failure within a fault domain. Beacon types are discussed in detail later in this chapter.

The next step is to isolate one of the two lobe areas as the source of failure. The easiest way to accomplish this is to remove one lobe area from the fault domain by actually removing one of the lobe cables from the MAU or wiring hub. Next, retest the ring.

If the failure symptom is gone, you have isolated the problem to the removed-lobe area. If the problem is still present, reconnect the first suspect lobe area, disconnect the second lobe area, and retest. The problem should not be present, and the failure will now be located to a specific lobe area.

Troubleshooting Lobe Areas

Sometimes network symptoms will point to a specific lobe area. This may be because you have already troubleshot an assigned fault domain and identified the failure to one of the lobe areas.

If the problem is isolated to a lobe area, the following components are possible failure causes:

- The RS NIC
- The RS
- The lobe cable
- The MAU or wiring hub

(In some cases a network file server problem can cause an RS to continuously insert and deinsert itself from the ring.)

To isolate the specific network failure component within a lobe area use the following logical process:

- Disconnect the lobe cable from its respective MAU port or wiring hub port and connect it to another MAU port or wiring hub port. Retest the ring. If the failure is gone, you have isolated the failure to the MAU port or wiring hub port. If the problem is still present, connect the lobe cable back to its original port. MAU and wiring hub troubleshooting are discussed further in the *MAU and Wiring Hub Problems* section later in this chapter.

- Next, if possible, attempt to verify the integrity of the lobe cable. Test the lobe cable with a time domain reflectometer (TDR) or a ring cable tester. If there are any clear cable failures, the lobe cable is most likely your problem. Another good troubleshooting method is to attach the RS to the same MAU or wiring hub port with another lobe cable. Sometimes this can be accomplished by bringing the RS into the wiring closet and attaching it to the MAU or wiring hub port via a test patch cable. (Try to have a cable set aside that you know is good.) Next retest the ring. If the ring tests okay, the original lobe cable is your problem. If the failure is still occurring, either the RS or the NIC is most probably the cause of failure.

- The failure cause now has to be identified as the RS or its respective NIC. The first step is to thoroughly double check the RS for proper configuration and good functionality. This is discussed in the *Ring Station Problems* section later in this chapter. If the RS is properly configured and is functionally okay, the NIC is the next assumed fault.

- If the NIC is targeted as the failure cause, the first step is to check all the NIC configuration settings and to test the NIC operation. NIC configuration and testing is discussed in *NIC Problems* later in this chapter. If all the NIC configuration settings are correct and the NIC tests okay, you can assume that the NIC has an intermittent failure. Swap the NIC with a known good NIC and thoroughly retest the ring.

- As mentioned earlier, in some instances a network file server problem will cause an RS to continuously insert and deinsert itself from the ring. When this occurs you can actually hear the MAU port continually clicking. This indicates some software incompatibility between the RS and the network file server. If you are dealing with a twisted pair wiring hub, you will not hear this clicking because there are no mechanical relays. In this case you need to run a protocol analysis session to verify this type of occurrence.

The sections that follow discuss how to troubleshoot each of the individual network components that may fail within an assigned fault domain, lobe area, or the overall Token Ring network. Remember that the problem reversal theory introduced earlier is an excellent problem verification method that can be applied to all the troubleshooting steps introduced below. This approach can be used across the fault-isolation spectrum and will provide you with conclusive testing results.

CABLE PROBLEMS

The most common failure within a Token Ring network is a cable fault. When a cable fault occurs, it is usually unexpected. The symptom typically appears as a mirage and exhibits itself as another network component failure. The symptom may appear as either a soft or a hard error condition on the ring. The worst thing about cable problems is that they can cause just one network area component to fail or they can bring the whole network to its knees. Cable problems can be both solid and intermittent.

Cable Failure Types and Causes

Several distinct problems can occur within a cable. Some TDRs may indicate that a cable is experiencing certain types of signal degradation such as crosstalk or noise. (*Crosstalk* can be defined as two or more internal cable conductors having common overlaying transmissions due to a magnetic field. Noise is the presence of unintentional outside signals infiltrating the cabling medium and causing interference that handicaps proper data communications.)

When signal degradation such as crosstalk or noise occurs, the actual cable failure usually fits into one of the following distinct problem categories:

- Open cables
- Shorted cable
- Crossed conductors
- Bad cable termination
- Bad connectors
- Improper cable placement

Open cables are the actual physical break of a cable conductor. A cable open problem is usually caused when a cable is crimped or bent. This can occur easily when a cable is improperly fed through a building area, such as a wall, a ceiling, or a conduit. A good suggestion is to use proper strain reliefs when running a cable; this can stop a cable from being stretched beyond its intended distance run.

A shorted cable occurs when two or more internal conductors are unintentionally physically connected to one another. This problem is usually caused when a cable is crimped or bent. If there is a unintentional crimp or strain put on a cable with twisted-pair conductors, it is more probable that a short will occur, rather than an open, because the pairs are physically crossed. Since the Token Ring cabling system uses twisted pair, shorts are a common cable failure type.

Crossed conductors occurs when two or more cable conductors are connected to the incorrect connector terminals. This problem can be quite deceiving, because it usually exhibits itself as a failed RS, MAU port, or another network device by attempting ring attachment. This can occur easily during installation of the cable connectors.

The best way to avoid this is to coordinate a color-coded connecter to a corresponding connector terminal. Most cables have internal color coding. The Token Ring cabling system usually uses a standard red, green, orange, and black color code for its internal conductors.

Bad cable termination is probably the most common type of cable problem in a Token Ring environment. Bad cable termination is the improper connection of the internal Token Ring cabling conductors to a corresponding Token Ring cabling connector. This can be categorized as loose conductors, disconnected conductors, an improper shielding connection, or even crossed conductors. The symptom of this type of problem can also be deceiving.

Bad connectors are sometimes the culprit of a suspected bad cable. Be aware that sometimes the IBM data connector shorting pins can break and cause cable failure or improper termination symptoms.

Improper cable placement can cause interference that can introduce noise into a cable. Cables should not be run or placed next to electrical sources, HVAC, certain lighting, or other possible sources of interference.

Next we discuss some ways to effectively troubleshoot cable problems that occur in the Token Ring environment.

Troubleshooting Cable Failures

Troubleshooting the Token Ring cabling system requires a different approach when compared to troubleshooting other LAN topologies such as EtherNet. This is because Token Ring is a physically star-wired network, versus EtherNet, which is a bus.

When there is a suspected cabling problem in a Token Ring cabling section (such as a lobe path cable), the proper approach is always to remove that particular cabling section from the ring and separately test that section. Because the network is a physical star, this usually does not affect the entire network, unless the suspected bad cable section is in the main ring path.

For troubleshooting suspected cabling problems in the Token Ring environment, you can think of two cabling areas: the lobe cables and the main ring path cabling.

Troubleshooting lobe cables. Later this chapter discusses how analyzing a low-level MAC frame can isolate a Token Ring problem to two lobe areas within a fault domain. Because cables do account for a high number of lobe path failures, if there is a suspected problem in a lobe area, the lobe cable should be the first component of the lobe path that you troubleshoot.

First, remove the lobe cable from the MAU port and the NIC. Next, test the particular lobe cable with either a TDR or a ring cable-specific tester, like the testing instruments discussed in Chapter 4. If there is a problem with the cable section, these devices should detect the problem and verify the problem type. If the TDR or ring cable tester detects no errors, chances are another network component—such as the MAU port, an RS, or a NIC in the suspected bad lobe path—is most probably at fault.

Troubleshooting main ring path cables. Sometimes a group of RSes or the whole Token Ring network is experiencing problems, such as an inability to connect to the ring, a crashing LAN network operating system (NOS), or a beaconing ring. In these cases, it's possible that the main ring path has an internal cable failure. As discussed in Chapter 5, if all of the MAUs are neatly organized in MAU racks and wiring closets, troubleshooting the main ring path will be relatively easy.

The proper way to approach a suspected main ring path cabling problem is to start with the first MAU and disconnect its RI and RO cables.

Next test the particular MAU by verifying that the RSes connected to it can properly perform Ring Insertion. If the MAU and NICs used in the network do not have specific MAU connection diagnostics, you will probably have to connect the ring file server to the MAU being tested and bring the NOS up so that the RSes can connect. This topic is discussed in more detail later in this chapter.

If the first MAU tests okay, connect the second MAU via an RO cable from the first MAU to the second MAU's RI port. (Note: If the network file server is up and RS shells are running, you should bring the network down before connecting the second MAU.) Next, test the two new MAU rings as described above.

Continue this troubleshooting method until a problem is encountered. What will usually occur is that a bad cable or MAU will be located by adding it to the ring and a problem will arise.

It really comes down to a basic elimination process. If your ring is functioning okay with the first three MAUs, and you add a fourth MAU and the ring will not come up properly, there is a problem in one of the following areas:

- The main ring cable connecting the RO and RI ports between MAU 3 and MAU 4

- The fourth MAU

- A network component connected to a MAU

At this point if a problem is located, put aside the suspected network problem area, reconnect the rest of the network, and test the new ring configuration. If there are still problems, start troubleshooting back from the last MAU that tested okay. There is always the possibility of more than one failure on a network.

If the network comes up okay, troubleshoot the defined problem area by first testing the main ring cable path section with either a TDR or a ring-specific tester, then testing the MAU, and finally testing any network components connected to the MAU.

When troubleshooting cable problems within the Token Ring topology, you may find that you encounter another problem or that the actual failure is due to another Token Ring network component. This is true across the spectrum of the network: You may be troubleshooting a suspected bad RS and find out that you actually have a bad cable. By being aware of how you are vectoring when troubleshooting, you can effectively isolate your problem to the correct network component.

MULTISTATION ACCESS UNIT AND WIRING HUB PROBLEMS

Troubleshooting a MAU or wiring hub problem can be relatively easy if the proper proactive measures are taken, meaning the MAU layout is properly configured in a standard MAU rack/wiring closet and, in the case of wiring hubs, the hub layout is centralized and properly documented. Generally, having all the proper network documentation available will be a great aid. All these proactive measures will make the troubleshooting task that much easier.

The physical star layout of lobes in a Token Ring network allows port changes to be made quite easily. This is critical to the next section, encountering suspected MAU and wiring hub problems. The next section presents certain types of MAU and wiring hub failure causes, along with some specific troubleshooting methods for MAU and wiring hub failures.

MAU and Wiring Hub Failure Symptoms, Causes, and Troubleshooting

There are really three types of problem situations in the Token Ring topology that may cause MAU or wiring hub failure. Note that the failure symptoms in these problem situations may appear as either soft or hard errors on the ring.

- MAU- or hub-specific port failures that will affect either just one lobe area or a fault domain

- Complete MAU or hub module faults that cause failure symptoms with just one MAU or hub module

- Complete MAU or hub module faults that cause either solid or intermittent failure symptoms to multiple MAUs, multiple hub modules, or the complete Token Ring network

Assume the following technical approach when troubleshooting MAU or wiring hub problems:

MAU- or hub-specific failures affecting one lobe area or fault domain. When a specific port on a MAU or wiring hub has a problem, the troubleshooting step is really quite straightforward. Because of the physical star layout, all you need to do is to verify that there is a port problem in the MAU or a port problem in a specific wiring hub module.

This can be done by simply moving the lobe cable from the suspected bad port to another port on the same MAU or wiring hub module. (Make sure that the new port is functioning.) Next retest the RS on the new port. If everything tests okay, the suspected bad port is at failure.

A good way to verify your testing results is to use the problem reversal theory and reverse the troubleshooting procedure by reconnecting the found bad port to a lobe cable to re-create the problem, and then putting the lobe cable back into the newly tested port. This will show that your testing results are correct. If a failure still exists with the same RS on a new port, troubleshoot the respective lobe area for that RS.

MAU or hub faults affecting only one MAU or hub. In the instance of a complete unit failure with a particular MAU or wiring hub module, the troubleshooting steps are also forthright. You should remove the MAU or wiring hub module from the ring configuration and then retest the ring. If no problems are encountered, the MAU or wiring hub module is probably at failure. Next replace the removed unit with another, and reconnect all the respective lobe cables.

The next step is to thoroughly retest the new ring configuration. If everything is okay, then the suspected bad MAU or wiring hub module is bad. Again, the testing results can be verified by reversing the troubleshooting procedure by reinserting the found bad MAU or wiring hub module into the ring configuration to re-create the problem.

MAU or hub faults affecting multiple MAUs or hubs. When you suspect that a MAU or a hub module failure is causing solid fault effects with either multiple MAUs, multiple hub modules, or the complete Token Ring network, the best procedure is to remove the MAU or wiring hub module from the ring configuration, and retest the ring. In essence follow the procedure as described in the paragraph above.

If the failure is intermittent, try a protocol analysis session. By running a comprehensive analysis session, integrated with the manual troubleshooting steps above, chances are you'll be able to isolate the problem.

It is important to mention that some MAU and wiring hub manufacturers include their own diagnostic tools with their products. Some manufacturers have designed specific diagnostic programs along with special hardware built in to the units for testing purposes. It's a good idea to refer to all of the vendor documentation to see if any specific diagnostic tools are available for the respective MAU or wiring hub.

One last note: Again, in the case of any intermittent problems that are suspected with MAUs or wiring hubs, always run a protocol analysis session to be thorough and conclusive.

NETWORK INTERFACE CARD (NIC) PROBLEMS

NIC problems can cause the most misleading Token Ring failures. This is true because the NIC is responsible for generating and receiving the final data signal that is transmitted on the ring cabling medium. NICs do not always fail solidly; sometimes a NIC will still operate in marginal condition. When this occurs a NIC can introduce numerous intermittent failures onto the ring.

If you review the Token Ring theory presented in Chapter 2 you'll see that the Token Ring topology employs sophisticated communication techniques. These communication techniques rely upon the NIC for accurate data transmission, data reception, data processing, and data timing. If a NIC fails even marginally, any of these important network processes can be impaired.

NIC Failure Symptoms and Causes

Token Ring NIC failure symptoms fall into three categories:

- They generate hard errors onto the network
- They generate soft errors onto the network
- Ring insertion failure

If a NIC encounters a solid internal fault or a solid fault in its holding RS, the NIC may generate a hard error such as a Beacon MAC frame onto the ring. Figure 6.1 shows a Network General Sniffer Advanced Token Ring Monitor depicting a beaconing ring.

In this case the particular RS, including the NIC, would be the network failure area of an assigned fault domain. If the result of

FIGURE 6.1
This Sniffer Analyzer trace shows a beaconing Token Ring network.

```
┌─ SUMMARY Delta ──────────────────────────────────────────────────┐
│     613  0.019  Broadcast  NwkGnlE004FA  MAC Claim Token          │
│     614  0.020  Broadcast  NwkGnlE004FA  MAC Claim Token          │
│     615  0.019  Broadcast  NwkGnlE004FA  MAC Claim Token          │
│     616  0.019  Broadcast  NwkGnlE004FA  MAC Claim Token          │
│     617  0.019  Broadcast  NwkGnlE004FA  MAC Claim Token          │
│     618  0.020  Broadcast  NwkGnlE004FA  MAC Claim Token          │
│     619  0.009  Broadcast  NwkGnlE002D0  MAC Beacon               │
│     620  0.020  Broadcast  NwkGnlE004FA  MAC Beacon               │
│     621  0.019  Broadcast  NwkGnlE004FA  MAC Beacon               │
└──────────────────────── Frame 619 of 828 ───────────────────────┘
┌─ DETAIL ─────────────────────────────────────────────────────────┐
│   MAC:  ---- MAC data ----                                        │
│   MAC:                                                            │
│   MAC:  MAC Command:                                              │
│   MAC:  Source: Ring station, Destination: Ring Station          │
│   MAC:  Subvector type: Beacon Type - Streaming signal, Claim Token│
│   MAC:  Subvector type: Physical Drop Number 00000000            │
│   MAC:  Subvector type: Upstream Neighbor Address NwkGnlE004FA   │
│   MAC:                                                            │
└──────────────────────── Frame 619 of 828 ───────────────────────┘
                        Use TAB to select windows
    1       2      3   4 ZOOM    5      6DISPLAY  7 PREV  8 NEXT   9    10 NEW
   HELP    MARK        IN     MENUS   OPTIONS   FRAME   FRAME         CAPTURE
```

troubleshooting the assigned RS and NIC is that the NIC is at failure, the problem is normally a NIC hardware failure. If the NIC has been operating for awhile without failure, usually the problem is hardware, but if it is a new RS installation or the RS has recently been reconfigured, it's possible that there may be an improper configuration setting.

The solid-failure-cause exceptions that are typically related to improper configuration are ring speed settings or NIC firmware microcode versions.

When a NIC generates a soft error onto the ring, it may be detecting a marginal internal failure. As discussed in Chapter 2, before an RS actually generates the soft error, it starts an internal NIC timer, T(Soft_Error_Report). The timer runs for two seconds to acquire soft error information.

There are various types of soft errors that can be accumulated and generated. The specific type of soft error may point to a potential cause of failure. Figure 6.2 shows a Network General Sniffer Analyzer trace that depicts a Token Ring soft error, "Internal Error," which may indicate that one of the NICs within a specific fault domain is in marginal operating condition. A complete soft

FIGURE 6.2
A Token Ring network "Internal Error," as captured here by the Network General Sniffer Analyzer.

```
┌─ SUMMARY Delta ─────────────────────────────────────────────┐
│  2 0.039 Error Mon. 000450196CE  MAC Report Soft Error        │
│  3 0.053 IBM    1229B6rteon045879  XNS SPP   D=AED8 S=9C01 NR=9329 │
│  4 0.003 Prteon045879BM 1229B6   XNS SPP A D=9C01 S=AED8 NR=9330 │
│  5 0.005 Prteon045879BM 1229B6   XNS SPP   D=9C01 S=AED8 NR=9330 │
│  6 0.005 IBM    1229B6rteon045879  XNS SPP A D=AED8 S=9C01 NR=9330 │
│  7 0.039 IBM    1229B6rteon045879  XNS SPP A D=AED8 S=9C01 NR=9330 │
│  8 0.091 Error Mon.  BM  1D2AF8  MAC Report Soft Error        │
│  9 0.422 Broadcast 000450196CE  BPDU S:Pri=8000 Port=8001 Root:P │
│ 10 0.200 Prteon045C14BM1D35F3  NET D=7908 S=E1B7 Data, 0 byte(s) │
│ ─────────────────────── Frame 2 of 20 ──────────────────────── │
├─ DETAIL ─────────────────────────────────────────────────────┤
│  MAC:  ---- MAC Data ----                                     │
│  MAC:                                                          │
│  MAC:  MAC Command: Report Soft Error                         │
│  MAC:  Source: Ring Station, Destination: Ring Error Monitor  │
│  MAC:  Subvector type: Isolating Error Counts                 │
│  MAC:      0 line errors,      2 internal errors,      0 burst errors │
│  MAC:      0 AC errors,        0 abort delimiters transmitted │
│  MAC:  Subvector type: Non-Isolating Error Counts             │
│  MAC:      0 lost frame errors,  0 receiver congestion,  0 FC errors │
│ ─────────────────────── Frame 2 of 20 ──────────────────────── │
│               Use TAB to select windows                       │
│   1      2    3  4 ZOOM   5    6DISPLAY  7 PREV  8 NEXT  9  10 NEW │
│  HELP   MARK     IN    MENUS OPTIONS  FRAME  FRAME      CAPTURE │
└───────────────────────────────────────────────────────────────┘
```

error breakdown is detailed later in this chapter. What is important to remember is that a NIC that generates certain types of soft errors may cause ring degradation that will in turn exhibit intermittent ring failure symptoms.

Ring insertion failure is the inability of a particular RS to enter the ring. The network area of failure is usually a specific lobe area. If after troubleshooting the lobe area you identify the failure component as definitely a specific NIC, the failure is usually caused by one of the following reasons:

- Actual NIC hardware failure

- Improper NIC configuration with respect to the following settings: I/O address; IRQ; DMA; Token Ring address; slot settings, 32- or 16- or 8-bit card; NIC microcode level; primary or secondary setting; speed settings

- Improper NIC software driver microcode or bad remote program load (RPL) PROM, specifically, the LAN drivers and their configuration or bad firmware in an RPL PROM chip

- Incompatibility with the particular RS, MAU, cable type, or the STP/UTP cabling connector

If any of these problems are present, the NIC will usually never successfully complete the Ring Insertion process.

The following section examines some of the effective ways to troubleshoot NIC problems that occur in a Token Ring network.

Troubleshooting NICs

In troubleshooting a suspected NIC failure, first categorize the problem as solid or intermittent. Next, research whether the NIC has been functioning properly and the failure is unexpected, or if this is a new or interim RS installation.

Observe the following logical guidelines for troubleshooting a NIC failure:

- If the NIC has been operating for a reasonable period of time and the problem is solid, chances are that the NIC has an internal hardware problem. Some NIC manufacturers include NIC diagnostics; if possible, run the diagnostics to confirm the NIC failure. If there are no diagnostics available, swap the NIC and run a protocol analysis session to check the ring integrity.

- If the NIC has been operating fine and the problem is intermittent, definitely run some type of NIC diagnostics. A thorough protocol analysis session is recommended because it may further confirm any intermittent failures by capturing soft errors generated from the NIC address in question. Document all test benchmark results from the protocol analysis session. Try both methods to confirm the NIC failure. If, after testing, there are still no conclusive results, attempt swapping the NIC and rerunning a protocol analysis. Thoroughly check all testing benchmarks. Sometimes by checking the previous test results against the new tests result, the failure cause will emerge.

- If the NIC is part of a new or interim RS installation and the problem is solid or intermittent, chances are that the NIC has a configuration problem. Some NIC diagnostics will help to isolate a configuration problem. But most of the time you will need to thoroughly check all the configuration settings, as listed in the "MAU and Wiring Hub Failure Symptoms, Causes, and Troubleshooting" section. If after you've checked and set all possible configurations there is still a NIC failure, the NIC may have an internal hardware problem and should be swapped. Then, to be conclusive, rerun a thorough protocol analysis on the ring.

Also keep in mind that some Token Ring NICs do use an RPL chip to accomplish the task of network software drivers. Because an RPL PROM chip contains the firmware code to go out on the ring and access the file server, this chip can sometimes fail and cause many of the same symptoms listed in this section. An RPL chip operation can fail for two reasons, either because it's bad or it's the wrong firmware revision needed to work with the current NOS. If you suspect a bad RPL chip, the best move is to swap the chip and retest the ring.

RING STATION PROBLEMS

When a user has a problem on any type of network, the first place the user points to is his or her own PC. With the Token Ring topology, the RS itself can be the source for a good number of problems.

Most of the time, if you suspect an RS of failure it's probably because you have already defined it as the specific network component containing the source of failure. This will most likely be the case because either the network user has complained of a problem or because the RS is part of a new installation or modification. RS failures are not usually the cause of soft errors being generated; this will normally be the NIC at fault. The next section outlines some of the common failures that occur with RSes on the Token Ring topology.

Ring Station Failure Symptoms and Causes

RS failure symptoms fall into three categories:

- RS failure and Ring Insertion failures due to hardware configuration or hardware failure

- RS failure and Ring Insertion failures due to software configuration or corruption

- RS failure and Ring Insertion failures due to RS-to-NIC incompatibility

Often when an RS fails or it cannot access the ring, it is because the station has recently been worked on. Sometimes a new PC option is added and the hardware configuration parameters get changed. There are hard failure occurrences, but they do not happen that often. Note that when they do occur, a soft or hard error condition may be present on the ring.

One of the most common failures with RSes is that their particular NIC drivers get placed in the wrong directories. Sometimes a particular path statement gets wiped out by a modification to the AUTOEXEC.BAT file. Another common occurrence is the CONFIG.SYS will be incorrect or is modified, and a Driver statement will be missing or the Files/Buffer statements will be incorrect or get changed. Sometimes actual software corruption occurs, but that happens infrequently. These conditions may generate a soft or hard error onto the ring.

RSes and NICs sometimes experience certain incompatibilities that cause RS failures or Ring Insertion failure. In certain instances this is due to a simple slot or setup configuration issue. Other times a particular PC will simply be incompatible with a certain NIC.

The following section offers some logical suggestions for troubleshooting RS problems.

Troubleshooting Ring Stations

With RS problems, again categorize the problem as solid or intermittent, and also research whether the RS has been operating okay for awhile or if it has recently been involved in a new installation or any hardware/software modifications.

As you troubleshoot an RS problem use the following logical guidelines:

- When a solid hardware failure occurs, the PC usually will indicate some sort of error during its self test. If you suspect a problem, attempt to run some sort of advanced local PC diagnostics. If a problem occurs, troubleshoot the PC by removing all I/O boards and retesting the RS.

  Next reverse this process by adding boards back into the PC one at a time and retesting. Sometimes a particular I/O board will cause a conflict in attaching to the ring. If a particular board is at fault, it should cause a failure when it is reinserted into the PC.

  If you don't have problems with any of the I/O boards, it's possible the PC has a hardware configuration problem. Check all necessary I/O and PC configurations. Sometimes the PC settings straighten out simply by you going through the configuration process. If none of these methods locate the failure, recheck the NIC as a possible cause of failure.

- Software configuration errors within a PC is one of the most frequent causes of Ring Insertion failure. All the necessary network files—including Token Ring NIC drivers, network shell drivers, AUTOEXEC.BAT, and CONFIG.SYS—must be in the correct file structure and must be uncorrupted.

  If a software configuration or corruption failure is suspected, first check to make sure that all the files are in the correct file structure as to their respective directory placement.

  If a file corruption is suspected, attempt to reload and reconfigure the particular file or files. Network documentation and vendor software manuals will be a key aid in this process. Always keep in mind that a simple incorrect statement in either AUTOEXEC.BAT or CONFIG.SYS can cause network failures. RS software problems can cause a significant number of failures in the Ring Insertion process or in an RS's ability to access the network file server.

Figure 6.3 shows a Network General Sniffer Analyzer trace depicting an RS attempting a normal ring insertion process.

- Especially with new installations and modifications, you'll encounter general RS-to-NIC incompatibilities that may cause RS failure or Ring Insertion failure. This problem really does fall into the new-installation category and will sometimes be quite deceiving.

  If this type of problem is suspected, attempt to run all available PC and NIC diagnostics and recheck all relevant documentation. Another good step is to call all the manufacturers involved to see whether they have any record of certified testing between the particular PC being used as an RS and the respective NIC.

  Many failure causes that appear to be within an RS revolve around the particular NIC. Keep in mind all the suggestions offered in the NIC and RS sections for a thorough troubleshooting process.

FIGURE 6.3
This trace shows
a Token Ring
network ring
station attempting
insertion into
the ring.

```
┌─ SUMMARY Delta ──────────────────────────────────────┐
│   1         Broadcast       estar000001  MAC  Active Monitor Present   │
│   2 0.020   Broadcast       00000000002  MAC  Standby Monitor Present  │
│   3 6.906   Broadcast       estar000001  MAC  Active Monitor Present   │
│   4 0.011   Broadcast       00000000002  MAC  Standby Monitor Present  │
│   5 6.916   Broadcast       estar000001  MAC  Active Monitor Present   │
│   6 0.012   Broadcast       00000000002  MAC  Standby Monitor Present  │
│   7 6.915   Broadcast       estar000001  MAC  Active Monitor Present   │
│   8 0.013   Broadcast       00000000002  MAC  Standby Monitor Present  │
│   9 1.028   Broadcast       estar000001  MAC  Ring Purge               │
│  10 0.000   400000000000100000000001  MAC  Duplicate Address Test      │
│  11 0.000   Broadcast       estar000001  MAC  Active Monitor Present   │
│  12 0.000   400000000000100000000001  MAC  Duplicate Address Test      │
│  13 0.010   Broadcast       00000000002  MAC  Standby Monitor Present  │
│  14 0.000   Config Srv       00000000001  MAC  Report SUA Change       │
│  15 0.015   Broadcast       00000000001  MAC  Standby Monitor Present  │
│  16 0.000   Param Server 00000000001  MAC  Request Initialization      │
│  17 0.000   Config Srv       estar0000001  MAC  Report SUA Change      │
│  18 0.000   Param Server 00000000001  MAC  Request Initialization      │
│  19 0.000   Param Server 00000000001  MAC  Request Initialization      │
│  20 0.000   Param Server 00000000001  MAC  Request Initialization      │
└──────────────────────── Frame 1 of 225 ──────────────┘
```

1	2	3	4	5	6DISPLAY	7 PREV	8 NEXT	9	10 NEW
HELP	MARK			MENUS	OPTIONS	FRAME	FRAME		CAPTURE

Remember that actively troubleshooting an RS problem by running a thorough protocol analysis session on the ring enables you to capture any network communication problems and any present soft or hard error conditions. This information can enable you to identify a specific RS failure cause. Also, to ensure network integrity, after taking any measures during troubleshooting an RS, rerun the protocol analysis session.

FILE SERVER PROBLEMS

A file server on a Token Ring network falls into the same category as a general RS: A file server basically has the same hardware and software modules as an RS. Because of this, the failure symptoms of communication processes and soft or hard error conditions that may be present on the ring may appear in the same way as they do with an RS.

Yes, a file server does contain different software and hardware LAN resources than a general RS—the NOS, database, bridging modules, and so on. But as far as the Token Ring architecture is concerned, it is just another Token Ring address. Most of the failure causes and troubleshooting guidelines also apply to a file server in a Token Ring network.

The next section has some extra notes for differentiating specific file server problems in the Token Ring topology.

File Server Failure Symptoms, Causes, and Troubleshooting Hints

This book concentrates specifically on the Token Ring topology, and does not discuss a specific NOS in detail. Thus this section is generic as to its discussion of NOSs. But note that whether you have Novell NetWare, IBM LAN Server, Microsoft LAN Manager, Banyan Vines, or any other NOS, the same failure causes and troubleshooting methods apply.

When you encounter a suspected file server problem, employ the following analytical guidelines:

- A file server contains the same important network files as an RS, such as the network shell software, CONFIG.SYS, and AUTOEXEC.BAT, with the addition of a NOS and its specialized configuration and drivers.

  As mentioned earlier in this chapter, a network file server problem can cause an RS to continually insert and deinsert itself from the ring. This is usually due to incompatibility between the NOS revision or configuration and the respective RS network shell software revision or configuration. When this type of problem occurs, attempt to focus closely on these possible causes. Your best aid will be the network software vendor documentation and the general network documentation.

- A frequent cause of problems on file servers is file structure configurations. For instance, a particular RS might be configured to look for certain files within a certain defined directory on the file server, but cannot find them because they are in another directory or are missing. The best suggestion here is to be methodical about checking for the directory structure as it relates to RS access.

• Security rights are a number one reason for Ring Insertion failure. If a particular RS inserts itself on to the LAN, attempts to log on to the file server, and is denied access, the RS may deinsert itself from the ring. Here the best suggestion is to check all the user rights. Security access at certain directory levels may also cause certain soft error messages due to increased traffic upon the ring.

• In general, network software file server problems can cause the Token Ring bandwidth to be eaten up with abnormal traffic between a certain RS and the file server. If you suspect this, the situation begs for a protocol analysis session.

With a protocol analyzer you will be able to capture this type of occurrence and to view the high-layer protocol communication between an RS and a network file server. This data will allow you to identify and troubleshoot the higher-layer communication processes. You will also be able to quickly identify any abnormal network bandwidth between a particular RS and the file server.

In figure 6.4 a Network General Sniffer Analyzer trace depicts a problem with a communication session between a Banyan file server and an RS. Notice the abnormal amount of redundant communication traffic between the RS and the file server. This topic is covered further in the *Troubleshooting High-Layer Communication Problems* and *Performance Testing* sections later in this chapter.

TOKEN RING NETWORK PERIPHERAL PROBLEMS

In any standard network there are peripherals such as printers and modems; in today's networks the peripherals are becoming much more sophisticated. All sorts of new products are hitting the marketplace, such as communication servers (modem pools with specialized network access hardware and software), network printers (printers with their own NIC card so they do not need to attach to an RS or file server), and fax servers (fax machines with internal NIC cards).

In taking this form, these devices are not simple peripherals any more—they are now actual nodes on the Token Ring network. Because they contain their own NICs, they also assume a unique Token Ring address, just like an RS. You can't troubleshoot these devices as simple peripherals anymore; you must view them as Token Ring nodes. The following section describes network peripheral operations, failure symptoms, and causes, and some troubleshooting methods.

FIGURE 6.4
A Sniffer Analyzer trace tracks communication problems between a file server and a network ring station.

```
┌─ SUMMARY Delta ──────────────────────────────────────────────┐
│  2  0.003  IBM      7976DBanyan Ser..  SMB R  OK               │
│  3  0.009  Banyan Ser..BM  7976DB      SMB C  F=0167 Read 161 at 66 │
│  4  0.003  IBM      7976DBanyan Ser..  SMB R  OK               │
│  5  0.008  Banyan Ser..BM  7976DB      SMB C  F=167 Close       │
│  6  0.002  IBM      7976DBanyan Ser..  SMB R  Closed            │
│  7  0.024  Banyan Ser..BM  7976DB      SMB C  Open \LEGAL\EVELYNP\WP\001 │
│  8  0.005  IBM      7976DBanyan Ser..  SMB R  F=0168 Opened      │
│  9  0.006  Banyan Ser..BM  7976DB      SMB C  F=0168 Seek to end  │
│ 10  0.002  IBM      7976DBanyan Ser..  SMB R  Seek to 1387       │
│ 11  0.010  Banyan Ser..BM  7976DB      SMB C  F=0168 Read 16 at 0 │
│ 12  0.002  IBM      7976DBanyan Ser..  SMB R  OK                │
│ 13  0.010  Banyan Ser..BM  7976DB      SMB C  F=0168 Read 16 at 0 │
│ 14  0.003  IBM      7976DBanyan Ser..  SMB R  OK                │
│ 15  0.008  Banyan Ser..BM  7976DB      SMB C  F=0168 Read 10 at 16 │
│ 16  0.003  IBM      7976DBanyan Ser..  SMB R  OK                │
│ 17  0.011  Banyan Ser..BM  7976DB      SMB C  F=0168 Read 50 at 16 │
│ 18  0.003  IBM      7976DBanyan Ser..  SMB R  OK                │
│ 19  0.010  Banyan Ser..BM  7976DB      SMB C  F=0168 Read 50 at 16 │
│ 20  0.003  IBM      7976DBanyan Ser..  SMB R  OK                │
│ 21  0.009  Banyan Ser..BM  7976DB      SMB C  F=0168 Read 158 at 66 │
└───────────────── Frame 12 of 24 ──────────────────────────────┘

   1       2      3     4      5      6DISPLAY  7 PREV   8 NEXT   9   10 NEW
 HELP    MARK                MENUS   OPTIONS   FRAME    FRAME        CAPTURE
```

Network Peripheral Operations

Again, when a network peripheral such as a printer contains its own Token Ring address, it has to be viewed as a unique Token Ring node, almost as if it were an RS. Some of the network peripherals access the Token Ring network with NIC and hardware/software components; others just use NIC hardware with firmware contained within PROM chips. Both configurations allow the assigned network peripheral to access the ring through standard Ring Insertion, and they both operate according to the Token Ring architecture operating-mode principles.

Network Peripheral Failure Symptoms, Causes, and Troubleshooting

Network peripheral failure symptoms are different from standard RS failure symptoms because a peripheral is actually a different device. For example, a standard RS cannot log on to the network file server if it cannot complete ring insertion, whereas a network printer may not be able to print because it cannot access the ring. It is important to note that a network peripheral failure can cause soft and hard error conditions to be generated on the ring.

Even though a network peripheral failure symptom is different than that of a standard RS, the network peripheral failure cause and RS failure cause are somewhat analogous. Both a network peripheral and a standard RS contain a NIC, and both access the ring through the 802.5 rules, so they both can be assumed to have some common failure causes.

For example, if a network printer cannot access the ring, the logical network area of fault is isolated to a lobe area containing the following components: a printer, a NIC, a lobe cable, and a MAU or hub port. If an RS cannot access the ring, then the lobe area components are a PC, a NIC, a lobe cable, and MAU or hub ports. The only major difference is that one lobe area contains a printer rather than a PC. But it is important to note that sometimes certain network peripheral failures may be related to either improper internal or external network configurations, because they sometimes rely upon and cooperate with other network devices to operate.

With all this in mind, try to approach troubleshooting a network peripheral with the standard lobe area troubleshooting methods discussed earlier in this chapter. One important difference for troubleshooting a network peripheral is that a protocol analysis session will be a key to resolving any problems. Because network peripherals are new entities to the standard Token Ring network configuration, a protocol analysis session is recommended. With a protocol analyzer you will be able to capture and view any network communication data traffic and soft or hard error conditions involving the assigned network peripheral.

BRIDGE, ROUTER, REPEATER, AND GATEWAY PROBLEMS

When you're troubleshooting a Token Ring internetwork, the bridges, routers, and repeaters will usually be involved. Because these devices separate the rings or ring route for their respective purposes (as discussed in Chapter 3), the actual troubleshooting of these devices requires a good understanding of their operational theory.

Chapter 3 is a good reference for the basic operation of bridges, routers, and repeaters in the Token Ring environment. For a more thorough understanding of a particular bridge, router, or repeater specification and operations, contact the particular manufacturer.

If a bridge, router, or repeater has a failure or improper configuration, most of the time the problem exhibits a fairly straightforward solid symptom. But there are also failure-cause instances that will make the problem symptom intermittent.

Whether the symptom is solid or intermittent, the failure symptom may be present in the form of a soft or hard error condition on the ring. This section describes some useful information for the failure symptoms, causes, and troubleshooting suggestions for bridges, routers, and repeaters in the Token Ring environment. The information is generic as to manufacturer type.

Bridge Failure Symptoms, Causes, and Troubleshooting

Because bridges connect rings at the Data Link level and are mainly used to segment traffic, a failure symptom will normally be clear. When a bridge failure occurs, the problem is usually evident. Some of the common bridge failure symptoms are as follows:

- No data traffic at all is able to get from one side of the bridge to the other.

- Partial traffic is unable to pass across the bridge and the problem is solid.

- Partial traffic is unable to pass across the bridge and the problem is intermittent.

- There are overloaded-bandwidth problems on a certain ring.

If no traffic is able to get from one side of the bridge to the other, the cause is usually a hardware configuration or hardware failure. The best way to approach troubleshooting this type of a problem is first to doublecheck the software and hardware configuration of the bridge. Configuration problems are common with new installations, network add-ons, and changes.

If the configuration does appear to be at fault, attempt to run some bridge diagnostics, if they are provided by the bridge manufacturer. The last and most comprehensive way to troubleshoot the problem is to run a protocol analysis session. Figure 6.5 depicts data passing across a particular bridge that was captured by a Network General Sniffer trace.

FIGURE 6.5
A protocol analysis session shows whether a bridge is successfully passing data.

```
┌─ DETAIL ─────────────────────────────────────────────────────────┐
│  DLC:  ─────── DLC Header───────                                   │
│  DLC:                                                              │
│  DLC:  Frame 99 arrived at 10:26:005.099; frame size is 90 (005A hex) bytes. │
│  DLC:  AC: Frame priority 0, Reservation priority 0, Monitor count 1 │
│  DLC:  FC: LLC frame, PFC attention code: None                     │
│  DLC:  FS: Addr recognized indicators: 11, Frame copied indicators: 11 │
│  DLC:  Destination = Functional address D50020808080              │
│  DLC:  Source      = Station 550020005008                         │
│  DLC:                                                              │
│  RI :  ─────── Routing Indicators ───────                          │
│  RI :                                                              │
│  RI :  Routing control = 6                                         │
│  RI :        110. . . . . = Single-route broadcast, all-routes broadcast return │
│  RI :        . . . 0 0110 = RI length is 6                         │
│  RI :  Routing control = 10                                        │
│  RI :        0. . . . . . . = Forward direction                    │
│  RI :        .001 . . . . = Largest frame is 1470                  │
│  RI :        . . . . 0000 = Reserved                               │
│  RI :  Ring number FE77 via bridge 7                               │
│  RI :  Ring number 777                                             │
│  RI :                                                              │
│  LLC:  ─────── LLC Header ───────                                  │
│  LLC:                                                              │
│  LLC:  DSAP = AA, SSAP = AA, Command, Unnumbered frame: UI         │
│  LLC:                                                              │
│  SNAP: ─────── SNAP Header ───────                                 │
│  SNAP:                                                             │
│  SNAP: Type = 6007 (DEC LAVC)                                      │
│  SNAP: [62 byte(s) of data]                                        │
│                                                                    │
├────────────────────────────────────────────────────────────────── │
│   1      2     3   4 ZOOM   5    6 DISPLAY  7 PREV  8 NEXT  9  10 NEW │
│  HELP   MARK       IN     MENUS  OPTIONS   FRAME   FRAME      CAPTURE │
└────────────────────────────────────────────────────────────────── ┘
```

If partial traffic will not pass and the problem is solid, the symptom is most probably related to a bridge table configuration or a source-routing problem with certain RSs. First, thoroughly check the bridge configuration. Next, run a protocol analysis session. Examine the Routing Information field of the frames that are not being passed through the bridge. A protocol analyzer will be the key in this instance. If a particular bridge addressing problem is found in the source-routing field, the originating RS may be a fault.

When partial traffic will not pass though the bridge and the problem is intermittent, the first and foremost step is to take out the protocol analyzer. Do a full capture and again examine all the routing information fields of the frames in question. Often an RS causes an intermittent bridge problem. Sometimes this can be due to a bad NIC, but most of the time the particular RS has a software application configuration problem in relation to its source-routing information for the particular bridge.

Figure 6.6 shows a frame sequence captured with a Network General Sniffer Analyzer. The frame sequence depicts a bridge forwarding source-routing information from a source ring to a destination ring.

Sometimes an incorrect bridge configuration parameter or source-routing problem with a specific RS can cause bandwidth problems in a multiple-ring environment. Certain bridges contain configuration parameters that can control the amount of traffic to be forwarded to another ring. This is an important setting, because the bandwidth of the destination ring can be seriously affected if an abnormal amount of traffic is being forwarded.

In a source-routing environment the problem may actually not lie with the bridge; it may be due to a particular software application configuration problem relating to source-routing information from a specific RS, but the problem is sometimes hard to identify. If certain rings in a multiple-ring configuration appear to have bandwidth problems, I cannot stress the importance of running a full protocol analysis session on the multiple-ring configuration.

Figure 6.7 shows the routing information screen from a Network General Sniffer Token Ring Advanced Monitor Analyzer, displaying data traffic from one ring to another. This particular screen capture depicts a source-routing overhead problem from one ring to another. The percentage of frames being forwarded is overloading the destination ring with traffic.

FIGURE 6.6
This trace depicts a bridge forwarding source-routing information to its destination ring.

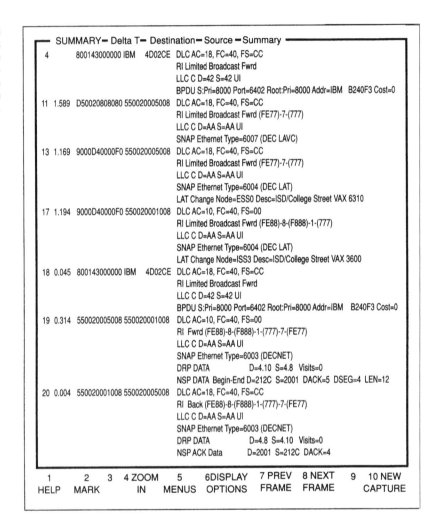

```
┌─ SUMMARY─ Delta T─ Destination─ Source ─Summary ──────────────┐
│  4        800143000000 IBM    4D02CE  DLC AC=18, FC=40, FS=CC                              │
│                                        RI Limited Broadcast Fwrd                            │
│                                        LLC C D=42 S=42 UI                                    │
│                                        BPDU S:Pri=8000 Port=6402 Root:Pri=8000 Addr=IBM  B240F3 Cost=0 │
│  11 1.589  D50020808080 550020005008   DLC AC=18, FC=40, FS=CC                              │
│                                        RI Limited Broadcast Fwrd (FE77)-7-(777)             │
│                                        LLC C D=AA S=AA UI                                    │
│                                        SNAP Ethernet Type=6007 (DEC LAVC)                    │
│  13 1.169  9000D40000F0 550020005008   DLC AC=18, FC=40, FS=CC                              │
│                                        RI Limited Broadcast Fwrd (FE77)-7-(777)             │
│                                        LLC C D=AA S=AA UI                                    │
│                                        SNAP Ethernet Type=6004 (DEC LAT)                     │
│                                        LAT Change Node=ESS0 Desc=ISD/College Street VAX 6310 │
│  17 1.194  9000D40000F0 550020001008   DLC AC=10, FC=40, FS=00                              │
│                                        RI Limited Broadcast Fwrd (FE88)-8-(F888)-1-(777)    │
│                                        LLC C D=AA S=AA UI                                    │
│                                        SNAP Ethernet Type=6004 (DEC LAT)                     │
│                                        LAT Change Node=ISS3 Desc=ISD/College Street VAX 3600 │
│  18 0.045  800143000000 IBM    4D02CE  DLC AC=18, FC=40, FS=CC                              │
│                                        RI Limited Broadcast Fwrd                            │
│                                        LLC C D=42 S=42 UI                                    │
│                                        BPDU S:Pri=8000 Port=6402 Root:Pri=8000 Addr=IBM  B240F3 Cost=0 │
│  19 0.314  550020005008 550020001008   DLC AC=10, FC=40, FS=00                              │
│                                        RI  Fwrd (FE88)-8-(F888)-1-(777)-7-(FE77)            │
│                                        LLC C D=AA S=AA UI                                    │
│                                        SNAP Ethernet Type=6003 (DECNET)                      │
│                                        DRP DATA          D=4.10 S=4.8  Visits=0             │
│                                        NSP DATA Begin-End D=212C S=2001 DACK=5 DSEG=4 LEN=12 │
│  20 0.004  550020001008 550020005008   DLC AC=18, FC=40, FS=CC                              │
│                                        RI  Back (FE88)-8-(F888)-1-(777)-7-(FE77)            │
│                                        LLC C D=AA S=AA UI                                    │
│                                        SNAP Ethernet Type=6003 (DECNET)                      │
│                                        DRP DATA          D=4.8 S=4.10  Visits=0             │
│                                        NSP ACK Data      D=2001 S=212C DACK=4               │
├─────────────────────────────────────────────────────────────┤
│  1      2      3   4 ZOOM   5      6DISPLAY  7 PREV  8 NEXT   9   10 NEW   │
│  HELP   MARK       IN    MENUS   OPTIONS  FRAME   FRAME       CAPTURE │
└─────────────────────────────────────────────────────────────┘
```

Router Failure Symptoms, Causes, and Troubleshooting

Router failure symptoms can be a little misleading. Sometimes the problem symptom will appear as a particular application, or the NOS will not work on certain rings. Note that software applications and NOSs rely on certain LAN communication protocols to communicate across the LAN. If a certain protocol is not being passed through a router, the application or NOS access may work on one ring and not another.

FIGURE 6.7
Token Ring-
specific protocol-
analysis tools
display useful
information, such
as the source-
routing overhead
problem shown
here.

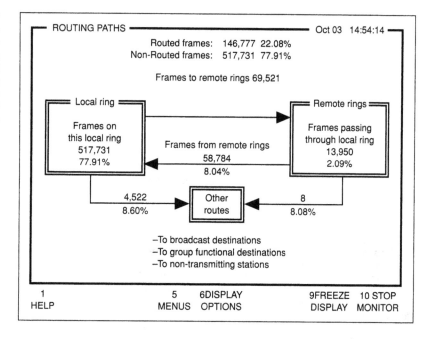

FIGURE 6.7
Token Ring-specific protocol-analysis tools display useful information, such as the source-routing overhead problem shown here.

Router failure symptoms fall into the following categories:

• They do not allow particular protocols to be passed through to another ring and the problem is solid.

• They do not allow particular protocols to be passed through to another ring and the problem is intermittent.

• They do not allow any data traffic to pass through and the problem is either solid or intermittent.

• There are overloaded bandwidth problems on a certain ring.

Because a router is used to segment traffic, many of the troubleshooting points discussed in the previous section also apply with a router, specifically, partial data transmission and destination ring overhead problems.

But because a router's main purpose is to connect rings that need to share the same protocols, they must understand and be configured for the protocol they are forwarding.

One of the main points to look for with a suspected router problem is incorrect configurations with the protocol routing table in the particular router. Sometimes these particular configurations are extremely complex and can be affected easily.

Figure 6.8 depicts a routing problem captured by a Network General Sniffer trace. The trace shows a summary view of a TCP/IP DNS packet that could not be forwarded across a router. Further decoding of various frames would show that the problem is there, because the router is not configured to forward TCP/IP DNS packets. This is a simple setting, but the problem denied all the users on the source ring access to a remote file server on the destination ring.

FIGURE 6.8
This Network General trace pinpoints a TCP/IP packet that was not forwarded across a router.

```
┌─ SUMMARY Delta ──────────────────────────────────────────────┐
│    1         Prteon045C14IBM  1D35F3        DSAP=E0, UI frame   │
│    2 0.002 IBM  1D35F3Prteon045C14          DSAP=E0, UI frame   │
│    3 0.184 Broadcast    Prteon046101 DNS C ID=2478 OP=REGISTER NAME=T│
│    4 0.001 IBM          61C09Wellfleet DNS C ID=2478 OP=REGISTER NAME=T│
│    5 0.338 Broadcast       Wellfleet BPDU S:Pri=8000 Port=8001 Root:P│
│    6 0.982 IBM  1229B6Prteon045879          DSAP=E0, UI frame   │
│    7 0.003 Prteon045879IBM  1229B6          DSAP=E0, UI frame   │
│    8 0.005 Prteon045879IBM  1229B6          DSAP=E0, UI frame   │
│    9 0.005 IBM  1229B6Prteon045879          DSAP=E0, UI frame   │
│   10 0.039 IBM  1229B6Prteon045879          DSAP=E0, UI frame   │
│   11 0.242 Prteon044525Prteon045C14         DSAP=E0, UI frame   │
│   12 0.005 Prteon045C14Prteon044525         DSAP=E0, UI frame   │
│   13 0.124 Broadcast    Prteon046101 DNS C ID=2478 OP=REGISTER NAME=T│
│   14 0.001 IBM          61C09Wellfleet DNS C ID=2478 OP=REGISTER NAME=T│
│   15 0.015 NetBIOS      Prteon046101        DSAP=E0, UI frame   │
│   16 0.311 Broadcast    IBM  1D2AF8 MAC Active Monitor Present  │
│   17 0.019 Broadcast    IBM  1CC749 MAC Standby Monitor Present │
│   18 0.013 Broadcast    Prteon045879 MAC Standby Monitor Present│
│   19 0.018 Broadcast    Prteon043A91 MAC Standby Monitor Present│
│   20 0.016 Broadcast    IBM  1CB7D8 MAC Standby Monitor Present │
│                    ── Frame 13 of 20 ──                         │
└───────────────────────────────────────────────────────────────┘

  1       2    3      4      5    6DISPLAY  7 PREV  8 NEXT   9   10 NEW
 HELP    MARK              MENUS  OPTIONS   FRAME   FRAME        CAPTURE
```

If the problem is that no data traffic is able to get from one side of the router to the other, the cause is usually a hardware configuration or hardware failure, as with a bridge.

Repeater Failure Symptoms, Causes, and Troubleshooting

Repeater failure symptoms are candid:

- When a repeater fails it will usually not allow data traffic to pass. Most of the time this occurrence will be solid, but sometimes it will be intermittent.

- Sometimes a repeater failure will simulate a main ring path failure symptom, and a hard error (such as beaconing or a wire fault condition) may arise.

A repeater failure is usually related to an internal hardware module failure, and at times the hardware configuration. There are instances when the physical placement of a repeater may be at fault due to the importance of the Token Ring cabling-length specifications. Also keep in mind that the cabling itself can cause a repeater failure symptom.

The first approach should be a TDR and, in the case of fiber, an OTDR. Also, use any repeater unit diagnostics, if the manufacturer offers them. One of the best overall methods of troubleshooting a suspected bad repeater is to remove the unit by bypassing it or relooping the cabling at the repeater entry point. Relooping the cabling can be done with patch cables for the specific cable type.

Gateway Failure Symptoms, Causes, and Troubleshooting

Gateway failure symptoms are rather direct. Usually you can access the gateway or you will not be able to access the gateway. At times a gateway session may seem slow or unresponsive, usually due to improper configuration in the LAN gateway design, but it can be related to a possible gateway failure. Also, at times, a LAN-to-host session may lock up intermittently, due to intermittent gateway hardware problems or an improper gateway configuration.

The failure causes can be a little more complex. Some of the most common failure causes are as follows:

- The host is not properly configured as to session setup for the particular gateway.

- The gateway itself is not properly configured in relation to hardware/software for access to the host or allowing ring stations access.

- A particular ring station or group of ring stations is unable to access the gateway, because they are not properly configured in relation to the software/hardware setup.

- An intermittent gateway hardware problem or an improper gateway configuration may cause a LAN-to-host session to intermittently lock up.

The recommended method for troubleshooting these types of problems is to first thoroughly check the gateway's configuration against the gateway manufacturer's hardware and software setup for use with the LAN and the respective host. Next verify that ring stations that need to access the gateway are configured properly according to the gateway manufacturer's specifications. Last, make sure that the respective host is properly configured as to session setup and port availability to handle communications to the respective gateway.

If there are any available diagnostics from the manufacturer, it's always a good idea to use them for gateway troubleshooting.

I also highly recommend that you fully reference the gateway manufacturer's instructions when working with any gateway issues.

PROTOCOL ANALYSIS

In Chapter 4 we defined and discussed protocol analysis methodology. This section provides an in-depth look at how to use a protocol analysis session to effectively troubleshoot a network problem within the Token Ring architecture.

As you read, keep in mind the prescribed approach for a general protocol analysis session: capture, view, analyze, check errors, benchmark performance, and focus. This generic approach overlays and directly interrelates with the specific methods of using protocol analysis to troubleshoot a Token Ring network.

It is important to mention that when approaching the Token Ring protocol model with protocol analysis, you must first analyze the lower layers of communication, then consecutively examine the higher-layer communication processes. This is because the low-level 802.5 Token Ring architectural communications must be at a normal operating state before you can conclusively examine any higher-layer protocols used by applications and NOSs. The integrity of the higher-layer protocol communication is based on proper and fluent low-layer protocol communications.

In performing any type of protocol analysis session on a Token Ring network, you must fully capture network data during peak and off-peak network usage periods. This means you cannot perform protocol analysis on a network in a quick or rushed fashion. The proper method is to use a full-capture approach and to run a protocol analysis session for at least a complete business day. This full-capture approach will give you a complete palette of events occurring on your network. In a multiple-ring environment, each ring should get the full-capture approach.

The next section introduces the proper approach for using protocol analysis to view and troubleshoot the low-level 802.5 communications layer, then leads into the higher-layer communication processes, and finally discusses performance testing on a Token Ring network.

EXAMINING AND TROUBLESHOOTING LOW-LEVEL 802.5 COMMUNICATIONS

To perform a protocol analysis session on the Token Ring topology, the proper approach is to establish a baseline of the network. A network baseline can be defined as the current state of a network's order of operation.

To establish an accurate baseline of your Token Ring network, it's always best to perform a protocol analysis session when your network is not experiencing any failures. Capturing a session of communication from the network when it is operating without any errors provides a true picture of its normal baseline. Then, when network failures do occur, you will be able to run a protocol analysis session and examine the captured data for any variation from the established normal network baseline.

Note that by examining any particular variations that occur, you may be able to pinpoint a failure cause within a specific network area or component. The following paragraphs cover how to use protocol analysis for measuring your network baseline and effectively troubleshooting any deviances from the norm.

802.5 frame communication. To establish a baseline or to troubleshoot a failure symptom, you should enter the protocol analysis session by focusing on the 802.5 base data frame communication processes. Chapter 2 discusses in detail all the MAC and LLC data frame formats. To recap, the data frame will carry the classification of either a MAC frame or an LLC frame.

The LLC frames carry the PDU (protocol data unit) that encases the actual high-level user data information that is transmitted on the ring. LLC frames involve multiple frame sequences such as addressing, control, and actual high-layer data information.

Because a defined LLC 802.5 data frame is primarily responsible for transferring the higher-layer data information among RSes, it is not considered responsible for establishing the base Token Ring medium access control communication sequencing. For this reason when encountering LLC frames you would normally concentrate on the higher-layer information that is enveloped with the LLC frame. The higher-layer communication processes are discussed in detail later in this section.

The 25 MAC frame types handle the actual Token Ring medium access control communication, and this is where you have to focus when examining the 802.5 low-level frame communication processes. When examining an 802.5 MAC data frame you have to correlate the MAC frame type with specific Token Ring communication processes. With a thorough understanding of the Token Ring communication process theory as discussed in Chapter 2, you should be able to capture a series of MAC frames and decipher what type of Token Ring communication process is currently occurring.

Once you understand these two important factors—the MAC frame and the current Token Ring communication process—you will be able to examine and troubleshoot the current state of low-level 802.5 frame communications for proper and fluent communication exchange between the network entities involved. Any deviances from a normal state of a low-level frame communication process may indicate a possible intermittent network component failure.

The following example describes a typical deviance from the normal state of a low-level MAC frame communication process. (Note: The Token Ring communication processes presented in Chapter 2 provide the necessary theory to fully understand the example.)

The Active Monitor Present MAC frame is supposed to be generated approximately every seven seconds to notify all standby monitors that an active monitor is on the ring. Because the Neighbor Notification process requires that the frame be generated every seven seconds, you should be able to see this frame present every seven seconds. If you do not, there is a deviance from the normal state of the MAC frame communication process.

You should be able to isolate a possible intermittent network component failure by examining the captured analysis trace for any deviance from this process, such as a Claim Token MAC frame being generated onto the ring by an RS that had its T(Receive_Notification) timer expire and is attempting to enter the Claim Token Transmit mode. This sequence would signify that the active monitor or a particular standby monitor has a problem and has dropped off the ring. When this occurs, the protocol analyzer may capture some soft errors present on the ring. The Network General Sniffer trace in figure 6.9 depicts an abnormal timing sequence on the ring in the generation of the Active Monitor Present MAC frame.

FIGURE 6.9
The individual pieces of the Token Ring Protocol model relate quite closely to the seven layers of the OSI model for LANs.

```
┌─ SUMMARY Delta ─────────────────────────────────────────────────┐
│  75   22.385   Broadcast   NwkGnlE004FA        DSAP=00, UI frame  │
│  76   22.995   Broadcast   NwkGnlE004F2        DSAP=00, UI frame  │
│  77   23.015   Broadcast   NwkGnlE002D0   MAC Active Monitor Present │
│  78   23.025   Broadcast   NwkGnlE004F2   MAC Standby Monitor Present │
│  79   23.038   Broadcast   NwkGnlE004FA   MAC Standby Monitor Present │
│  80   23.465   Broadcast   NwkGnlE004F2   MAC Claim Token        │
│  81   23.468   Broadcast   NwkGnlE004FA   MAC Claim Token        │
│  82   23.488   Broadcast   NwkGnlE004FA   MAC Claim Token        │
│  83   23.508   Broadcast   NwkGnlE004FA   MAC Claim Token        │
│  84   23.508   Broadcast   NwkGnlE004FA   MAC Ring Purge         │
│  85   23.512   Broadcast   NwkGnlE004FA        DSAP=00, UI frame  │
│  86   23.512   Config Srv  NwkGnlE004FA   MAC Report New Monitor │
│  87   23.512   Broadcast   NwkGnlE004FA   MAC Active Monitor Present │
│  88   23.513   Config Srv  NwkGnlE004F2   MAC Report SUA Change  │
│  89   23.525   Broadcast   NwkGnlE004F2   MAC Standby Monitor Present │
│  90   23.998   Broadcast   NwkGnlE004F2        DSAP=00, UI frame  │
│  91   24.515   Broadcast   NwkGnlE004FA        DSAP=00, UI frame  │
│  92   25.000   Broadcast   NwkGnlE004F2        DSAP=00, UI frame  │
│  93   25.518   Broadcast   NwkGnlE004FA        DSAP=00, UI frame  │
│  94   26.003   Broadcast   NwkGnlE004F2        DSAP=00, UI frame  │
└───────────────────── Frame 94 of 127 ──────────────────────────┘
   1       2      3     4      5      6DISPLAY  7 PREV   8 NEXT   9    10 NEW
  HELP    MARK               MENUS  OPTIONS   FRAME    FRAME         CAPTURE
```

The important thing to note is that by applying the approach displayed in the example above to other 802.5 low-level frame communication processes, you should be able to troubleshoot other network failures and isolate a failure cause within a specific network area or component.

After examining the 802.5 low-level frame communication processes, the next step is to examine the captured data from the protocol analysis session for any soft or hard error conditions that may have been recorded.

Error recording. During a protocol analysis session, the particular analyzer may capture certain soft and hard errors if they occur on the ring. Depending on the protocol analyzer or network-monitoring tool being used, the process may be automatic or it may need to be initiated. All the protocol analysis and monitoring tools mentioned in Chapter 4 dynamically collect most soft and hard errors that occur on a Token Ring network.

Some of the analyzer and monitoring devices allow your captures to be selective by filtering certain specified error patterns; they also allow you to categorize the particular errors in different formats. This is a recommended approach for troubleshooting, because it allows you to gather conclusive and organized testing results.

When you're performing error recording, set alarm triggers for some of the more serious errors or a particular error that you want to observe more closely. Most of the analyzer and monitoring tools mentioned in Chapter 4 offer error alarm triggering.

The next paragraphs describe in detail the soft and hard error conditions that can occur on a Token Ring network, and their respective failure causes, along with some recommended troubleshooting methods using protocol analysis.

Soft error breakdown. As discussed in Chapter 2, soft errors are the less-critical type of errors that can occur on the ring, and they usually only temporarily disturb the normal mode of ring communication.

To recap, when soft errors occur, an RS collects the errors and sends them to the functional REM address. When an RS encounters a soft error it increments its internal soft error counter and starts a Token Ring protocol timer T(Soft_Error_Report). After two seconds the timer expires and the RS generates a Report Soft Error MAC frame.

High occurrences of certain soft errors can cause ring performance degradation and initiate the Ring Recovery process. When the Ring Recovery process occurs the ring is reset back to a stable mode of operation. This process involves reinitiating all the basic ring startup processes, such as the Token Claiming process and the Neighbor Notification process. As these processes take place unexpectedly, you can see how ring performance degradation may occur.

Some soft errors are considered more serious than others. When recording soft errors you must be aware of the level of seriousness and the possible failure cause for each type of soft error. Certain soft errors actually point to a possible network component as the failure cause. The Report Soft Error MAC frame that is transmitted contains the soft error type, the reporting RS's NIC address, and its respective NAUN's NIC address.

When performing a protocol analysis session for the purpose of error recording, the proper way to examine a Report Soft Error MAC frame is to note the type of soft error and any associated addresses in the MAC frame; with this information you can identify certain possible network components as the cause of specific network failures.

As mentioned, the Report Soft Error MAC frame contains the soft error type. The type is indicated by the byte that is set in the soft error counter field of the Report Soft Error MAC frame. The soft error counter field is a 12-byte field: 10 of the bytes represent soft error types; the other two bytes are reserved for future use. The hexadecimal value of a particular soft error byte indicates the actual soft error count for the soft error type. Figure 6.10 displays a soft error report captured by the IBM LAN Manager program.

The soft error types are divided into two different categories, isolating error types and non-isolating error types.

Isolating error types are specific errors the reporting RS internal error counter collected and could isolate to an assigned fault domain. Isolating error types can point to an actual fault domain because the RS that first detects the error is the station that originated the error, and it counts, collects, and generates the Report Soft Error MAC frame.

Non-isolating error types are errors that a certain nonspecific reporting RS may detect, collect, and generate, without any specific, defined error source information. Because the particular reporting

RS is not defined as the station that originated the error, the station and its NAUN cannot be conclusively considered part of an assigned fault domain.

FIGURE 6.10
The IBM LAN
Manager reports
on varous Token
Ring conditions,
including the soft
error report
shown here.

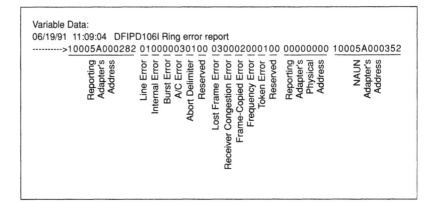

The following is a description of isolating error types, their possible associated failure causes, and the recommended troubleshooting methods:

- **Internal Error.** These errors signify that the reporting RS has encountered a recoverable internal error. If this particular error is recorded frequently, the reporting station NIC may be operating in marginal condition. Any available diagnostics should be run on the particular RS, and you can remove the station from the ring and rerun a protocol analysis session to be conclusive.

- **Burst Error.** These errors signify that the reporting RS has encountered a signal error detected in the Token Ring cabling medium. Normally these errors occur when RSes leave or enter the ring, which will cause ring reconfigurations. If the error is due to a ring reconfiguration, you should be able to check the protocol analysis session trace for the Neighbor Notification process occurring directly before the

burst error; for example, you should see a Report
NAUN Change MAC frame present before the
error.

If this particular error is recorded frequently
and no ring reconfigurations are occurring, it is
possible that the cabling medium has a problem. In
this case, troubleshoot the fault domain involved as
described earlier in this chapter.

• **Line Error.** These errors signify that the reporting
RS checksum process has detected a checksum error
in a specific received data frame or token, after
transmission of the respective token or data frame.
When this error occurs, it is usually related to ring
recoveries or simple ring reconfiguration. There are
times when the presence of a line error can be due
to a failure cause located in the reporting station's
NAUN.

If these errors arise often, test the reporting
station's NAUN. This can be done with diagnostics
or by removing the station from the ring and
rerunning a protocol analysis session.

• **Abort Delimiter Transmitted Error.** This error
signifies that the reporting RS has encountered a
recoverable internal error that forced it to transmit
an Abort Delimiter frame. If this error is recurrent,
the reporting station NIC may be operating in
marginal condition. Again, in this instance,
diagnostics should be run on the particular RS, and
also the station can be removed from the ring and a
protocol analysis session run, to be conclusive.

• **AC Error.** This error indicates that the reporting
RS's NAUN could not successfully set the address
recognized or frame copied bits in the newly
transmitted frame, even though it has actually
completed the copy of the bits on its last frame
received. If this error is happening often it is
possible that the reporting station's NAUN has a
failure. Again the NAUN can be tested with
diagnostics or by removing the station from the ring
and rerunning a protocol analysis session.

The following is a description of non-isolating error types and their possible associated failure causes and recommended troubleshooting methods:

- **Lost Frame Error.** This error indicates that an originating RS generated a frame onto the ring to a specific address and did not receive the frame back. This error may be detected by either the active monitor or the originating RS. Because the RS did not receive the frame back it cannot release the token, which causes the active monitor to initiate ring recovery and issue a new token. Also, because the station did not receive the frame back, the source that may have caused the frame to become lost is not directly identifiable.

  If this type of error occurs frequently, attempt to troubleshoot the fault domain surrounding the reporting RS, and also continue to rerun the protocol analysis session to identify any repetitive patterns of this error.

- **Receiver Congestion Error.** This error indicates that the reporting RS could not receive a frame addressed to its address. This usually occurs because of lack of buffer space within the NIC on the destination RS. There is always a chance that the destination station NIC is at fault, but most of the time this error occurs because a specific network software application is causing the particular destination RS to be flooded with data too frequently.

  This type of error occurs often on certain network file servers. If the cause is related to the flooding of data and is a frequent occurrence, and something is not eventually done to alleviate the problem, the NOS may have operational failures. This problem can usually be remedied in either of two ways: The network software application access can be redesigned, or a NIC with larger buffer space can be installed in the particular destination RS.

- **Frame Copied Error.** This error signifies that the reporting RS has copied a frame that may have the same address as its own address, in other words a duplicate address. It is also possible that the frame did get corrupted on the ring. If this error occurs frequently and there is not an assigned duplicate Token Ring address on the ring, check the reporting RS's adapter.

- **Frequency Error.** This error signifies that the reporting RS is attempting to receive a frame that does not contain the proper ring clock frequency. Since the active monitor is responsible for maintaining the Ring Master Clock, it is possible that the active monitor has encountered an error. If this error occurs frequently, check the active monitor and the reporting RS's respective NAUN. Again run any available diagnostics, remove any suspected RS from the ring, and rerun a protocol analysis session.

- **Token Error.** A token error is only generated by the active monitor in the event that it does not detect a token on the ring. Because the active monitor cannot pinpoint the reason for the token being lost, the cause cannot be directly associated with any particular network component. The active monitor will initiate ring recovery and issue a new token. Also, when a token error occurs because of the ring recovery process, it is highly possible that other RSes will detect and generate burst, line, and lost frame errors onto the ring. If token errors occur frequently, continue to run a protocol analysis session to identify any repetitive patterns of this error.

Note that when soft errors occur on a Token Ring network, they are not always caused by an actual failure on the network. As discussed in some of the error descriptions above, sometimes these errors are triggered by a simple ring reconfiguration. Because of the Token Ring architecture's intricacies, it was also designed with a sophisticated scheme for error handling. This scheme allows the Token Ring architecture to recover from some of the less-serious operational failures.

The key in approaching soft errors is to be aware of high occurrences and the associated ring performance degradation that can occur. Again, with a thorough approach to protocol analysis, you should be able to be conclusive as to your testing results by identifying any clear communication trends involving soft errors.

Hard error breakdown. Hard errors are the more-critical category of errors that can occur on the ring. A hard error is an actual solid failure with a specific network component. On a Token Ring network a hard error will take the form of a failure symptom by the beaconing process. When a hard error occurs the fault area must usually be bypassed in order for the ring to operate. The bypass may occur dynamically due to the inherent beaconing process built into the Token Ring architecture.

To recap, when an RS detects a hard error, it enters the beaconing process to attempt a dynamic ring recovery. But there are times when the fault area that is causing the hard error cannot be bypassed, and the specific fault area (such as a defined fault domain, lobe area, or network component) must be removed from the ring configuration in order to reestablish normal ring operation.

When performing a protocol analysis session on a ring, you will most likely be able to identify any hard errors quickly. All the protocol analysis and ring monitoring devices mentioned in Chapter 4 can detect the beaconing process and locate the network fault area to a specified fault domain, lobe area, or network component. Some protocol analysis and ring monitoring devices can actually enter a beaconing ring, allowing you to troubleshoot and quickly identify any hard errors that are causing a ring to experience failure.

If you encounter a hard error in a protocol analysis session, the first step is to examine the Beacon MAC frame. The Beacon MAC frame contains three important fields related to fault isolation: the reporting RS, the reporting station's NAUN, and the beacon type. The reporting RS and the NAUN are the logical assigned fault domain. The beacon type field further identifies the most likely failure cause within the fault domain. There are four beacon types:

- **Ring Recovery mode set.** This indicates that the ring is already in ring recovery.

- **Signal loss error.** This beacon type indicates that there is most likely a cable fault in the cabling medium internal to the assigned fault domain. If this beacon type reoccurs, troubleshoot the assigned fault domain cabling medium as discussed earlier in this chapter.

- **Streaming Signal/Not Claim Token MAC frame.** This beacon type indicates that there is most likely a failure with one of the RSes involved in the fault domain. The error is inconclusive as to which RS may be at fault. The best bet here is to troubleshoot the complete assigned fault domain as discussed earlier in this chapter.

- **Streaming Signal/Claim Token MAC frame.** This beacon type also signifies that there is a failure with one of the RSes in the assigned fault domain. It is also inconclusive as to which RS may be at fault. Again, troubleshoot the complete assigned fault domain as discussed earlier in this chapter.

Again, the second step when troubleshooting a hard error is to first isolate the failure cause to one of the two lobe areas defined in the assigned fault domain, and then finally to a specific network component.

In summary, the proper approach for troubleshooting hard errors in a Token Ring network is to focus on the assigned fault domain addresses and beacon type by using protocol analysis, then to integrate the manual fault-isolation methods for troubleshooting an assigned fault domain and lobe areas, as detailed earlier in this chapter.

Examining and Troubleshooting High-Layer Communication Problems

Once you have verified that the 802.5 base frame communication processes are proper and fluent, and the ring has been analyzed for soft and hard error occurrences, the next step is to examine the higher-layer communication processes.

When using a protocol analyzer to troubleshoot the higher-layer communication processes, first perform a full-capture session. Next, view the high-layer protocol communication that occurs concurrently between general RSes and the communication between general RSes and the network file server.

What you will actually be examining is the application and NOS communication process between the respective RSes. All applications and NOSs use a predefined protocol for exchanging information. These are unique (to the application or NOS) protocol methods and nomenclature for communication among network nodes. You have to become familiar with the involved application or NOS protocol for communicating. Also be aware that certain applications may use multiple layers of the Token Ring protocol model for transmission.

For example, the IBM PC LAN program uses the Session layer for the NetBIOS protocol and then sets up at the Application layer a communication channel for the IBM SMB protocol to communicate on. When analyzing this type of communication session you will have to examine the NetBIOS and SMB communication processes. This requires that you be aware and understand the respective protocol communication commands for each of the assigned high-layer protocols.

Whatever application protocol is involved, there are some common determiners as to file access between all application and NOS protocols. Everything that occurs between network nodes at the higher layers concerning application and NOS communication is based on some sort of file access process. In other words, there are only so many things you can do with a particular application or NOS in relation to file access: You can open a file, read a file, write to file, close a file, create a file, delete a file, and so on.

Once you understand the basic processes that occur with file access, you can apply them to protocol analysis. If during protocol analysis you see an RS attempting to open a file, and it continually is denied access, you may be able to clearly identify the problem as a security problem. Or you may see an RS that is encountering a write-to-file error due to lack of available disk space on the file server. The same analysis approach can be applied to many different file access scenarios.

The Network General Sniffer Analyzer trace in figure 6.11 depicts a bindery error relating to a file access problem on a Novell file server.

Once you understand the application/NOS protocols involved in your network and their basic file access communication processes, you will be able to use a protocol analyzer to examine the higher layers in the Token Ring protocol model for proper and fluent communication processes.

FIGURE 6.11
The Sniffer
Analyzer shows a
bindery error on a
Novell NetWare
file server.

```
┌─ SUMMARY Delta ──────────────────────────────────────────────┐
│   4 0.001 IBM    25D10ANovell Ser.. NCP R  Bindery error      │
│   5 0.057 Novell Ser..IBM  3A5AFC   NCP C  F=BAB6 Read 1024 at 410603 │
│   6 0.002 IBM    3A5AFCNovell Ser.. NCP R  OK 1024 bytes read │
│   7 0.003 Novell Ser..IBM  3A5AFC   NCP C  F=BAB6 Read 1024 at 410603 │
│   8 0.002 IBM    3A5AFCNovell Ser.. NCP R  OK 1024 bytes read │
│   9 0.010 Novell Ser..IBM  3A5AFC   NCP C  F=BAB6 Read 4 at 73 │
│  10 0.000 IBM    3A5AFCNovell Ser.. NCP R  OK 4 bytes read    │
│  11 0.023 Novell Ser..IBM  3A5AFC   NCP C  F=BAB6 Read 4 at 73 │
│  12 0.000 IBM    3A5AFCNovell Ser.. NCP R  OK 4 bytes read    │
│                        Frame 4 of 47                          │
├─ DETAIL ──────────────────────────────────────────────────────┤
│    NCP:  ---- Service a Queue Job Reply ----                  │
│    NCP:                                                        │
│    NCP:  Request/sub-function code = 23,113 (reply to frame 3)│
│    NCP:                                                        │
│    NCP:  Completion code = D5 (Bindery error)                 │
│    NCP:  Connection status flags = 00 (OK)                    │
│    NCP:  [Normal end of NetWare "Service a Queue Job Reply" packet.] │
│    NCP:                                                        │
│                                                               │
│                        Frame 4 of 47                          │
│                   Use TAB to select windows                   │
│   1      2      3  4 ZOOM   5    6 DISPLAY  7 PREV  8 NEXT  9  10 NEW │
│  HELP   MARK      IN    MENUS  OPTIONS    FRAME   FRAME      CAPTURE  │
└───────────────────────────────────────────────────────────────┘
```

Performance Testing

Abnormal high network bandwidth usage can cause considerable performance degradation on a Token Ring network. The performance degradation may present itself in the form of several different failure symptoms, a specific network application operating slowly, the whole network operating slowly, log-on failures, or by soft or hard error conditions arising.

When benchmarking the actual performance of a Token Ring network, the first step is to monitor the network bandwidth utilization at an overall baseline view and then to measure the network bandwidth used by each of the individual RSes.

Most of the protocol analyzers and ring-monitoring tools mentioned in Chapter 4 allow you to look at the overall baseline network bandwidth and at individual RS levels. Some of the units offer both graphical and numeric display modes for network bandwidth. Figure 6.12 shows the "Absolute Traffic Statistics for Single Stations" screen from the Network General Sniffer Advanced Token Ring Monitor.

FIGURE 6.12
The Sniffer
Advanced Token
Ring Monitor
"Absolute Traffic
Statistics for
Single Stations"
screen.

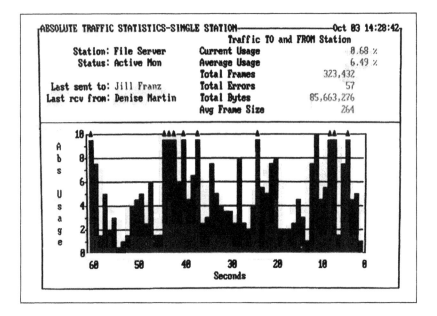

When using a protocol analyzer or a ring-monitoring tool to view the overall baseline network bandwidth, you have to first be aware of the actual maximum bandwidth available on the Token Ring cabling medium. For instance, if the network is running at 4Mbps, the maximum available bandwidth is about 4500 bytes; if your network is running at 16Mbps, the maximum available bandwidth is about 18000 bytes.

Once you are aware of the maximum available bandwidth you can determine how much of the available network bandwidth is being consumed overall by network traffic. It is important to remember that if you are viewing network bandwidth you must apply the full-capture method (discussed earlier in this chapter) for monitoring the network during peak and off-peak network usage periods to get conclusive testing results.

This is extremely important when measuring network bandwidth, because your network bandwidth is a usage factor that will fluctuate frequently throughout the business day. For example, there may be certain network failures that occur due to a large number of users attempting to access a specific network application at the same time. This type of occurrence will typically occur at certain times of the business day. In monitoring the network with a full-capture approach, you will most probably capture this type of network access trend if it is present on the network.

Overall, if you are experiencing any abnormal high network bandwidth usage that is causing performance problems, the cause is usually either a network application problem or is related to a specific RSes experiencing a failure.

Once you have benchmarked the network bandwidth utilization at an overall baseline view, the next step is to benchmark the network bandwidth usage of each individual RS. Because you have established the overall baseline of the consumed network bandwidth, you can now use the protocol analyzer or ring monitoring tool to look at the individual RS. By looking closely at individual RSes you may be able to identify any network bandwidth abnormalities with particular stations. As discussed earlier, certain RSes may absorb an abnormal amount of network bandwidth due to redundant communication traffic between the RS and the file server. Sometimes these failures are related to the application or the NOS, or the particular RS may have an internal failure causing the problem.

The best approach to use if you encounter a particular RS absorbing abnormal bandwidth is to first troubleshoot the 802.5 low layer and then the high-layer communication processes for normal and fluent communication, as described earlier. If you suspect that the RS is the failure cause, use the methods discussed earlier in this chapter.

Another approach is to load the network. This technique is discussed next, and is extremely useful in intermittent network failure situations.

Loading the network. When you are experiencing intermittent problems on a Token Ring network, one of the most useful troubleshooting approaches is to use one of the traffic-generation features to load the network with additional traffic. By carefully loading the network with additional network traffic you can benchmark its tolerance and performance in response to additional traffic, for performance-tuning purposes. This testing technique can also be used to flush out certain types of intermittent failure causes; by generating additional network traffic you can stress the network enough to cause certain marginal network component failures to surface.

You have to be careful when using this technique. First you must be aware of the current network usage and any possible impacts to the network user community. Second, you really have to understand all the Token Ring network bandwidth considerations mentioned earlier, including the actual maximum bandwidth available, the overall network bandwidth baseline view, and individual RS bandwidth consumption.

If you use this technique properly it can be extremely useful for both troubleshooting Token Ring network problems and for performing performance tuning. Figure 6.13 shows the Network General Sniffer Analyzer "Traffic Generator" screen displaying traffic being generated onto a Token Ring network.

The next chapter presents a series of comprehensive and detailed Token Ring network troubleshooting flow guides that encompass some of the troubleshooting approaches introduced in this chapter.

FIGURE 6.13
Generating additional network traffic, as depicted in this Sniffer Analyzer screen, sometimes aids in troubleshooting.

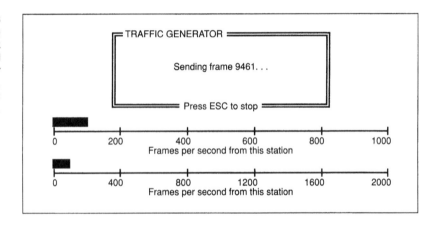

chapter 7 TROUBLESHOOTING FLOW GUIDES

As you saw in Chapter 6, there are many fault symptoms and causes associated with failures of fault domains, lobe areas, and network components. When attempting to troubleshoot these areas in the Token Ring architecture, you must make many decisions in correctly vectoring to the path that leads to your failure cause. Your troubleshooting skills will become more effective as your vectoring decisions become more astute and precise.

The flows guides that were developed for Chapter 7 will help your vectoring decision process by artificially simulating the correct thought process for fault-isolation vectoring when troubleshooting a Token Ring network. The simulation process is automated by the disk included in the back of this book. The disk is coded with artificial intelligence software that will allow you to load the disk into your PC and dynamically follow a semiautomatic PC screen flow guide that replicates the troubleshooting steps in this chapter.

Take the time to carefully read and follow each step before you take any of the defined actions in a flow guide you are currently following. Also make sure to thoroughly read any "NOTE" in the flow guides.

While you're using the flow guides, it's a good idea to take memos on your troubleshooting steps and results.

7.1 NETWORK PROBLEM ENTRY FLOW GUIDE

The network problem entry flow guide is the entry point for approaching the specific network area or component flow guides included in this chapter. From the 14 main network failure symptom choices below, attempt to decide which one most closely relates to the failure symptom you've encountered in the particular network area, and follow the vector to the respective chapter section. If for some reason you feel that your particular failure symptom lies with a certain network component, you can at your discretion vector directly to the respective flow guide.

While deciding, also note whether the failure symptom fits logically into one of the following network areas:

- All network users
- A group of network users
- One network user

In addition, note whether the failure symptom is classified as solid or intermittent.

Main Network Failure Symptoms

1. A ring station, group of ring stations, or the complete network is hanging or freezing.

   (Vector to flow guide 7.6)

2. A ring station or group of ring stations cannot access any ring resources, such as the main network file server.

   (Vector to flow guide 7.4)

3. The network is encountering a specific soft or hard error on the network.

   (Vector to flow guide 7.15)

4. The network is experiencing any of the following failures: the whole network is operating slowly, a specific network application is operating slowly, or there are network log-on failures.

(Vector to flow guide 7.15)

5. Problem accessing or using a particular application/group of applications, or certain directories/files, on the network file server.

(Vector to flow guide 7.14)

6. A particular network operating system feature or set of NOS features on the network file server is not working.

(Vector to flow guide 7.14)

7. A network peripheral cannot be used or accessed.

(Vector to flow guide 7.10)

8. A network printer or printers cannot be used or accessed.

(Vector to flow guide 7.12)

9. Problems accessing or using a network server other than the main network file server, such as database, fax, communication, or print server.

(Vector to flow guide 7.14)

10. Problem accessing or using other rings in an internetwork that are connected to the local ring via a bridge.

(Vector to flow guide 7.7)

11. Problem accessing or using other rings in an internetwork that are connected to the local ring via a router.

(Vector to flow guide 7.8)

12. Problem accessing or using a host connection that is connected via a gateway on the local ring or a ring in an internetwork.

(Vector to flow guide 7.13)

13. The complete network is hanging or freezing, and the problem appears to be related to a repeater.

(Vector to flow guide 7.9)

14. A network-sharable or non-sharable modem cannot be used/accessed, or there is a problem accessing the ring from a remote modem connection.

(Vector to flow guide 7.11)

7.2 FAULT DOMAIN AND LOBE AREA PROBLEM FLOW GUIDES

Is the failure symptom isolated to a fault domain (for example, two lobe areas/two respective ring stations or network devices)?

(Vector to sub-flow guide 7.2.1)

Is the failure symptom already located to a specific lobe area?

(Vector to sub-flow guide 7.2.2)

7.2.1 Failure symptom is located to a fault domain

Remove one of the lobe cables involved in the fault domain from the MAU or wiring hub. Retest the ring.

Is the failure symptom gone?

[YES] You have located the problem to the removed lobe area.

——-> Vector to sub-flow guide 7.2.2 and troubleshoot the removed lobe area.

NOTE: If there are still problems present after following sub-flow guide 7.2.2, vector back up to this sub-flow guide (7.2.1), then go directly to the next step to troubleshoot the other lobe area in the fault domain as a possible fault.

[NO] Reconnect the first suspect lobe area cable and disconnect the second lobe area cable and retest.

Is the failure symptom gone?

[YES] You have located the problem to the removed lobe area.

——-> Vector to sub-flow guide 7.2.2 and troubleshoot the removed lobe area.

[NO] If there are still problems, first attempt restarting at the beginning of sub-flow guide 7.2.1. If you end up back at this same point, then vector to flow guide 7.15.

NOTE: Remember that if you defined this fault domain from data captured during a protocol analysis session, the Beacon MAC Frame should be examined. If the Beacon type field is classified as a "Signal Loss Error," a cable involved in the fault domain may be at fault.

7.2.2 Failure symptom is located to a specific lobe area

Disconnect the suspected lobe cable from its original MAU or wiring hub port and connect it to another MAU or wiring hub port. Retest the ring.

Is the failure symptom gone?

[YES] The original specific MAU or wiring hub port is bad. Troubleshoot the specific MAU or wiring hub port by vectoring to flow guide 7.4, *MAU*.

[NO] Test the lobe cable with a TDR or a ring cable tester. If there are any faults found with the cable, verify the cable fault by vectoring to flow guide 7.3, *Cable*. If there are no cable faults, go to the next step.

Have you thoroughly troubleshot the ring station or network peripheral involved in this lobe area?

[YES] Troubleshoot the respective NIC by vectoring to flow guide 7.5, *NIC*.

[NO] Troubleshoot the respective ring station or network peripheral by vectoring to either flow guide 7.6, *Ring Station*, or 7.10, *Network Peripheral*.

NOTE: If you have tried troubleshooting all the network components in the respective lobe area—ring station, network peripheral, NIC, MAU or wiring hub, and cabling—and the failure symptom is still present on the ring, attempt to gather more conclusive fault isolation data by vectoring to flow guide 7.15.

7.3 CABLE PROBLEM FLOW GUIDES

Does the failure symptom you are troubleshooting in a specific lobe area appear to be related to a lobe cable?

(Vector to flow guide 7.3.1)

Does the failure symptom you are troubleshooting with a group of ring stations/network peripherals or the complete Token Ring network appear to be related to the main ring path?

(Vector to flow guide 7.3.2)

7.3.1 A lobe cable appears to be causing a failure symptom in a lobe path

Remove the lobe cable from the MAU or wiring hub port and the NIC. Test the lobe cable with either a TDR or a ring cable-specific tester.

Did testing the cable find any faults in the cable?

[YES]   The suspected bad cable is faulty. Take the necessary action to resolve the problem by replacing the respective lobe cable in the lobe area, and retest the ring station or network peripheral for proper operation. If the failure symptom is gone, record the problem in the network maintenance and service log. If there are still problems present, go to the next step.

[NO]   If no faults are found by testing the lobe cable, then another network component—such as the MAU or wiring hub port, ring station, network peripheral, or a NIC in the suspected bad lobe area—is most probably at fault. Reattach the original lobe cable into the lobe path and retroubleshoot the respective lobe path by vectoring to flow guide 7.2.

NOTE: If you definitely feel the original lobe cable has a problem, it may be best to keep the newly replaced lobe cable attached, rather than replacing the original lobe cable, before resuming troubleshooting by vectoring to flow guide 7.2. This is going to be a judgment call on your part.

7.3.2 The main ring path cabling appears to be causing a problem with a group of ring stations or the complete Token Ring network

Does the ring contain a repeater?

[YES] If you have not troubleshot the repeater, and you feel it may be introducing a problem into the main ring path, vector to flow guide 7.9. If you're confident it is not the problem, go to the next step.

[NO] Disconnect the first MAU in the MAU rack from the ring by disconnecting its RI and RO cables.

NOTE: If your main ring path is configured in such a way that your MAUs are spread out, and are not properly centrally located in a MAU rack, the following procedure may be more difficult.

NOTE: Also, in the case of a wiring hub you may have to take a unique approach, such as removing the respective wiring hub modules from the wiring hub. It is recommended that you reference the manufacturer's instructions. Check for any available specific MAU connection diagnostics.

Next, test the first MAU by verifying that the ring stations connected to it can properly perform ring insertion.

Did the first MAU test OK?

[YES] Disconnect the second MAU from the ring and connect it to the first MAU. Next test the new ring configuration operation (first and second MAU) by verifying that the ring stations connected to it can properly perform ring insertion.

NOTE: Continue to use this troubleshooting method of disconnecting the next physical MAU in the MAU rack from the original ring configuration and adding it to the new ring configuration until a problem is encountered.

If adding a network component, such as a MAU or main ring path cabling section, to the new ring configuration causes a problem, then go to the next step. If no problems are found in any of the main ring path components, vector to flow guide 7.15.

[NO] Replace both the MAU and main ring path cabling sections that were added to the new ring configuration and that caused the failure symptom to arise. Retest the ring.

NOTE: Retesting the ring should be done by putting aside the suspected bad MAU and main ring cabling path section and then reconnecting the rest of the network to the new ring configuration.

If no problems are encountered, record the problem in the network maintenance and service log. If there are still problems present, restart troubleshooting back from the last MAU that tested OK. There is always the possibility of more than one failure on the network. If you continue to arrive back at this point, vector to flow guide 7.15.

7.4 MULTISTATION ACCESS UNIT (MAU) AND WIRING HUB PROBLEM FLOW GUIDES

Does the failure symptom that is occurring appear to be related to a specific MAU or hub port failure?

(Vector to sub-flow guide 7.4.1)

Are the failure symptoms that appear to be related to a suspected bad MAU or wiring hub module occurring with multiple users or the complete Token Ring network?

(Vector to sub-flow guide 7.4.2)

NOTE: Because this flow guide is generic as to the MAU and wiring hub manufacturer, for some of the troubleshooting steps mentioned in this flow guide, I highly recommend that you also reference the respective manufacturer's documentation for any special predefined methods for checking configuration and for diagnostic testing.

NOTE: In the case of some wiring hubs, you may have certain diagnostics available which will help you locate a specific problem. If this type of diagnostics is available, attempt to use them for fault isolation.

7.4.1 A specific MAU or hub port appears to be encountering a failure

Move the lobe cable from the suspected bad port to another port on the same MAU or wiring hub module. Before you move the lobe cable, make sure the new port is functioning. Next, retest the respective ring station or network peripheral on the new MAU or wiring hub port.

Did physically changing the port get rid of the failure symptom?

[YES]   The suspected bad port is bad. Replace the respective MAU or hub module and retest the ring station or network peripheral for proper operation. If the failure symptom is gone, record the problem in the network maintenance and service log. If there are still problems, go to the next step.

[NO]   If a failure still exists with the same ring station or network peripheral, reattach the lobe cable to the original port and troubleshoot the respective lobe area for the assigned MAU or wiring hub port by vectoring to flow guide 7.2.

7.4.2 A suspected bad MAU or wiring hub module appears to be causing failure symptoms with multiple users or the complete Token Ring network

Whether the failure symptom is solid or intermittent, remove the suspected bad MAU or wiring hub module and associated main ring path cabling sections from the ring configuration, then retest the ring.

Are the failure symptoms now gone?

[YES]   The respective MAU, wiring hub module, or a main ring path cabling section is at failure. Replace the removed unit and cables with another unit and cables. Retest the new ring configuration. If no problems are encountered, record the problem in the network maintenance and service log. If there are still problems present, go to the next step.

NOTE: Even if your problem is now fixed, if you feel that one of the main ring path cabling sections did cause the problem, you can verify the problem by vectoring to flow guide 7.3. If you want to verify the MAU or wiring hub failure, you can do so with any available manufacturer diagnostics.

[NO]   If failure symptoms are still present, reinsert the original MAU or wiring hub module and respective cables into the ring configuration.

Have you troubleshot and verified the integrity of the main ring path cabling?

[YES]   Run a protocol analysis session to gain more conclusive fault isolation data by vectoring to flow guide 7.15.

[NO]   Troubleshoot the main ring path cabling by vectoring to flow guide 7.3.

7.5 NIC PROBLEM FLOW GUIDES

Did you arrive at this flow guide because of NIC failure indications from running a protocol analysis session?

(Vector to sub-flow guide 7.5.1)

Did you arrive at this flow guide after troubleshooting a lobe area, ring station, network file server, MAU/wiring hub, cable, or network peripheral?

(Vector to sub-flow guide 7.5.2)

NOTE: Because this flow guide is generic as to the NIC manufacturer, for some of the troubleshooting steps mentioned in this flow guide I highly recommend that you also reference the NIC manufacturer's documentation for any special predefined methods for checking NIC configuration and for bridge testing.

7.5.1 Error indication in a protocol analysis session

Whether the error is a hard error indicated by a Beacon MAC frame or a soft error that indicates a possible NIC failure, swap the respective NIC and rerun another thorough protocol analysis session on the ring.

After swapping the NIC and rerunning the new protocol analysis session, did the error go away?

[YES]   Leave the newly replaced NIC in the ring station or device and record the problem in the network maintenance and service log.

[NO]   Replace the original NIC back into the ring station or network peripheral, vector to flow guide 7.15, and rerun a protocol analysis session on the ring. Sometimes when you rerun a protocol analysis session, the failure cause will become more clear by moving to another Token Ring address.

If after you rerun another protocol analysis session the error does not move to another device and is still identifying the particular NIC address as a failure cause, troubleshoot the assigned lobe area for the respective NIC by vectoring to flow guide 7.2.

7.5.2 Vectoring from lobe area, ring station, network file server, MAU/wiring hub, cable, or network peripheral flow guide

Is the failure symptom that led you to this flow guide classified as solid or intermittent?

[SOLID]   ——>   Go to S1.

[INTERMITTENT]   ——>   Go to S2.

[S1]   *Solid.* Thoroughly check all the following areas:

1. Check all NIC hardware/software configuration parameters:

- I/O address

- IRQ

- DMA

- Token Ring address

- Slot settings (32-, 16-, or 8-bit card)

- NIC microcode level

- Primary or secondary setting

- Speed settings

2. Check the ring station for the respective NIC for proper NIC software driver microcode and a good RPL PROM.

3. Check for possible NIC incompatibilities with the particular ring station, MAU, cable type, or the STP/UTP cabling connector.

Did you find any problems in any of the three areas?

[YES] Take the necessary action to resolve the problem and retest the ring station or network peripheral for proper operation. If the failure symptom is gone, record the problem in the network maintenance and service log. If the problem is still there after retesting, go to the next step.

[NO] Run any available NIC diagnostics from the NIC manufacturer or from elsewhere to be conclusive. Whether the diagnostics pinpoint a failure or not, swap the original NIC in the ring station or network device and retest the ring station or network peripheral for proper operation, vector to flow guide 7.15, and rerun a protocol analysis session on the ring. If the failure symptom goes away, record the problem in the network maintenance and service log.

If, after rerunning another protocol analysis session, an error occurs with the assigned ring station or network peripheral, and the specific failure symptom does not go away, replace the original NIC, then troubleshoot the assigned lobe area for the respective NIC by vectoring to flow guide 7.2.

NOTE: If you definitely feel the original NIC has a problem, it may be best to keep the newly replaced NIC in the respective ring station (rather than replacing the original NIC) before resuming troubleshooting by vectoring to flow guide 7.2. This is going to be a judgment call on your part.

[S2]   *Intermittent.* In the case of an intermittent problem with a NIC, first attempt to run any available NIC diagnostics. Then, regardless of the diagnostic testing results, swap the original NIC in the ring station or network peripheral and check its general operation. Also vector to flow guide 7.15 and rerun a protocol analysis session on the ring.

If the protocol analysis session does not record any errors associated with the Token Ring address involved, and the intermittent problem does not reappear, record the problem in your network maintenance and service log.

If after you swap the NIC the failure symptom is still present, replace the original NIC and troubleshoot the assigned lobe area for the respective NIC by vectoring to flow guide 7.2.

NOTE: If you definitely feel the original NIC has a problem it may be best to keep the newly replaced NIC in the respective ring station rather than replacing the original NIC, before resuming troubleshooting by vectoring to the main menu and choosing 7.2. This is going to be a judgment call on your part.

7.6 RING STATION PROBLEM FLOW GUIDES

Are all the ring stations on the network experiencing the failure symptom?

(Vector to sub-flow guide 7.6.1)

Is just a group of ring stations experiencing the failure symptom?

(Vector to sub-flow guide 7.6.2)

Is just one ring station experiencing the failure symptom?

(Vector to sub-flow guide 7.6.3)

NOTE: This flow guide is generic as to the ring station/PC manufacturer. For some of the troubleshooting steps mentioned in this flow guide, I highly recommend that you also reference the PC manufacturer's documentation for any special predefined methods for checking PC configuration and for PC testing.

7.6.1 All the ring stations are having the symptom

Are all the ring stations running the same application or using the same directories or files on a particular file server when experiencing the symptom?

[YES] Vector to flow guide 7.14 and troubleshoot possible file server application or directory/file problems.

[NO] Go to the next step.

Have you troubleshot and verified the integrity of the main ring path cabling?

[YES] Run a protocol analysis session to gather more conclusive results by vectoring to flow guide 7.15.

[NO] Troubleshoot the main ring path cabling by vectoring to flow guide 7.3, *Cable*.

7.6.2 A group of ring stations is having the symptom

Is the group of ring stations running the same application or using the same directories or files on a particular file server when experiencing the symptom?

[YES] Vector to flow guide 7.14 and troubleshoot possible file server application or directory/file problems.

[NO] *Is the group of users located on the same MAU or wiring hub module?*

[YES] Troubleshoot a possible MAU or wiring hub failure by vectoring to flow guide 7.4.

[NO] Recheck the ring stations involved for proper software and hardware configuration setup and requirements.

- Make sure all the necessary directories and files are on the local drives in the ring stations and are set up correctly.
- Make sure all the necessary hardware is installed in the ring stations and is configured correctly.

NOTE: Check the network operating system manuals for station setup concerning both software and hardware prerequisites.

Are there any identifiable hardware or software configuration setup problems with the involved ring stations?

[YES] Take the necessary action to resolve the configuration problem and retest the ring stations for proper operation. If the failure symptom is gone, record the problem in the network maintenance and service log. If a failure symptom is still present, go to the next step.

[NO] If the problem strongly appears to be network file server-to-ring station related as to ring insertion, vector to flow guide 7.14.

If you cannot be conclusive, vector to flow guide 7.15 and run a protocol analysis session on the ring.

7.6.3 One ring station is having the symptom

Is the ring station always running the same application or using the same directory or file on a particular file server when experiencing the symptom?

[YES] Vector to flow guide 7.14 and troubleshoot possible file server application or directory/file problems.

[NO] Move the ring station to another port on the MAU or wiring hub and recheck the ring station operation.

Did moving the ring station to another port resolve the problem?

[YES] Vector to flow guide 7.4 and troubleshoot possible MAU or wiring hub problems.

[NO]   Troubleshoot the respective lobe cable involved by vectoring to flow guide 7.3. If troubleshooting the lobe cable does identify any problems with the lobe cable, vector back to this flow guide by choosing flow guide 7.6, then vector to sub-flow guide 7.6.3 and jump directly to the next step.

Next, test the respective ring station for proper software and hardware configuration setup and requirements.

- Make sure all the necessary directory and files are on the local drive in the ring station and are set up correctly.

- Make sure all the necessary hardware is installed in the ring station and is configured correctly.

NOTE: Check the network operating system manuals for station setup concerning both software and hardware prerequisites.

Did rechecking the ring station software and hardware requirements locate any incorrect configuration setup problems?

[YES]   Take the necessary action to resolve the configuration problem and retest the ring station for proper operation. If the failure symptom is gone, record the problem in the network maintenance and service log. If the problem is still present and it strongly appears to be network file server-to-ring station related as to ring insertion, vector to flow guide 7.15 and troubleshoot the high-level communication process. If it does not appear to be file server related, go to the next step.

[NO]   Attempt to run any available PC diagnostics. Also try to troubleshoot the PC for any I/O board conflicts as discussed in the *Ring Station Problems* section of Chapter 6.

Did running the diagnostics or troubleshooting the PC find any problems?

[YES]   Take the necessary action to resolve the problem and retest the ring station for proper operation. If the failure symptom is gone, record the problem in the network maintenance and service log. If the problem is still there after retesting, go to the next step.

[NO] Vector to flow guide 7.5 and troubleshoot the respective ring station for a NIC problem.

NOTE: A lot of new ring stations are being manufactured with internal NICs within the PC motherboard hardware architecture. If the ring station you are troubleshooting has this configuration, you should just attempt replacing the motherboard rather than vectoring to 7.5 and troubleshooting the NIC.

7.7 BRIDGE PROBLEM FLOW GUIDES

Is the failure symptom that no data traffic is able to get from one side of the bridge to the other, or is data intermittently getting corrupted when passing through the bridge?

(Vector to sub-flow guide 7.7.1)

Is the failure symptom that only partial data traffic is able to pass across the bridge?

(Vector to sub-flow guide 7.7.2)

Is the failure symptom that an overloaded bandwidth condition is present on a certain ring?

(Vector to sub-flow guide 7.7.3)

NOTE: This flow guide is generic as to the bridge manufacturer. For some of the troubleshooting steps mentioned in this flow guide, I highly recommend that you also reference the bridge manufacturer's documentation for any special predefined methods for checking bridge configuration and for bridge testing.

7.7.1 No data traffic is able to get from one side of the bridge to the other, or data is intermittently getting corrupted when passing through the bridge

Thoroughly check the software and hardware configuration of the bridge.

Are there any incorrect configuration parameters present in the bridge?

[YES]   Take the necessary action to resolve the problem and retest the bridge for proper operation. If the failure symptom is gone, record the problem in the network maintenance and service log. If the problem is still there after retesting, go to the next step.

[NO]   Attempt to run bridge diagnostics.

Did running the diagnostics produce any errors that identify a bridge failure?

[YES]   Take the necessary action to resolve the problem and retest the bridge for proper operation. If the failure symptom is gone, record the problem in the network maintenance and service log. If the problem is still there after retesting, go to the next step.

[NO]   There may still be a problem with the bridge, but to get more conclusive fault isolation data, vector to flow guide 7.15.

NOTE: If after using this flow guide you cannot conclusively locate the problem, and you continue to find failure symptoms that point to a bridge problem, reference the manufacturer's instructions.

7.7.2 Only partial data traffic is able to pass across the bridge

Thoroughly check the software and hardware configuration of the bridge.

Are there any incorrect configuration parameters in the bridge?

[YES]   Take the necessary action to resolve the problem and retest the bridge for proper operation. If the failure symptom is gone, record the problem in the network maintenance and service log. If the problem is still there after retesting, go to the next step.

[NO]   Check the ring for source-routing problems with certain ring stations. Thoroughly examine the Routing Information field of the frames that are not being passed through the bridge.

NOTE: Keep in mind that particular ring stations can have a software application configuration problem in relation to the source-routing field that they are directly transmitting.

Did examining the ring for source-routing problems locate any specific problems with a certain ring station's Routing Information field?

[YES] Take the necessary action to resolve the source-routing problems with the respective ring station's source-routing parameters, then retest the bridge for proper operation. If the failure symptom is gone, record the problem in the network maintenance and service log. If the problem is still there after retesting, go to the next step.

[NO] Attempt to gather more conclusive fault-isolation data by thoroughly examining the Routing Information field from all the frames that are not being passed through the bridge. Vector to flow guide 7.15.

NOTE: If after using this flow guide you cannot conclusively locate the problem, and you continue to find failure symptoms that point to a bridge problem, reference the manufacturer's instructions.

7.7.3 An overloaded bandwidth condition is present on a certain ring

Thoroughly check the bridge for any incorrect configuration parameters that can control the amount of traffic to be forwarded to another ring.

Are there any incorrect configuration parameters present in the bridge?

[YES] Take the necessary action to resolve the problem and retest the bridge for proper operation. If the failure symptom is gone, record the problem in the network maintenance and service log. If the problem is still there after retesting, go to the next step.

[NO] Check the source ring for source-routing problems with certain ring stations. Thoroughly examine the Routing Information field of the frames that are possibly causing bandwidth problems in the destination ring.

NOTE: Keep in mind that a particular ring station can have a software application configuration problem in relation to the source-routing field that it is directly transmitting.

Did examining the ring for source-routing problems locate any specific problems with a certain ring station's Routing Information field?

[YES]   Take the necessary action to resolve the source-routing problems with the respective ring station's source-routing parameters, then retest the bridge for proper operation. If the failure symptom is gone, record the problem in the network maintenance and service log. If the problem is still there after retesting, go to the next step.

[NO]   Attempt to gather more conclusive fault-isolation data by vectoring to flow guide 7.15.

NOTE: Thoroughly examine the Routing Information field from all the frames for incorrect addressing information for source routing that may be causing an overhead problem from one ring to another. Look closely at the percentage of frames being forwarded that are overloading the destination ring with traffic.

NOTE: If after using this flow guide, you cannot conclusively locate the problem, and you continue to find failure symptoms that point to a bridge problem, reference the manufacturer's instructions.

7.8 ROUTER PROBLEM FLOW GUIDES

Is the failure symptom that particular protocols are not being passed through to another ring?

(Vector to sub-flow guide 7.8.1)

Is the failure symptom that no data traffic is able to get from one side of the router to the other, or that data is intermittently getting corrupted when passed through the router?

(Vector to sub-flow guide 7.8.2)

Is the failure symptom that only partial data traffic is able to pass across the router?

(Vector to sub-flow guide 7.8.3)

Is the failure symptom that an overloaded bandwidth condition is present on a certain ring?

(Vector to sub-flow guide 7.8.4)

NOTE: This flow guide is generic as to the router manufacturer. For some of the troubleshooting steps mentioned in this flow guide, I highly recommend that you also reference the router manufacturer's documentation for any special predefined methods for checking router configuration and for router testing.

7.8.1 Particular protocols are not being passed through to another ring

Thoroughly check the router's software and hardware configuration, as related to the router's protocol-routing table.

Are there any incorrect configuration parameters present in the router's protocol-routing table, as related to the specific protocol that is not properly being passed through to the destination ring?

[YES]   Take the necessary action to resolve the problem and retest the router for proper operation. If the failure symptom is gone, record the problem in the network maintenance and service log. If the problem is still there after retesting, go to the next step.

[NO]   Attempt to run router diagnostics.

Did running the diagnostics produce any errors that identify a router failure?

[YES]   Take the necessary action to resolve the problem and retest the router for proper operation. If the failure symptom is gone, record the problem in the network maintenance and service log. If the problem is still there after retesting, go to the next step.

[NO]   There may still be a configuration problem with the router, but to get more conclusive fault-isolation data, vector to flow guide 7.15.

NOTE: When running a protocol analysis session on the ring, keep in mind that a router's main purpose is to connect rings that need to share the same protocols; they must understand and be configured for the protocol that they are forwarding.

NOTE: If after using this flow guide you cannot conclusively locate the problem, and you continue to find failure symptoms that point to a router problem, reference the manufacturer's instructions.

7.8.2 No data traffic is able to get from one side of the router to the other, or data is intermittently getting corrupted when passed through the router

Thoroughly check the software and hardware configuration of the router.

Are there any incorrect configuration parameters present in the router?

[YES]   Take the necessary action to resolve the problem and retest the router for proper operation. If the failure symptom is gone, record the problem in the network maintenance and service log. If the problem is still there after retesting, go to the next step.

[NO]   Attempt to run router diagnostics.

Did running the diagnostics produce any errors that identify a router failure?

[YES]   Take the necessary action to resolve the problem and retest the router for proper operation. If the failure symptom is gone, record the problem in the network maintenance and service log. If the problem is still there after retesting, go to the next step.

[NO]   There may still be a problem with the router, but to get more conclusive fault-isolation data, vector to flow guide 7.15.

NOTE: If after using this flow guide, you cannot conclusively locate the problem, and you continue to find failure symptoms that point to a router problem, reference the manufacturer's instructions.

7.8.3 Only partial data traffic is able to pass across the router

Thoroughly check the software and hardware configuration of the router.

Are there any incorrect configuration parameters present in the router?

[YES]   Take the necessary action to resolve the problem and retest the router for proper operation. If the failure symptom is gone, record the problem in the network maintenance and service log. If the problem is still there after retesting, go to the next step.

[NO]   Check the ring for source-routing problems with certain ring stations. Thoroughly examine the Routing Information field of the frames that are not being passed through the router.

NOTE: Keep in mind that a particular ring station can have a software application configuration problem in relation to the source-routing field that they are directly transmitting.

Did examining the ring for source-routing problems locate any specific problems with a certain ring station's Routing Information field?

[YES]   Take the necessary action to resolve the source-routing problems with the respective ring station's source-routing parameters and then retest the router for proper operation. If the failure symptom is gone, record the problem in the network maintenance and service log. If the problem is still there after retesting, go to the next step.

[NO]   Attempt to gather more conclusive fault-isolation data by thoroughly examining the Routing Information field from all the frames that are not being passed through the router. Vector to flow guide 7.15.

NOTE: If after using this flow guide you cannot conclusively locate the problem, and you continue to find failure symptoms that point to a router problem, reference the manufacturer's instructions.

7.8.4 An overloaded bandwidth condition is present on a certain ring

Thoroughly check the router for any incorrect configuration parameters that can control the amount of traffic to be forwarded to another ring.

Are there any incorrect configuration parameters present in the router?

[YES] Take the necessary action to resolve the problem and retest the router for proper operation. If the failure symptom is gone, record the problem in the network maintenance and service log. If the problem is still there after retesting, go to the next step.

[NO] Check the source ring for source-routing problems with certain ring stations. Thoroughly examine the Routing Information field of the frames that are possibly causing bandwidth problems in the destination ring.

NOTE: Keep in mind that a particular ring station can have a software application configuration problem in relation to the source-routing field that it is directly transmitting.

Did examining the ring for source-routing problems locate any specific problems with a certain ring station's Routing Information field?

[YES] Take the necessary action to resolve the source-routing problems with the respective ring station's source-routing parameters, then retest the router for proper operation. If the failure symptom is gone, record the problem in the network maintenance and service log. If the problem is still there after retesting, go to the next step.

[NO] Attempt to gather more conclusive fault-isolation data. Vector to flow guide 7.15.

NOTE: Thoroughly examine the Routing Information field from all the frames for incorrect addressing information for source routing that may be causing an overhead problem from one ring to another. Look closely at the percentage of frames being forwarded that are overloading the destination ring with traffic.

NOTE: If after using this flow guide, you cannot conclusively locate the problem, and you continue to find failure symptoms that point to a router problem, reference the manufacturer's instructions.

7.9 REPEATER PROBLEM FLOW GUIDE

Is the failure symptom that no data traffic is able to get from one side of the repeater to the other, or that a hard error such as a beaconing condition is present on the ring?

(Vector to sub-flow guide 7.9.1)

NOTE: This flow guide is generic as to the repeater manufacturer. For some of the troubleshooting steps mentioned in this flow guide, I highly recommend that you also reference the repeater manufacturer's documentation for any special predefined methods for checking repeater configuration and for repeater testing.

7.9.1 No data traffic is able to get from one side of the repeater to the other, or a hard error such as a beaconing condition is present on the ring

NOTE: If a repeater is the suspected problem, first attempt to troubleshoot the problem by testing the main ring path cabling section that normally passes through the repeater. Do this by disconnecting the attached cable sections and relooping the cabling sections at the repeater entry points with patch cables. With fiber this may be more difficult.

Bypass the repeater and test the main ring path cabling segments with a TDR (or OTDR in the case of fiber).

With the repeater disconnected, did testing the cable produce any cable faults?

[YES]   There is most probably a problem with the main ring path cabling. If you are not sure what portion of the main ring path section is bad, vector to flow guide 7.3.

   If you can be conclusive as to which portion of the main ring cabling path section is bad, replace the respective main ring path cabling section. Then reattach the repeater and retest the ring. If the failure symptom is gone, record the problem in the network maintenance and service log. If the problem is still there after retesting, go to the next step.

[NO]   Attempt to run any available repeater diagnostics.

Did running the diagnostics produce any errors that identify a repeater failure?

[YES]   Take the necessary action to resolve the problem and retest the repeater for proper operation. If the failure symptom is gone, record the problem in the network maintenance and service log. If the problem is still there after retesting, go to the next step.

[NO]   Thoroughly check the repeater configuration.

Are there any incorrect configuration parameters present in the repeater?

[YES]   Take the necessary action to resolve the problem and retest the repeater for proper operation. If the failure symptom is gone, record the problem in the network maintenance and service log. If the problem is still there after retesting, go to the next step.

[NO]   Check the actual physical placement of the repeater, with respect to its specification for distance requirements within the Token Ring cabling system.

NOTE: There are instances when the physical placement of a repeater may cause failure symptoms that point to the main ring path cabling being at fault. Consult the repeater manufacturer for instructions as to distance requirements.

Is the repeater incorrectly placed as to its specifications?

[YES] Take the necessary action to resolve the problem and retest the repeater for proper operation. If the failure symptom is gone, record the problem in the network maintenance and service log. If the problem is still there after retesting, go to the next step.

[NO] There may still be a problem with the repeater, but to get more conclusive fault-isolation data, vector to flow guide 7.15.

NOTE: If, after using this flow guide, you cannot conclusively locate the problem and you continue to find failure symptoms that point to a repeater problem, reference the manufacturer's instructions.

7.10 NETWORK PERIPHERAL PROBLEM FLOW GUIDES

NOTE: If devices such as modems, printers, or fax boards are connected to a ring station or a file server, they are not actually considered network peripherals, because they do not contain their own NICs. If the peripheral you are troubleshooting does not contain its own internal NIC, then vector to the applicable flow guide. (For example, suppose a modem or printer is connected to a ring station or file server, and the ring station or file server contains the NIC. In this instance you would vector to either the modem or printer problem flow guide.) But if the device does contain its own internal NIC, this flow guide is applicable.

Did you arrive at this flow guide because of NIC failure indications from running a protocol analysis session?

(Vector to sub-flow guide 7.10.1)

Did you arrive at this flow guide because you have identified a failure symptom that appears to be directly related to a problem with a specific network peripheral?

(Vector to sub-flow guide 7.10.2)

NOTE: As discussed in Chapter 6, a network peripheral failure symptom is usually different from that of a standard ring station. But, because both a network peripheral and a standard ring station contain a NIC, and both access the ring through the 802.5 rules, they both can be assumed to have the same logical network area of fault components, which is the respective network peripheral's lobe area, specifically the network peripheral, the NIC, the lobe cable, and the MAU or hub port.

NOTE: Some of the network peripherals access the Token Ring network with NIC and hardware/software components; others just use NIC hardware with firmware contained within PROM chips. Both configurations allow the assigned network peripheral to access the ring through standard ring insertion, and they both operate according to the Token Ring architecture operating-mode principles.

NOTE: This flow guide is generic as to the network peripheral manufacturer. For some of the troubleshooting steps mentioned in this flow guide, I highly recommend that you also reference the network peripheral manufacturer's documentation for any special predefined methods for checking network peripheral configuration and for network peripheral testing.

7.10.1 Error indication in a protocol analysis session

Whether the error is a hard error indicated by a Beacon MAC frame or a soft error that indicates a possible NIC failure in the network peripheral, swap the respective NIC and rerun another thorough protocol analysis session on the ring.

NOTE: Some types of network peripherals have a NIC physically built in to the motherboard. If this is the case, then you may have to replace the whole unit. I recommend that you reference the manufacturer's instructions.

After you swapped the NIC and reran a protocol analysis session, did the error go away?

[YES]   Leave the newly replaced NIC in the network peripheral and record the problem in the network maintenance and service log.

[NO]   Return the original NIC back into the network peripheral, vector to flow guide 7.15, and rerun a protocol analysis session on the ring. Sometimes, by rerunning a protocol analysis session the failure cause will become more clear by moving to another Token Ring address.

NOTE: If after rerunning a protocol analysis session the error does not move to another device and is still identifying the particular NIC address as a failure cause, troubleshoot the assigned lobe area for the respective NIC by vectoring to flow guide 7.2.

NOTE: If after using this flow guide you cannot conclusively locate the problem, and you continue to find failure symptoms that point to a network peripheral problem, reference the manufacturer's instructions.

7.10.2 A failure symptom appears to be directly related to a problem with a specific network peripheral

Is the network peripheral involved in some network communications with a particular application or is it using the same directory or file on a particular file server when experiencing the symptom?

[YES] Vector to flow guide 7.14 and troubleshoot a possible file server application or directory/file problem that may be related to the network peripheral operation.

[NO] Move the network peripheral to another port on the MAU or wiring hub and recheck the network peripheral operation.

Did moving the network peripheral to another port resolve the problem?

[YES] Vector to flow guide 7.4 and troubleshoot a possible MAU or wiring hub problem.

[NO] Troubleshoot the respective lobe cable involved by vectoring to flow guide 7.3. If troubleshooting the lobe cable does not identify any problems with the lobe cable, vector back to this flow guide (7.10), then vector to sub-flow guide 7.10.2 and jump directly to the next step.

Next, test the respective network peripheral for proper software and hardware configuration setup and requirements.

- If the network peripheral has local disk storage, make sure all the necessary directories and files for the network peripheral are set up correctly.

- Make sure all the necessary hardware is installed in the network peripheral and that it is configured correctly.

NOTE: Check the network operating system manuals for network peripheral setup concerning both software and hardware prerequisites.

Did rechecking the network peripheral software and hardware requirements find any incorrect configuration-setup problems?

[YES] Take the necessary action to resolve the configuration problem and retest the network peripheral device for proper operation. If the failure symptom is gone, record the problem in the network maintenance and service log. If the problem is still present, go to the next step.

[NO] Attempt to run any available network peripheral diagnostics. Also try to troubleshoot the network peripheral for any I/O board conflicts.

Did running the diagnostics or troubleshooting the network peripheral find any problems?

[YES] Take the necessary action to resolve the problem and retest the network peripheral for proper operation. If the failure symptom is gone, record the problem in the network maintenance and service log. If the problem is still there after retesting, go to the next step.

[NO] Has the NIC in the assigned network peripheral been troubleshot?

[YES] There may be a network file server-to-network peripheral related problem as to ring insertion or protocol communication. Perform a protocol analysis session and focus closely on the communication between the network file server and the assigned network peripheral. Vector to flow guide 7.15.

[NO] Vector to flow guide 7.5 and troubleshoot the respective network peripheral station for a NIC problem.

NOTE: A lot of network peripherals are being manufactured with internal NICs within the respective logic board hardware architecture. If the network peripheral you are troubleshooting has this configuration, just attempt replacing the motherboard rather than vectoring to 7.5 and troubleshooting the NIC.

NOTE: If after using this flow guide, you cannot conclusively locate the problem, and you continue to find failure symptoms that point to a network peripheral problem, reference the manufacturer's instructions.

7.11 MODEM PROBLEM FLOW GUIDES

Are you having a problem accessing or using a modem that is connected to the ring as a shared modem?

(Vector to sub-flow guide 7.11.1)

Are you having a problem accessing or using a modem that is connected to a specific ring station or file server as an unshared modem?

(Vector to sub-flow guide 7.11.2)

Are you having a problem accessing or using a modem that is connected to a ring from a remote location?

(Vector to sub-flow guide 7.11.3)

NOTE: If the respective modem is connected to a ring station or a file server, it is not actually considered a network peripheral because it does not contain its own NIC. In this case, the following flow guide is applicable.

If the modem does contain its own NIC, you should troubleshoot the problem as a network peripheral by vectoring to flow guide 7.10. If, after troubleshooting the problem as a network peripheral, you feel that the modem or modem-sharing software may be at fault, vector back to this flow guide (7.11).

NOTE: This flow guide is generic as to the modem and modem network-sharing software manufacturer. For some of the troubleshooting steps in this flow guide, I highly recommend that you also reference the manufacturer's documentation for any special predefined methods for checking configuration and for testing.

7.11.1 Problem accessing or using a modem that is connected to the ring as a shared modem

Check the ring station or file server that the modem is connected to and the modem itself to make sure they are configured with all the proper hardware and software components and the correct configuration parameters. Also check the network file server for all the correct modem-sharing software and proper configuration.

Are there any incorrect configuration parameters present in either the respective ring station, modem, or network file server?

[YES]   Take the necessary action to resolve the problem, and retest the modem for proper operation. If the failure symptom is gone, record the problem in the network maintenance and service log. If the problem is still there after retesting, go to the next step.

[NO]   Attempt to run any available modem diagnostics and troubleshoot the modem link cables and phone lines.

Did running the diagnostics, checking the link, or checking the phone lines produce any errors?

[YES]   Take the necessary action to resolve the problem and retest the modem for proper operation. If the failure symptom is gone, record the problem in the network maintenance and service log. If the problem is still there after retesting, go to the next step.

[NO]   There may still be a configuration problem with the modem, or the modem network-sharing software. Reference the respective modem and modem-software manufacturers' instructions.

7.11.2 Problem accessing or using a modem that is connected to a specific ring station or file server as an unshared modem

Check the ring station or file server that the modem is connected to and the modem itself to make sure they are configured with all the proper hardware and software components and the correct configuration parameters.

Are there any incorrect configuration parameters present in either the respective ring station, file server, or modem?

[YES]   Take the necessary action to resolve the problem and retest the modem for proper operation. If the failure symptom is gone, record the problem in the network maintenance and service log. If the problem is still there after retesting, go to the next step.

[NO]   Attempt to run any available modem diagnostics and troubleshoot the modem link cables and phone lines.

Did running the diagnostics, checking the link, or checking the phone lines produce any errors?

[YES]   Take the necessary action to resolve the problem and retest the modem for proper operation. If the failure symptom is gone, record the problem in the network maintenance and service log. If the problem is still there after retesting, go to the next step.

[NO]   There may still be a configuration problem with the modem. Reference the respective modem manufacturer's instructions.

7.11.3 Problem accessing or using a modem that is connected to a ring from a remote location

Check the local and host ring stations that the modems are connected to and the modems themselves to make sure they are configured with all the proper hardware and software components and the correct configuration parameters. Also check the host network file server for all the correct modem-sharing software and proper configuration.

Are there any incorrect configuration parameters present in either the respective ring stations, modems, or host network file server?

[YES]   Take the necessary action to resolve the problem and retest the modems for proper operation. If the failure symptom is gone, record the problem in the network maintenance and service log. If the problem is still there after retesting, go to the next step.

[NO] Attempt to run any available modem diagnostics and troubleshoot the host and remote modems, link cables, and phone lines.

Did running the diagnostics, checking the link cables, or checking the phone lines produce any errors?

[YES] Take the necessary action to resolve the problem and retest the modems for proper operation. If the failure symptom is gone, record the problem in the network maintenance and service log. If the problem is still there after retesting, go to the next step.

[NO] There may still be a configuration problem with the modems or the modem network-sharing software. Reference the respective modem and modem-software manufacturers' instructions.

7.12 PRINTER PROBLEM FLOW GUIDES

Are you having a problem accessing or using a printer that is connected to the ring as a shared printer?

(Vector to flow guide 7.12.1)

Are you having a problem accessing or using a printer that is connected to a specific ring station or file server as an unshared printer?

(Vector to flow guide 7.12.2)

NOTE: If this printer is connected to a ring station or a file server, it is not actually considered a network peripheral because it does not contain its own NIC. In this case, the following flow guide is applicable.

If it does contain its own NIC, you should troubleshoot the problem as a network peripheral by vectoring to flow guide 7.10. If after troubleshooting the problem as a network peripheral you feel that the printer or printer-sharing software may be at fault, vector back to this flow guide (7.12).

NOTE: This flow guide is generic as to the printer and printer network-sharing software manufacturer. For some of the troubleshooting steps in this flow guide, I highly recommend that you also reference the manufacturer's documentation for any special predefined methods for checking configuration and for testing.

7.12.1 Problem accessing or using a printer that is connected to the ring as a shared printer

Check the ring station, file server, or print server that the printer is connected to, and the printer itself, to make sure they are configured with all the proper hardware and software components and the correct configuration parameters. Also check the network file server or print server for all the correct printer-sharing software and proper configuration.

Are there any incorrect configuration parameters present in either the respective ring station, network file server, print server, or printer?

[YES]   Take the necessary action to resolve the problem and retest the printer for proper operation. If the failure symptom is gone, record the problem in the network maintenance and service log. If the problem is still there after retesting, go to the next step.

[NO]   Attempt to run any available printer diagnostics and test the printer cabling.

Did running the diagnostics and testing the printer cabling produce any errors?

[YES]   Take the necessary action to resolve the problem and retest the printer for proper operation. If the failure symptom is gone, record the problem in the network maintenance and service log. If the problem is still there after retesting, go to the next step.

[NO]   There may still be a configuration problem with the printer or the printer network-sharing software. Reference the respective printer and printer-software manufacturers' instructions.

7.12.2 Problem accessing or using a printer that is connected to a specific ring station or file server as an unshared printer

Check the ring station or file server that the printer is connected to and the printer itself to make sure they are configured with all the proper hardware and software components and the correct configuration parameters.

Are there any incorrect configuration parameters present in either the respective ring station or the printer?

[YES] Take the necessary action to resolve the problem and retest the printer for proper operation. If the failure symptom is gone, record the problem in the network maintenance and service log. If the problem is still there after retesting, go to the next step.

[NO]   Attempt to run any available printer diagnostics and test the printer cabling.

Did running the diagnostics and testing the printer cabling produce any errors?

[YES] Take the necessary action to resolve the problem and retest the printer for proper operation. If the failure symptom is gone, record the problem in the network maintenance and service log. If the problem is still there after retesting, go to the next step.

[NO]   There may still be a configuration problem with the printer or the printer network-sharing software. Reference the respective printer and printer-software manufacturers' instructions.

7.13 GATEWAY PROBLEM FLOW GUIDES

Is the whole network having a problem accessing or using a host gateway that is connected to a local ring?

(Vector to sub-flow guide 7.13.1)

Is just one ring station or a group of ring stations having a problem accessing or using a host gateway that is connected to a local ring?

(Vector to sub-flow guide 7.13.2)

Is there a problem accessing or using a host gateway from a nonlocal ring that is bridged, routed, or connected through a remote connection?

(Vector to sub-flow guide 7.13.3)

Is the failure symptom that gateway sessions appear to be running slowly or unresponsively?

(Vector to sub-flow guide 7.13.4)

Are LAN-to-host sessions intermittently locking up or freezing?

(Vector to sub-flow guide 7.13.5)

NOTE: This flow guide is generic as to the gateway and gateway-sharing software manufacturers. For some of the troubleshooting steps mentioned in this flow guide, I highly recommend that you also reference the manufacturer's documentation for any special predefined methods for checking configuration and for testing.

7.13.1 The complete network is having a problem accessing or using a host gateway that is connected to a local ring

Thoroughly check the gateway's configuration as to the gateway manufacturer's hardware and software setup for use with the LAN and the respective host.

Are there any incorrect configuration parameters present in the gateway's configuration as to the hardware and software setup for use with the LAN or the host?

[YES]   Take the necessary action to resolve the problem and retest the gateway for proper operation. If the failure symptom is gone, record the problem in the network maintenance and service log. If the problem is still there after retesting, go to the next step.

[NO]   Check all the ring stations that need to access the gateway for the proper configuration as to the gateway manufacturer's specifications.

Are there any incorrect configuration parameters present in the ring station's configuration as to hardware and software setup for use with the gateway?

[YES]   Take the necessary action to resolve the problem and retest the gateway for proper operation. If the failure symptom is gone, record the problem in the network maintenance and service log. If the problem is still there after retesting, go to the next step.

[NO]   Check the host to make sure that it is properly configured as to session setup and port availability to handle communications to the respective gateway.

Are there any incorrect configuration parameters present in the host's configuration as to hardware and software setup for use with the LAN ring stations or the gateway?

[YES]   Take the necessary action to resolve the problem and retest the gateway for proper operation. If the failure symptom is gone, record the problem in the network maintenance and service log. If the problem is still there after retesting, go to the next step.

[NO]   Attempt to run any available gateway diagnostics.

Did running the diagnostics produce any errors?

[YES]   Take the necessary action to resolve the problem and retest the gateway for proper operation. If the failure symptom is gone, record the problem in the network maintenance and service log. If the problem is still there after retesting, go to the next step.

[NO]   There may still be a configuration problem with the gateway or the LAN gateway software. Reference the respective gateway and gateway software manufacturers' instructions.

7.13.2 Just one ring station or just a group of ring stations is having a problem accessing or using a host gateway that is connected to a local ring

Check all the ring stations that are experiencing the problem for the proper configuration as to the gateway manufacturer's specifications.

Are there any incorrect configuration parameters present in any of the ring stations' configuration as to the hardware and software setup for use with the gateway?

[YES]   Take the necessary action to resolve the problem and retest the gateway for proper operation. If the failure symptom is gone, record the problem in the network maintenance and service log. If the problem is still there after retesting, go to the next step.

[NO]   Check the host to make sure that it is properly configured as to session setup and port availability to handle communications for all the ring stations that are experiencing the problem.

Are there any incorrect configuration parameters present in the host's configuration as to the hardware and software setup for use with the LAN ring stations?

[YES]   Take the necessary action to resolve the problem and retest the gateway for proper operation. If the failure symptom is gone, record the problem in the network maintenance and service log. If the problem is still there after retesting, go to the next step.

[NO]   Attempt to run any available gateway diagnostics.

Did running the diagnostics produce any errors?

[YES]   Take the necessary action to resolve the problem and retest the gateway for proper operation. If the failure symptom is gone, record the problem in the network maintenance and service log. If the problem is still there after retesting, go to the next step.

[NO]   There may still be a configuration problem with the gateway or the LAN gateway software. Attempt to get more conclusive fault-isolation data on the communication between the gateway and the ring stations experiencing the problem. Vector to flow guide 7.15.

NOTE: If after using this flow guide you cannot conclusively locate the problem, and you continue to find failure symptoms that point to a gateway problem, reference the manufacturer's instructions.

7.13.3 Problem accessing or using a host gateway from a nonlocal ring that is bridged, routed, or connected through a remote connection

First, verify that the particular bridge, router, or remote connection link is functioning properly. If necessary, vector to the respective flow guide for the particular device: flow guides 7.7 *Bridge*; 7.8 *Router*; and 7.11 *Modem*.

Are there any problems with the linking devices, specifically the bridge, router, or communication (modem) devices/links?

[YES] Take the necessary action to resolve the problem and retest the gateway for proper operation. If the failure symptom is gone, record the problem in the network maintenance and service log. If the problem is still there after retesting, go to the next step.

[NO] If there are no problems that can be conclusively located to those respective devices, attempt to get more conclusive fault-isolation data on the complete LAN communication process relating to the gateway by vectoring to flow guide 7.15.

7.13.4 The gateway sessions appear to be running slowly or unresponsively

Check all the gateway's operational-mode configurations for the proper configuration as to the gateway manufacturer's specifications.

Are there any incorrect configuration parameters in any of the gateway's configurations for the hardware and software setup for use with the LAN/host?

[YES] Take the necessary action to resolve the problem and retest the gateway for proper operation. If the failure symptom is gone, record the problem in the network maintenance and service log. If the problem is still there after retesting, go to the next step.

[NO] Check the host to make sure its session setup and port availability are properly configured to handle communications for all the ring stations that are experiencing the problem.

Are there any incorrect configuration parameters present in the host's configuration as to session and port capacity for use with the LAN layout of ring stations that are set up to use the gateway?

[YES]   Take the necessary action to resolve the problem and retest the gateway for proper operation. If the failure symptom is gone, record the problem in the network maintenance and service log. If the problem is still there after retesting, go to the next step.

[NO]   Attempt to run any available gateway diagnostics.

Did running the diagnostics produce any errors?

[YES]   Take the necessary action to resolve the problem and retest the gateway for proper operation. If the failure symptom is gone, record the problem in the network maintenance and service log. If the problem is still there after retesting, go to the next step.

[NO]   There may still be a configuration problem with the gateway or the LAN gateway software. Attempt to get more conclusive fault-isolation data on the communication between the gateway and the ring stations that are experiencing the problem. Vector to flow guide 7.15.

NOTE: If after using this flow guide you cannot conclusively locate the problem, and you continue to find failure symptoms that point to a gateway problem, reference the manufacturer's instructions.

7.13.5 LAN-to-host sessions are intermittently locking up or freezing

Attempt to run any available gateway diagnostics.

Did running the diagnostics produce any errors?

[YES]   Take the necessary action to resolve the problem and retest the gateway for proper operation. If the failure symptom is gone, record the problem in the network maintenance and service log. If the problem is still there after retesting, go to the next step.

[NO]   There may still be a configuration problem with the gateway or the LAN gateway software.

Thoroughly check the gateway's configuration as to the gateway manufacturer's hardware and software setup for use on the LAN and the respective host.

Are there any incorrect configuration parameters present in the gateway's configuration as to the hardware and software setup for use with the LAN or the host?

[YES]   Take the necessary action to resolve the problem and retest the gateway for proper operation. If the failure symptom is gone, record the problem in the network maintenance and service log. If the problem is still there after retesting, go to the next step.

[NO]   Attempt to get more conclusive fault-isolation data on the communication between the gateway and the ring stations that are experiencing the problem. Vector to flow guide 7.15.

NOTE: If after using this flow guide you cannot conclusively locate the problem, and you continue to find failure symptoms that point to a gateway problem, reference the manufacturer's instructions.

7.14 FILE SERVER PROBLEM FLOW GUIDE

Is there a problem with a ring station, group of ring stations, the complete network, or a network peripheral accessing or using a particular application/group of applications, or certain directories/files, on the network file server?

(Vector to sub-flow guide 7.14.1)

Is a particular network operating system (NOS) feature or set of NOS features on the network file server not working?

(Vector to sub-flow guide 7.14.2)

Is there a problem accessing or using an extra network server other than the main network file server (for example, database, fax, communication, print server)?

(Vector to sub-flow guide 7.14.3)

Does there appear to be a problem with abnormal network bandwidth between a particular ring station/group of ring stations, or network peripheral and the network file server?

(Vector to sub-flow guide 7.14.4)

NOTE: This flow guide is generic as to the network operating system (such as Novell, IBM LAN Server, Microsoft LAN Manager, and Banyan VINES). When you reference some of the troubleshooting steps in this flow guide, I highly recommend that you also reference the NOS manufacturer's documentation for any special predefined methods for checking NOS configuration, hardware/software requirements, and for NOS diagnostics and testing.

7.14.1 There is a problem with a ring station, a group of ring stations, the complete network, or a network peripheral accessing or using a particular application/group of applications, or certain directories/files on the network file server

First, check the network file server and any symptomatic ring stations for the following software and hardware configuration setup parameters and requirements.

- Make sure that the NOS network shell software, NOS NIC drivers, CONFIG.SYS, AUTOEXEC.BAT, and all the necessary network operating system files are set up for the respective NOS specialized configuration and NOS hierarchical directory structure.

- Check the NOS directory structure as it relates to the ring station and any respective network peripheral access.

- Check all the NOS security rights configurations.

- Make sure all the necessary directory/files for any NOS applications on the network drive and ring station drives are set up correctly.

- Make sure all the necessary hardware is installed in the file server/ring stations, is configured correctly, and is functioning OK.

NOTE: Check the respective NOS manuals for file server setup concerning network-software-vendor requirements for both software and hardware prerequisites and their respective configurations.

Are there any identifiable hardware or software configuration setup problems with the network file server?

[YES] Take the necessary action to resolve the configuration problem and retest the ring for proper operation. If the failure symptom is gone, record the problem in the network maintenance and service log. If failure symptom is still present, go to the next step.

[NO] If there appears to be no problem with the file server or its setup, attempt to gather more conclusive fault-isolation data by running a protocol analysis session on the ring. Vector to flow guide 7.15 and focus on the problem by capturing and viewing the high-layer communication processes.

NOTE: If after using this flow guide, you cannot conclusively locate the problem, and you continue to find failure symptoms that point to the network file server problem, reference both the NOS software and the particular file server/hardware manufacturers' instructions.

7.14.2 A particular network operating system (NOS) feature or set of NOS features on the network file server is not working

First, fully reference the respective NOS manuals for operation of the NOS feature or features.

In checking the NOS manuals, were you able to find any operational instructions to resolve your problem?

[YES]   Take the necessary action to resolve the problem and retest the NOS feature for proper operation. If the failure symptom is gone, record the problem in the network maintenance and service log. If the failure symptom is still present, go to the next step.

[NO]   Check the NOS manuals for file server setup concerning network-software-vendor requirements for both software and hardware prerequisites and their respective configurations.

Are there any identifiable hardware or software configuration setup problems with the network file server?

[YES]   Take the necessary action to resolve the configuration problem and retest the NOS feature for proper operation. If the failure symptom is gone, record the problem in the network maintenance and service log. If the failure symptom is still present, go to the next step.

[NO]   Contact your NOS support channel for assistance in using and configuring this particular NOS feature.

7.14.3 There is a problem accessing or using an extra network server other than the main network file server (for example, database, fax, communication, or print server)

Is the file server that is involved on a nonlocal ring that is bridged, routed, or connected through a remote connection?

[YES]   ————>   Go to S1.

[NO]   ————>   Go to S2.

[S1]   *File server is on a nonlocal ring that is bridged, routed, or connected through a remote connection.* First, verify that the particular bridge, router, or remote connection link is functioning properly. If necessary, vector to the respective flow guide for the particular device: flow guides 7.7 *Bridge*; 7.8 *Router*; 7.11 *Modem*.

Are there any problems with the linking devices, specifically the bridge, router, or communication (modem) devices/links?

[YES]   Take the necessary action to resolve the problem and retest the respective network file server for proper operation. If the failure symptom is gone, record the problem in the network maintenance and service log. If the problem is still there after retesting, go to the next step.

[NO]   Go to S2 and follow the troubleshooting steps as though the remote file server were actually located on the local ring.

[S2]   *File server is on the local ring.* First, check the network file server for the following software and hardware configuration setup parameters and requirements.

• Make sure that the NOS network shell software, NOS NIC drivers, CONFIG.SYS, AUTOEXEC.BAT, and all the necessary network operating system files are set up for the respective NOS specialized configuration and NOS hierarchical directory structure.

• Check the NOS directory structure as it relates to ring station and any respective network peripheral access.

• Check all the NOS security rights configurations.

• Make sure all the necessary directory/files for any NOS applications on the network drive are set up correctly.

• Make sure all the necessary hardware is installed in the file server, is configured correctly, and is functioning OK.

NOTE: Check the respective NOS and software application manuals for file server setup concerning network-software-vendor requirements for both software and hardware prerequisites and their respective configurations.

Are there any identifiable hardware or software configuration setup problems with the network file server?

[YES]   Take the necessary action to resolve the configuration problem and retest the ring for proper operation. If the failure symptom is gone, record the problem in the network maintenance and service log. If failure symptom is still present, go to the next step.

[NO]   If there appears to be no problem with the file server or its setup, attempt to gather more conclusive fault-isolation data by running a protocol analysis session on the ring. Vector to flow guide 7.15 and focus on the problem by capturing and viewing the high-layer communication processes.

NOTE: If after using this flow guide you cannot conclusively locate the problem, and you continue to find failure symptoms that point to the network file server problem, reference both the NOS software and the particular file server/hardware manufacturers' instructions.

7.14.4 There appears to be a problem with abnormal network bandwidth between a particular ring station/group of ring stations, or network peripheral, and the network file server

First, check the network file server for the following software and hardware configuration setup parameters and requirements.

- Make sure that the NOS network shell software, NOS NIC drivers, CONFIG.SYS, AUTOEXEC.BAT, and all the necessary network operating system files are set up for the respective NOS specialized configuration and NOS hierarchical directory structure.

- Check the NOS directory structure as it relates to ring station and any respective network peripheral access.

- Check all the NOS security rights configurations.

- Make sure all the necessary directory/files for any NOS applications on the network drive are set up correctly.

- Make sure all the necessary hardware is installed in the file server, is configured correctly, and is functioning OK.

NOTE: Check the respective NOS and software application manuals for file server setup concerning network-software-vendor requirements for both software and hardware prerequisites and their respective configuration.

Are there any identifiable hardware or software configuration setup problems with the network file server?

[YES] Take the necessary action to resolve the configuration problem and retest the ring for proper operation. If the failure symptom is gone, record the problem in the network maintenance and service log. If the failure symptom is still present, go to the next step.

[NO]   Check the file server NIC buffer space specifications to see if they meet the NOS and software application manufacturers' requirements for the ring user population and access.

Is the file server's NIC low on required buffer space for the NOS or particular application's operation?

[YES]   Take the necessary action to resolve the problem and retest the ring for proper operation. If the failure symptom is gone, record the problem in the network maintenance and service log. If the failure symptom is still present, go to the next step.

[NO]   Attempt to gather more conclusive fault-isolation data by running a protocol analysis session on the ring. Vector to flow guide 7.15 and focus on the problem by capturing and viewing the high-layer communication processes and the baseline network bandwidth.

NOTE: If after using this flow guide you cannot conclusively locate the problem, and you continue to find failure symptoms that point to a network file server problem, reference both the NOS software and the particular file server/hardware manufacturers' instructions.

7.15 PROTOCOL ANALYSIS FLOW GUIDES

Did you arrive at this flow guide because you need to troubleshoot a network failure symptom that requires running a protocol analysis session to examine the low-layer 802.5 frame communication processes?

(Vector to sub-flow guide 7.15.1)

Did you arrive at this flow guide because you are encountering a specific soft or hard error on the network, or the network is freezing or hanging?

(Vector to sub-flow guide 7.15.2)

Did you arrive at this flow guide because you need to troubleshoot a network failure symptom that requires running a protocol analysis session to examine the high-layer network frame communication processes?

(Vector to sub-flow guide 7.15.3)

Is the network experiencing any of the following failure symptoms: The whole network is operating slowly, a specific network application is operating slowly, or log-on failures?

(Vector to sub-flow guide 7.15.4)

NOTE: While using these flow guides, keep in mind the prescribed approach for a general protocol analysis session: capture, view, analyze, check errors, benchmark performance, and focus.

7.15.1 Performing a protocol analysis session to examine the low-layer 802.5 frame communication processes

First, start the protocol analysis session by establishing the network baseline of operations. Set up the protocol analyzer to perform a full capture.

NOTE: If the higher-layer protocols are clouding your testing results, you can filter them out, so as to focus more closely on the low layers.

Closely examine the 802.5 low-level frame communication processes. Interrogate all the base 802.5 MAC data frames as to how they respectively correlate with the time-related Token Ring communication processes captured in the protocol analysis session.

Scrutinize the current state of low-level 802.5 frame communications exchange between the network entities involved, for proper and fluent protocol exchange. Specifically, if you are troubleshooting a certain network component, such as a gateway, router, bridge, ring station, file server, network peripheral, and so on, look for the low-level 802.5 frame communication processes associated with that specific network device's Token Ring address.

In other words, are there any noticeable deviances from a normal state of low-level frame communication process that may indicate a possible failure within a fault domain or a specific network component?

NOTE: You may need to reference the Token Ring communication processes presented in Chapter 2.

Did you find any deviances from the normal state of low-level 802.5 frame communication processes that indicate a possible failure within a fault domain or a specific network component failure?

[YES]   Take the necessary action to resolve the problem by vectoring to the flow guide for that particular specific network component (such as 7.6 *Ring Station*, 7.10 *Network Peripheral*, 7.14 *File Server*, and so on).

      If you are not completely conclusive as to a specific network component that may be related to the failure symptom, vector to flow guide 7.2 and troubleshoot the respective Token Ring addresses associated in the frames (that is, the possible fault domain) that deviate from the normal state of communication

      If, after vectoring to the respective fault domain, network area, or network component, you find a problem, resolve the problem and retest the ring by vectoring back to this flow guide (7.15). Rerun another baseline session to test the ring. If there are no more deviances from the normal state of operations, record the problem in the network maintenance and service log. If the problem is still there after rerunning another session, go to the next step.

[NO]   Vector down to the next sub-flow guide, 7.15.2.

7.15.2 Encountering specific soft or hard errors on the network or the whole network is freezing or hanging

NOTE: Keep in mind that abnormal high network bandwidth usage can cause performance degradation on the network which can present itself in the form of soft or hard error conditions. If you immediately suspect high bandwidth as a problem, first vector down to sub-flow guide 7.15.4 and analyze the network bandwidth. If at this point you feel that the bandwidth is within normal parameters, continue with the following steps.

NOTE: Remember that by using any available error alarm triggering features with your protocol analyzer, you may be able to observe more dynamically any particular errors as they occur.

Examine the captured data from the respective protocol analysis session for any recorded soft or hard error conditions.

If any soft errors are recorded, Go to S1.

If any hard errors are recorded, Go to S2.

[S1]   *Soft Error Vectoring*

NOTE: Keep in mind that soft errors are the less-critical type of errors that can occur on the ring, and they do not always indicate a definite problem with any associated network component via a Token Ring address. But they may indicate a marginal failure with that network component. So when following any recommended vectors in the following soft error vectors, use your own logical thought processes as to the degree of seriousness of the failure symptom that is occurring, before taking any corrective action.

NOTE: When examining the type of soft error captured during the protocol analysis session, look closely at the Report Soft Error MAC frame for the following information and take appropriate notes: the type of soft error, and both associated addresses in the MAC frame.

NOTE: Remember that the Report Soft Error MAC frame contains the soft error counter field, which is a 12-byte field: 10 of the bytes actually represent soft error types, and the other two bytes are reserved for future use. The hexadecimal value of a particular soft error byte indicates the actual soft error count for the soft error type.

Next, examine the respective Report Soft Error MAC frame that was captured during the protocol analysis session for the type of soft error and both associated addresses in the MAC frame.

Place your captured soft error type into one of the following 10 soft error type categories, then go to that soft error type. Next, use the address information along with the presented isolation solution to identify the soft error failure cause.

10 Soft Error Types

1. Internal Error
2. Burst Error
3. Line Error
4. Abort Delimiter Transmitted Error

5. AC Error

6. Lost Frame Error

7. Receiver Congestion Error

8. Frame Copied Error

9. Frequency Error

10. Token Error

Internal Error. Troubleshoot the addresses in the assigned fault domain by vectoring to flow guide 7.2. Keep in mind that the reporting station NIC may be the failure cause.

Burst Error. Keep in mind these errors can occur when ring stations leave or enter the ring, causing ring reconfigurations, which are not of a serious nature. Check the protocol analysis session trace for ring reconfigurations occurring directly before the burst error. If no ring reconfigurations are occurring, troubleshoot the addresses in the assigned fault domain by vectoring to flow guide 7.2.

Line Error. These errors can also occur when ring stations leave or enter the ring, which will cause ring reconfigurations, or because of simple ring recoveries. Check the protocol analysis session trace for the ring reconfigurations occurring directly before the line error. If no ring reconfigurations or ring recoveries are occurring, troubleshoot the addresses in the assigned fault domain by vectoring to flow guide 7.2. Keep in mind that the presence of a line error can be due to a failure cause located in the reporting station's NAUN.

Abort Delimiter Transmitted Error. Troubleshoot the addresses in the assigned fault domain by vectoring to flow guide 7.2. Keep in mind that the reporting station NIC may be the failure cause.

AC Error. Troubleshoot the addresses in the assigned fault domain by vectoring to flow guide 7.2. Keep in mind that the presence of an AC error can be due to a failure cause located in the reporting station's NAUN.

Lost Frame Error. Troubleshoot the addresses in the assigned fault domain by vectoring to flow guide 7.2.

Receiver Congestion Error. Troubleshoot the addresses in the assigned fault domain by vectoring to flow guide 7.2. Keep in mind that a receiver congestion error usually occurs because of lack of buffer space within the NIC on the destination ring station.

Frame Copied Error. Check the ring for a duplicate address as related to the reporting ring station's adapter. If no duplicate address is found, troubleshoot the addresses in the assigned fault domain by vectoring to flow guide 7.2.

Frequency Error. Troubleshoot the ring station that is assigned the active monitor role and the reporting ring station's NAUN for a possible failure by vectoring to flow guide 7.6.

Token Error. Troubleshoot the addresses in the assigned fault domain by vectoring to flow guide 7.2.

NOTE: Remember that when experiencing intermittent problems such as soft errors on a Token Ring network, you can use traffic-generation techniques to load the network with additional traffic to flush out certain types of intermittent failure causes. By generating additional network traffic you can stress the network enough to cause certain marginal network component failures to surface.

NOTE: If a particular soft error occurs frequently, and you have thoroughly analyzed the respective soft error and followed the recommended troubleshooting steps yet cannot conclusively locate a failure cause for the error, vector down to sub-flow guide 7.15.4 and analyze the network bandwidth.

[S2]   *Hard Error Vectoring*

NOTE: Remember that hard errors are the more critical category of errors that can occur on the ring. They are actual solid failures with a specific network component and take the form of a failure symptom by the beaconing process.

If you encounter a hard error in a protocol analysis session, the first step is to examine the Beacon MAC frame for the following information:

• The assigned fault domain addresses: reporting ring station and the reporting station's NAUN

• The Beacon type

When a hard error occurs and a Beacon MAC frame is captured, troubleshoot the addresses in the assigned fault domain by vectoring to flow guide 7.2. Keep in mind that if the Beacon type is a "signal loss error," the failure cause is most likely a cable fault in the cabling medium internal to the assigned fault domain.

NOTE: If a hard error occurs frequently, and you have thoroughly analyzed the Beacon MAC frame and followed the recommended troubleshooting steps for the fault domain and yet cannot conclusively locate a failure cause for the error, vector down to sub-flow guide 7.15.4 and analyze the network bandwidth.

7.15.3 Performing a protocol analysis session to examine the high-layer network frame communication processes

Have you verified that the 802.5 base frame communication processes are proper and fluent as to low-level protocol exchange?

[YES]   Go to S1.

[NO]   Vector back to sub-flow guide 7.15.1 and troubleshoot the low-level 802.5 base communication processes.

[S1]   First, perform a full-capture session. Next view the high-layer protocol communication that occurs concurrently between the network components—the ring stations, network peripherals, gateways, bridges, routers, file servers, and so on—that are involved in the high-layer communication processes that you are troubleshooting. Closely examine the application and network operating system communication process between the respective network components.

NOTE: Keep in mind that certain applications may use multiple layers of the Token Ring protocol model for transmission. Check all the higher layers.

Are the involved network components and their respective application/network operating system communication processes exchanging the correct assigned protocol?

[YES]   Reference the NOS and software application manufacturers and if necessary contact your NOS and software support channel for assistance with troubleshooting any suspected high-layer communication process.

[NO]   *Does the incorrect protocol exchange appear to be related to some sort of file access process problem with a particular NOS or software application?*

[YES]   Reference the NOS and software application manufacturers and if necessary contact your NOS and software support channel for assistance with troubleshooting any suspected high-layer communication process.

[NO]   Check the network components involved in the specific high-layer communication process that you are troubleshooting for a possible failure by vectoring to the flow guide for that particular specific network component (for example 7.6 *Ring Station*, 7.10 *Network Peripheral*, 7.14 *File Server*, and so on).

If you are not completely conclusive as to a specific network component that may be related to the failure symptom, vector to flow guide 7.2 and troubleshoot the respective Token Ring addresses associated in the high-layer frames that appear to be involved with failure symptoms.

If, after vectoring to the respective fault domain, network area, or network component, you find a problem, resolve the problem and retest the ring by vectoring back to this flow guide (7.15) and rerun another baseline session to test the ring. Then reexamine the high-layer communication processes for any deviances from the previous testing results.

If everything appears normal, record the problem in the network maintenance and service log. If the problem is still present, contact your NOS and software support channel for assistance with troubleshooting any suspected high-layer communication process.

7.15.4 The network is experiencing one or more of the following failure symptoms: The whole network is operating slowly, a specific network application is operating slowly, or log-on failures

First, set up the protocol analyzer or network monitoring tool to monitor the network bandwidth utilization at an overall baseline view.

Is the overall network baseline within normal operating levels of a previously established baseline for your network?

NOTE: If you do not have a previously established baseline for your network, attempt to identify that a reasonable portion of the available maximum bandwidth is still available for use.

[YES] Vector back to the beginning of this flow guide (7.15) and follow the subsections of this complete flow guide. (That is, examine the low-layer 802.5 frame communication processes, check for specific soft or hard errors on the network, and examine the high-layer network frame communication processes.)

[NO] Check the overall baseline network bandwidth as to individual ring stations and all other network components' level usage. Attempt to locate a particular ring station or other network component that may be absorbing abnormal bandwidth.

Can you locate any particular ring stations or other network components that may be absorbing abnormal bandwidth?

[YES] If you have not troubleshot the high-level communication process on the ring, vector back to sub-flow guide 7.15.3 and thoroughly troubleshoot the high-level communication process for any NOS or application communication processes that may be absorbing abnormal bandwidth. After analyzing the high-layer communication process, vector back to this sub-flow guide (7.15.4) and remeasure the baseline network bandwidth.

If you have troubleshot the high-level communication processes, go to the next step.

[NO] Even though you cannot specifically locate any particular ring stations or other network components that may be absorbing abnormal bandwidth, still check any ring stations or network components that are suspect by vectoring to the flow guide for that particular specific network component (for example, 7.6 *Ring Station*, 7.10 *Network Peripheral*, 7.14 *File Server*, and so on).

If you are not completely conclusive as to a specific network component that may be related to the failure symptom, vector to flow guide 7.2 and troubleshoot the respective Token Ring addresses associated with high bandwidth usage.

If after vectoring to the respective fault domain, network area, or network component you find a problem, resolve the problem and retest the ring by vectoring back to this flow guide (7.15) and vector directly back to sub-flow guide 7.15.4. Rerun another baseline bandwidth test session to reexamine the ring for bandwidth usage.

If everything appears normal, record the problem in the network maintenance and service log. If the problem is still present, contact your NOS and software support channel for assistance with troubleshooting any suspected network bandwidth issues.

NOTE: If you have benchmarked the network bandwidth utilization at overall baseline view and usage of the individual ring stations and other network components and you still have a bandwidth problem that you cannot locate, contact your NOS and software support channel for assistance with troubleshooting any suspected bandwidth problem.

chapter **8** SUMMARY

Well, you've reached the end of road. This chapter leaves you with some closing remarks and important recommendations so that you can use the knowledge you gained from this book.

DOCUMENT YOUR PROBLEMS

As you wind down the Token Ring troubleshooting paths, as you run through the NICs and onto the cabling medium, step through MAUs, and jump across bridges and routers and into other NICs, you will make multiple maneuvers in multiple directions before you reach the place in which your treasure chest of failure causes is hidden.

While you are expending all that effort to locate the failure cause that relates to your failure symptom, it is extremely important that you take accurate notes on all the steps you take in troubleshooting a problem.

You can jot down your troubleshooting steps on a piece of paper, or you can enter notes into a PC software notepad. But the important thing to remember is to document your troubleshooting failure symptoms, failure causes, action steps, and action results.

Do not forget to document your troubleshooting results in the network maintenance and service log as described in Chapter 5.

Keep in mind the troubleshooting approach discussed in Chapter 6. To recap, always approach any Token Ring network problem from the symptom. Attempt to conclusively define the problem that is occurring as a specific symptom.

Next, attempt to logically locate the failure cause into one of the three logical network areas: the complete network, a group of network users, or an individual network user or specific network component.

After you define the symptom and the area of the network that is experiencing the symptom, remember to categorize the symptom as a solid problem or an intermittent problem.

By remembering the proper troubleshooting approach—first, define the symptom; second, place the symptom in a specific network area; third, define the symptom as solid or intermittent— you will have the key to start the troubleshooting shuttle that will enable you to resolve your Token Ring network problems quickly and efficiently.

USE THE TROUBLESHOOTING FLOW GUIDES

The flow guides in Chapter 7 give you a simple and swift route to resolving any Token Ring network problems you encounter. These flow guides help artificially simulate the accurate fault-isolation vector process maneuvers for troubleshooting a Token Ring network.

Also keep in mind that the Token Ring architecture as presented in Chapter 2 will be your main reference library for information relating to Token Ring architectural processes. You may need to reference this information if you are making your vectoring decisions during the troubleshooting process.

The icing on the cake in assisting you with your fault-isolation vectoring decisions is the disk that is coded with artificial intelligence software. The disk was developed in exact correlation with the troubleshooting steps presented in the sections of Chapter 7. It is intended to give you an easier and faster path to resolving the Token Ring problems you encounter.

The flow guides in Chapter 7 and the coded disk will greatly assist your troubleshooting efforts.

With these last notes and a wave of the magic Token Ring wand, you are on your way to becoming an official Token Ring associate wizard.

appendix A

ADDRESSES OF COMPANIES MENTIONED IN THIS BOOK

3Com Corp.
5400 Bayfront Plaza
Santa Clara, CA 95052
(800) NET-3COM
(408) 764-5000

AICorp Inc.
138 Technology Drive
Waltham, MA 02254-9748
(617) 893-8826

Andrew Corp.
2771 Plaza Del Amo
Torrance, CA 90503
(213) 320-7126

Antel Optronics Inc.
1701 North Greenville Ave.
Suite 203
Richardson, TX 75081
(214) 690-5200

Apple Computer, Inc.
20525 Mariani Ave.
Cupertino, CA 95014
(800) 635-9550

AT&T Computer Systems
1 Speedwell Ave.
Morristown, NJ 07960
(800) 247-1212

Banyan Systems Inc.
120 Flanders Rd.
Westboro, MA 01581
(800) 828-2404
(508) 898-1000

Brightwork Development Inc.
766 Shrewsbury Ave.
Jerral Center West
Tinton Falls, NJ 07724
(201) 530-0440
(800) 552-9876

Bytex Corp.
Southborough Office Park
120 Turnpike Rd.
Southborough, MA 01772-1886
(800) 227-1145
(508) 480-0840

ProTools Inc.
14976 NW Greenbrier Pkwy.
Beaverton, OR 97006-5733
(503) 645-5400
(800) 743-4335

Spider Systems Inc.
12 New England Executive Park
Burlington, MA 01803
(617) 270-3510

SynOptics Communications Inc.
4401 Great America Pkwy.
P.O. Box 58185
Santa Clara, CA 95052-8185
(800) PRO-NTWK
(800) 544-1340

Triticom
P.O. Box 11536
St. Paul, MN 55111
(612) 937-0772

OTHER REFERENCE MATERIAL

1. IBM Token-Ring Network Architecture Reference, Document SC30-3374-02.

2. IBM Token-Ring Network Problem Determination Guide, Document SX27-3710-3.

3. IBM Cabling System Planning and Installation Guide, Document GA27-3361-5.

4. IBM Token-Ring Network Installation Guide, Document GA27-3578-2.

5. The Institute of Electrical and Electronic Engineers, Inc., Token Ring Access Method and Physical Layer Specifications, IEEE STD 802.5-1989.

ACRONYM LIST

AM	Active monitor
AMP	Active monitor present
APPC	Advanced Program-to-Program Communication (IBM)
ARL	Adjusted ring length
AWG	American Wire Gauge
BPDU	Bridge Protocol Data Unit
CAU	Controlled access unit (IBM)
CRC	Cyclic redundancy check
CRS	Configuration report saver
CSFS	Cable signal fault signature
CSU	Channel service unit
DDE	Dynamic Data Exchange
DLC	Data link control
DMA	Direct memory access
DOD	Department of Defense
DSAP	Destination service access point
DSU	Data service unit
EISA	Extended Industry Standard Architecture
ETR	Early token release

FDDI	Fiber Data Distributed Interface
FS	File server; frame status
HCL	Hop count limit
IBMNMIBM	Network Management
IEEE	Institute of Electrical and Electronic Engineers
IRQ	Interrupt request
ISO	International Organization for Standardization
LAM	Lobe attachment module
LAN	Local area network
LBS	LAN bridge server
LED	Light-emitting diode
LL	Length identifier
LLC	Logical link control
LRM	LAN reporting mechanism
LU	Logical unit (SNA)
MAC	Medium access control
MAU	Multistation access unit
Mbps	Megabits per second
MCA	Micro Channel Architecture
MTTR	Mean time to repair
MVID	Major vector ID
NAUN	Nearest active upstream neighbor
NetBIOS	Network Basic Input/Output System (IBM)
NIC	Network interface card
NOS	Network operating system
OSI	Open Systems Interconnection
OTDR	Optical time domain reflectometer
PDU	Protocol data unit

PROM	Programmable read-only memory
PU	Physical unit (SNA)
REM	Ring error monitor
RI	Ring in; routing information
RO	Ring out
RPL	Remote program load
RPS	Ring parameter server
RS	Ring station
SA	Source address
SDLC	Synchronous Data Link Control
SM	Standby monitor
SMB	Server Message Block (IBM)
SMP	Standby monitor present
SNA	Systems Networking Architecture (IBM)
SNMP	Simple Network Management Protocol
SR	Source routing
SSAP	Source service access point
SSCP	Systems Service Control Point (SNA)
STA	Spanning tree algorithm
STP	Shielded twisted pair (cabling)
T	Token Ring protocol timer
TB	Transparent bridging
TCP/IP	Transmission Control Protocol/ Internetwork Protocol
TDR	Time domain reflectometer
UNA	Upstream neighbors address
UTP	Unshielded twisted pair (cabling)
WAN	Wide-area network
XNS	Xerox Networking System

10BASE-T. The IEEE 802.3 specification for unshielded twisted-pair EtherNet.

16Mbps. A Token Ring-specified speed for data transmission that uses frame sizes of approximately 18000 bytes, along with ETR.

4Mbps. A Token Ring-specified speed for data transmission that uses frame sizes of approximately 4500 bytes.

802.5. An IEEE standard for the Token Ring access method and Physical layer specifications.

Abort sequence frame. A frame sequence used to clear the ring when there is a problem with a frame.

Active monitor (AM). The main communication manager on the ring, the AM is responsible for maintaining key transfer of data and control information balanced between all stations on the ring.

Adjusted ring length (ARL). The final maximum length of certain cabling segments in the Token Ring topology, derived by calculations involving distance in relation to the number of MAUs, repeaters, and wiring closets in the network.

Advanced Program-to-Program Communications (APPC). Part of the SNA protocol, establishing the conditions that enable programs to communicate across the network. This capability, involving LU6.2 and its associated protocols, allows communication between two or more processes in an SNA network without the involvement of a common host system or of terminal emulation.

AppleTalk. A set of communication protocols used to define networking on an AppleShare network. Based on the OSI model, AppleTalk is comparable to other communication protocols, in that they specify communications that range from application interfaces to media access.

AUTOEXEC.BAT file. A special file used to customize the DOS workstation environment.

Baseband transmission. A form of data transmission used to send unmodulated digital pulses over the network cabling by sending only one signal frequency over the line at a time.

Beaconing. A Token Ring communication process that occurs when a ring station generates a warning signal onto the ring if it sees a hard error occur with itself or its NAUN.

BPDU (hello bridge protocol data units). A protocol used by the spanning tree algorithm to control transmission of data.

Bridge. A device that connects local area networks via the Data Link layer of the OSI model.

Broadcasting. An addressing method by which a station on the ring communicates to one or more stations through a common address that the destination stations share.

Building blueprints. A set of documents that shows the physical layout of a particular building.

Cabling. The physical medium that connects transmission points within a local area network.

Cabling connector. A physical link that connects two points within the cabling section of a local area network.

CONFIG.SYS file. A special file used to configure the DOS workstation environment.

Configuration report server (CRS). A ring management server role whose main responsibility is to collect important statistical information from the ring and to forward that information to the LAN Manager console.

CPU (Central Processing Unit). The part of a computer containing the circuits required to interpret and execute instructions.

CSU (Channel Service Unit). A device that interfaces a T1 line to a local loop.

Cyclic redundancy check (CRC). A 32-bit sequence within a Token Ring data frame which is an error-checking method that involves a calculation of the bit transmission at the sending and receiving ends of each ring station.

Data frame. A variable-length frame that carries either ring control or data information. The frame will then carry the designation of either a MAC frame (control) or an LLC frame (data).

DECnet. A set of networking protocols developed by Digital Equipment Corp. and used in their VAX family of computers for data exchange. Although DECnet is currently a proprietary protocol, DEC is merging its protocols with OSI protocols.

Destination ring station. A station that is the intended receiver of a particular frame generated and transmitted by an originating ring station.

Differential Manchester Encoding. A form of data transmission that is communicated on the ring medium using a specialized bit-encoding scheme.

DLC.LAN. The portion of the Data Link layer of Token Ring that encodes, decodes, and routes MAC and LLC information.

DLC.LANMGR. A manager function that resides within the DLC.LAN and is responsible for managing the control of information between both the LLC and MAC layers at the Data Link level.

Downstream. The normal direction of data flow on the Token Ring network.

DSU (Data Service Unit). A device that converts RS232 terminal signals to line codes for local loop transmission.

Duplicate address. An address that is the same as the address of another active ring station on the ring.

Early Token Release (ETR). A ring-access technique that allows two data frames to travel on the ring at the same time.

EtherNet. A network cable and access protocol scheme originally developed by DEC, Intel, and Xerox, but now marketed primarily by DEC and 3Com.

Fault domain. The logical area of a fault error as determined by the Token Ring architecture.

Fault isolation vectoring. The art of deciding what is the correct direction to follow when troubleshooting a LAN problem.

Fiber Data Distributed Interface (FDDI). A network topology that runs at 100Mbps. The topology is a token-passing network very similar to IEEE 802.5.

Fiber optic cabling. Cable that uses light instead of electricity to transfer information.

Flow guide. A logical, nongraphical, written troubleshooting flow chart.

Functional addressing. An addressing method by which a station that has widely used functions can be assigned a predefined address, so other stations can communicate with it.

Gateway. A hardware/software package that runs on the OSI Application layer and enables incompatible protocols to communicate. Includes X.25 gateways. Usually connects PCs to a host machine, such as an IBM mainframe.

Group addressing. An addressing method by which one or more stations are addressed.

Hard errors. The more serious type of errors that can occur on the ring. A hard error is considered an actual solid failure and impairs the normal mode of ring operation.

IBM cabling types. A set of cabling types designed for the Token Ring topology as specified by IBM.

IBM data connector. The IBM standard data connector that has internal self-shorting bars, which automatically loop the cabling back to form an electrical ring.

IBM NetView. Network-monitoring software for SNA networks.

IBM Network Management (IBMNM) protocol. A specific communication protocol that is used to communicate among the Token Ring architectural ring management roles.

IBM Server Message Block (SMB). A distributed file-system network protocol from IBM and Microsoft that enables one computer to use the files and peripherals of another as if they were local.

IBM Systems Network Architecture (SNA). An IBM network architecture defined in terms of its functions, formats, and protocols.

IBM Token Ring planning forms. A set of IBM forms for planning and maintaining Token Ring network configurations.

Individual addressing. An addressing method by which each station is addressed uniquely across the ring.

Institute of Electrical and Electronics Engineers (IEEE). A body that creates networking standards for cabling, electrical topology, physical topology, and access schemes.

Intermittent failure. A failure symptom that cannot be re-created at will; it may occur at any time.

Internetwork. Two or more networks connected by an internal or external router.

Internetwork Package Exchange (IPX). A Novell NetWare protocol that enables the exchange of message packets on an internetwork.

I/O board. Hardware that enables the transfer of data into and out from a computer.

Jumper cables. Cables that are usually used between ports on a patch panel.

LAN Bridge Server (LBS). A ring management server role whose main responsibility is to monitor important statistical information about data routed between two or more rings that are connected by a bridge.

LAN drivers. Software or firmware that translates operating system requests (such as input/output requests) into a format that is recognizable by specific hardware, such as adapters.

LAN Reporting Mechanism (LRM). A ring management server function that is responsible for maintaining communication between a LAN Manager console and remote management servers.

Lobe. The complete composite of network components in a specific lobe area that physically connects to a specific MAU or wiring hub.

Lobe area. One logical arm of a specified network node, including specific network components, such as a ring station, a NIC, a lobe cable, and a MAU or wiring hub port.

Lobe cable. The section or sections of cable that attach a ring station or network device to a MAU or wiring hub.

Lobe path. Same as lobe area.

Local administration. The means of assigning ring stations unique individual addresses defined by a group or person other than the IEEE.

Local area network (LAN). A system that links computers together to form a network, usually with a wiring-based cabling scheme. LANs connect personal computers and electronic office equipment, enabling users to communicate, to share resources, such as data storage and printers, and to access remote hosts or other networks.

Logical Link Control (LLC). The data sequence used within Token Ring data frames that contains information that is actual user data information to be transmitted.

Main ring path. The logical path that interconnects a series of network components and cabling sections to form the logical ring.

Main ring path cabling. The cabling sections that make up the physical path that forms the main ring path.

MAU charger. An IBM device used to open relays in the IBM MAU.

MAU rack layout. A document that depicts the physical and logical layout of a MAU rack.

Maximum lobe length. The maximum length to which a lobe cable can extend without losing its transmission quality and capability.

Medium Access Control (MAC). The data sequence used within Token Ring data frames that contains the information used to manage the flow of traffic on the ring.

Memory. The active part of computer storage used when a computer runs a program or a command.

Modem. A device that enables the transmission and reception of digital information over telephone lines.

Multistation Access Unit (MAU). An access device used to connect the main cabling structure to the devices in use on a Token Ring network.

Nearest Active Upstream Neighbor (NAUN). The first active upstream ring station from any particular active ring station.

Neighbor Notification. A Token Ring communication process that involves a logical consecutive procedure enabling every ring station to be informed of its NAUN's address.

NetBIOS (Network Basic Input/Output System). A programmable entry into the network that allows systems to communicate over network hardware using a generic networking interface which can run over multiple transports or media.

Network architecture. The design of the way the network topology is integrated with the network protocols.

Network area. Any particular logically defined area of the network, such as a group of ring stations, a set of MAUs, and so forth.

Network component. Any specific hardware or software device that is connected to the network or is part of a specific network area.

Network documentation. The necessary documents to maintain a reference of the hardware and software components within a LAN layout.

Network documentation software tools. A software package that can gather LAN statistics (such as hardware and software configurations) and create automated records on the gathered information.

Network file server. A computer on the network capable of recognizing and responding to client requests for services. These services can range from basic file and print services to support for complex, distributed applications. For example, a distributed database management system can create a single logical database across multiple servers.

Network file server and ring station documentation. A series of written or automated records that maintains an overview of the components of both the file server and ring stations in a Token Ring network environment.

Network interface card (NIC). A logic card that uses electronic circuitry and software routines to connect a ring station to the cabling medium through a specified access method.

Network maintenance and service logs. A written or automated record that maintains an historical log of any problems that occur within a Token Ring network environment.

Network operating system (NOS). A set of software programs that manages the use of data and resources on a network of connected workstations.

Network peripherals. Network devices that physically connect to the network via their own internal NIC, without needing to be attached to a ring station or a file server.

Network protocol. An orderly, predefined method by which devices on a LAN communicate with each other.

Network shell software. The software programs at each individual workstation that enable the workstation to take advantage of the network's data and resources.

NIC Agent. A set of routines within the Token Ring chipset on the NIC that interpret and route all the data frames that are transferred between the device and the network.

Open System Interconnection (OSI). A model for network communications, consisting of seven layers that describe what happens when computers communicate with one another.

Optical time domain reflectometer (OTDR). A device that operates in the same manner as a TDR, except by using a laser for a light source to generate optical pulse signals and by using an optical receiver.

Originating ring station. A ring station that generates and transmits a particular frame onto the Token Ring cabling medium.

Patch cables. Cables used between a ring station and a wall plate.

Patch panel. A physical panel, usually contained within a wiring closet, that is used as a patch board for running a group of cables to one area, and providing the flexibility to move lobe cables from one MAU to another easily.

Patch panel layout. A document that depicts the physical layout and logical cable wiring scheme of a patch panel.

Performance tuning. The process of using the statistics gathered in a protocol analysis session and making any necessary modifications to either the software or hardware design components of a LAN, for the purpose of improving its operational performance.

Phantom DC current. A current that is generated during Ring Insertion by an NIC to a specific MAU port to open the MAU port relay.

Physical star. A network topology with a central hub and radiating spokes.

Priority access. A Token Ring communication process that involves a qualifying method by which all ring stations attain a certain priority for their turn to gain control of the token.

Problem Reversal Theory. A troubleshooting theory based on taking known testing results and reversing the respective troubleshooting procedure to re-create the problem for problem verification, before finally implementing the newly tested network component into the network.

Protocol analysis. The process of capturing, viewing, and analyzing how a communication protocol is operating within a particular network architecture.

Protocol analysis session. A specific instance of using a protocol analyzer to capture, decode, and examine data involved with communication across a live network.

Protocol analyzer. A device that can capture, decode, and display packets containing data from a network.

Remote program load (RPL) PROM. A PROM that enables a diskless ring station to attach to a network file server.

Repeater. A device that amplifies, then regenerates a signal to extend the distance of a local area network.

Ring cable tester. A device designed specifically for testing the Token Ring topology cabling.

Ring error monitor (REM). A ring management server role whose main responsibility is to collect soft and hard errors from all stations that generate any errors on the ring.

Ring In (RI). The port on the left side of the MAU, used for access from another MAU and the associated ring cabling section. This is also termed as the entrance method to another MAU or wiring hub module.

Ring Insertion. The five-phase process that a ring station must go through to actively attach itself to a Token Ring network.

Ring Out (RO). The port on the right side of the MAU, used to access another MAU and the associated ring cabling section. This is also termed as the exit method from one MAU or wiring hub module to another.

Ring parameter server (RPS). A ring management server role whose main responsibility is to communicate ring initialization parameters to all new ring stations attaching to the ring.

Ring Purge. A Token Ring communication process that can be defined as the attempted resetting of the ring to Normal Repeat mode.

Ring station (RS). A PC that contains the necessary hardware, software, and functions to enable it to access a Token Ring network as a node.

Router. A software and hardware connection between two or more networks, usually of similar design, that enables traffic to be routed from one network to another on the basis of the intended destinations of that traffic. A router can connect networks that use different network adapters or transmission media as long as both sides of the connection use the same protocols. If a router is located in a server, it is called an internal router; if located in a workstation, it is called an external router.

RS232. A set of interface standards that dictates how asynchronous devices, such as PCs and terminals, communicate over telephone wire. Based on a 25-pin architecture that permits 19.2Kbps data transfer.

Shielded twisted pair (STP). A cable consisting of two twisted-pair conductors that are insulated by a metal-backed mylar substance.

Simple Network Management Protocol (SNMP). Developed for TCP/IP networks.

Soft errors. The less-serious type of errors that can occur on the ring. They usually do not impair the normal mode of ring operation.

Solid failure. A failure symptom that can be recreated at will.

Source routing. A means of data transmission by which the node that is generating the transmission will determine the route that the data will follow.

Source routing bridge. A bridge that can understand and forward frames with source-routing data fields.

Spanning tree algorithm (STA). A method to determine a packet's best path when there are multiple path routes within an internetwork.

Standby monitors (SM). All general ring stations (RSes) on the ring.

Synchronous Data Link Control (SDLC). An IBM-defined link-control protocol that is code-independent.

Time domain reflectometer (TDR). A device that generates and transmits a specific signal down a cable, then monitors the cable for a signal reflection.

Token claiming. A Token Ring communication process that occurs when standby monitors go into contention to win the active monitor role.

Token frame. A three-byte frame that circulates the ring as a control signal.

Token Ring. A network that employs a ring topology and uses a token-passing method for ring access.

Token Ring addressing schemes. Set addressing methods that are dictated by the Token Ring architecture.

Token Ring architecture management roles. Management ring station roles predefined by the Token Ring architecture.

Token Ring protocol timers. A set of clock utilities included in the Token Ring architecture and used for synchronizing the protocols that interrelate on the ring.

Topology. The physical layout of a network.

Transmission Control Protocol/Internet Protocol (TCP/IP). A protocol suite developed for the U.S. Department of Defense (DoD) specifically to permit different types of computers to communicate and exchange information with one another. TCP/IP is currently mandated as an official DoD protocol and is also widely used in the UNIX community.

Universal administration. The means of assigning ring stations unique individual addresses defined by the IEEE.

Unshielded twisted pair (UTP). A cable consisting of two twisted-pair conductors that are not insulated; common telephone wire.

Upstream. The direction on a Token Ring network that is contrary to the normal direction of data flow (that is, downstream).

Wall plate. A plate that is usually used for mounting an internal building cable connector on a physical wall.

Wiring closet. A room that usually contains the patch panel and MAU racks. Some large Token Ring installations require multiple wiring closets.

Wiring hubs. Access devices that also connect the main cabling structure to the devices used on the network, but that typically use a cage construction and allow multiple topologies and cabling types to be intermixed through specialized hardware and software.

XNS (Xerox Networking System). A set of transmission protocols developed by Xerox.

X.25. CCITT recommendations that define a protocol for communication between packet-switched public data networks and user devices in the packet-switched mode.

Some definitions provided by Novell Inc.

Index

www.ingramcontent.com/pod-product-compliance
Lightning Source LLC
Chambersburg PA
CBHW062104050326
40690CB00016B/3195